D0824820

The Bird

CALGARY PUBLIC LIBRARY

AUG - 2014

Also by Doug Wilson

Fred Hutchinson and the 1964 Cincinnati Reds

The Bird

The Life and Legacy of Mark Fidrych

DOUG WILSON

THOMAS DUNNE BOOKS
ST. MARTIN'S GRIFFIN
NEW YORK

Dedicated to the little boy who loves baseball inside all of us

THOMAS DUNNE BOOKS.
An imprint of St. Martin's Press.

THE BIRD. Copyright © 2013 by Doug Wilson. All rights reserved. Printed in the United States of America. For information, address St. Martin's Press, 175 Fifth Avenue, New York, N.Y. 10010.

www.thomasdunnebooks.com
www.stmartins.com

Designed by Omar Chapa

The Library of Congress has cataloged the hardcover edition as follows:

Wilson, Doug. 1961–
    The Bird: the life and legacy of Mark Fidrych / Doug Wilson.—First edition.
        p. cm.
    Includes bibliographical references and index.
    ISBN 978-1-250-00492-5 (hardcover)
    ISBN 978-1-250-02114-4 (e-book)
I. Title

                                                        2013474057

ISBN 978-1-250-04845-5 (trade paperback)

St. Martin's Griffin books may be purchased for educational, business, or promotional use. For information on bulk purchases, please contact Macmillan Corporate and Premium Sales Department at 1-800-221-7945, extension 5442, or write specialmarkets@macmillan.com.

First St. Martin's Griffin Edition: April 2014

10 9 8 7 6 5 4 3 2 1

Contents

Prologue   1

1. Northboro   5
2. Bristol   31
3. Lakeland, Montgomery, and Evansville   47
4. Detroit   61
5. Birdmania   98
6. "Slow Down"   153
7. The Long Road Back   178
8. Pawtucket   203
9. Northboro Redux   215

   Epilogue   242
   Acknowledgments   249
   Notes   253
   Bibliography   293
   Index   295

Prologue

They had never seen anything like it. For a month stories had been leaking out of Detroit of a curious phenomenon—a twenty-one-year-old rookie pitcher, who seemingly came out of nowhere, who was as wildly popular and flaky as he was talented. He not only filled stadiums and won games, he manicured the mound on his hands and knees and talked to the ball before pitching. His name was Mark Fidrych, but he was known as *The Bird* because he looked like Big Bird, that large, yellow, curly headed Muppet that was all the rage at the time on the kid's show *Sesame Street*.

Baseball in 1976 was in dire straights. The reserve clause had been struck down and the Pandora's Box of free agency had been opened. A large number of players were openly talking of playing out their options at the end of the season and defecting—abandoning their teams for the highest bidder. The owners had locked out the players in spring training due to squabbles over the player agreement contract. Fans, disheartened by the greed that had taken over the game, were sick of hearing about lawyers, agents, and astronomical salaries.

In the seventies, baseball fans got to see two, and only two, nationally televised games each week: the traditional NBC Saturday afternoon *Game of the Week* and the newer *Monday Night Baseball* on ABC. There was no cable; no ESPN. That was it—two games a week. And everybody watched them. Some smart network guy decided that the late-June matchup in Detroit between the division-leading Yankees and the Tigers would be a good game to put on. This young Bird guy was scheduled to pitch; might be interesting television. Interesting television indeed. That night the country was treated to nothing short of a cultural iconoclastic event. Witnesses would forever remember it as part of the times—the baseball equivalent of the Beatles on the *Ed Sullivan Show*.

The powerful Yankees would go to the World Series that October for the first of three consecutive years, but on this night, they were merely straight men: Washington Generals to The Bird's Globetrotters. The 18 million viewers across the country were treated to The Bird's full array of antics. They saw him hopping excitedly out of the dugout to congratulate teammate Rusty Staub after a first-inning home run. They saw him sprinting on and off the field between innings, like he couldn't wait to get there, then couldn't wait to get back and tell everyone how much fun he had. They saw him rush over to shake hands with fielders after routine plays. Twice the cameras showed him patting down the mound, carefully arranging the dirt. "That's not a member of the Detroit ground crew you see," said announcer Warner Wolf the first time. "That's Mark Fidrych."

The Bird's exuberance and joy were plainly evident. This guy was actually enjoying himself—having fun playing baseball, like we all used to when we were kids. And, what's more, the camera repeatedly caught him between pitches, standing on the mound, his hands together with the ball in his glove held out in front of his face—with his lips moving. He was talking. Talking to the ball. The total package was just too much. The unexpected pleasure of it all mesmerized both the television audience at home and the announcers in the booth, and they were swept up in the emotion of the night as it built to the finish.

When the Yankees came to the plate in the top of the ninth,

down 5-1 with The Bird still on the mound, the fans were delirious. The atmosphere was electric. "I've seen a lot of ball games
played and I've caught a few," said announcer Bob Prince, "but I
don't think I've ever seen a pitcher this keyed up in the ninth inning of a ball game, or all through the ball game. You'd think this
guy would be running out of gas by now, but he is just starting to
heat it up."

"He's giving me duck bumps," added Wolf.

With the fans on their feet, screaming, "Let's go Mark," the
kid mowed down the Yankees in the final inning. After the last
out, an easy ground ball to second, Fidrych ran all over the field,
shaking his teammates' hands. He grabbed the umpire's hand and
pumped it. Who shakes hands with an umpire? "And the Tigers act
like Fidrych has just won the seventh game of the World Series,"
the announcer intoned.

And then, the most remarkable thing of the whole evening occurred: nobody went home. Even after the players had filed through
the dugout into the clubhouse and the field was empty, nobody
went home. The fans remained standing, screaming, "We want
The Bird! We want The Bird!" Five, ten minutes after the game had
ended, the camera panned through the stadium, and it was still
completely filled with standing, screaming fans. In 1976, the curtain call was not in vogue in baseball—but it was about to make a
dramatic comeback.

Fidrych was pushed out of the dugout by his teammates and
the stadium exploded. He stood in his socks, shrugging, smiling,
and flapping his arms. He waved to the crowd, tipped his cap, and
then covered his head with both hands like an embarrassed third
grader who has just realized everyone is looking at him. With incredible, unmistakable joy on his face, he shook hands with his
teammates and tried to get them to come out with him, but they
stayed in the dugout, understanding that the moment belonged to
Mark. He leaned over the roof of the dugout and shook hands with
fans. He shook hands with the cop standing next to the dugout.
Who shakes hands with a cop? Announcer Bob Uecker grabbed
the kid for an interview and introduced him to the nation. Mark's
face glowed. He radiated enthusiasm and happiness. As he talked

about the game he sounded like a ten-year-old describing his first trip to Disney World. "You've got a home here," said Uecker nodding to the fans who were still cheering madly. "I love it," the kid gushed. And the best part of it all was that it was real. It wasn't an act.

This one evening would ignite an unprecedented frenzy that would play out over the next three months. The nation would fall in love with The Bird's enthusiasm, spontaneity, genuineness, celebrated goofiness, and the fact that he was happy doing it all for the major league minimum of $16,500 a year. Fans and the media simply would not be able to get enough of him. He would achieve a level of cross-over popularity that has not been approached by a baseball player since. He would appear on the covers of *Sport, Sports Illustrated, Baseball Digest,* the *Sporting News,* the *New York Times Saturday* magazine, *Parade* magazine, and would become the first athlete ever to grace the cover of *Rolling Stone.* He would be the starting pitcher in the All-Star Game and dominate the media coverage of that event like few ever had before. He would bring almost a million people to stadiums around the country in his twenty-nine starts that season and, more importantly, would cause millions more, young and old, to become baseball fans. He would be held up as an example of all that was right with baseball, the savior of the game, the answer to the greed that had threatened the national pastime. A rival manager would state, "Babe Ruth never created this much attention on his best day," and no one would doubt him. The commissioner of baseball would coin the term "The Mark Fidrych Syndrome" as a symbol of hope for future generations of baseball fans. In his meteoric streak across the consciousness of America, Mark "The Bird" Fidrych would become as much of a 1970s pop cultural icon as Evil Knievel, *Saturday Night Fever, Jaws, The Six Million Dollar Man,* and, dare we say it, Fonzie before he jumped the shark.

That would all come later, however. On this night, as the fans and The Bird celebrated the moment, the announcers, try as they might, seemed at a loss to find the correct words to sum up what they were seeing. But they all agreed on one thing: they had never seen anything like it.

1

Northboro

The story of Mark Fidrych is unique to the annals of baseball history. It's easy now to look back and wonder how it all could have happened; to be amazed at the innocence and lack of technologic sophistication of the era. How could a baseball player suddenly emerge from absolute obscurity and capture the nation's affection so completely over such a short period of time? Of course, in this present day of media overload—of Web sites that rate the best prepubescent players in the country, of a multitude of national baseball tournaments for kids from the time they are able to first play the game, of agents who squeeze every dollar out of teams before signing the first contract—it could never happen. But back then, there was a small window of opportunity; just the right ingredients.

Fans had not yet lost every ounce of optimistic naiveté due to endless stories of selfish multimillion-dollar athletes involved in one scandal after another. It was a time when people not only believed in miracles, they *wanted* to believe in miracles. It was a time of exploding cultural change, when people held a fascination for things new and unusual, while at the same time others held an unmistakable anxiety over the irretrievable loss of certain values—and it was a time when a player with a one-of-a-kind personality and talent could show up and unwittingly satisfy both. The remarkable story of Mark Fidrych, how he achieved his fantastic level of popularity, and what he did afterward is worth revisiting, because it is unlikely to ever occur again. To understand it all, it is necessary, of course, to start at the beginning.

Before Mark Fidrych was The Bird, he was Fid. Fid from Northboro. Just one of the guys growing up in a small town. There is no mystery to the source of Mark Fidrych. Everything he would become later had its roots in this setting, which gave him the outlook on life and values that endured over time: the solid foundation of a blue-collar work ethic and the trinity that marked his life of family, friends, and fun. Everything about Mark that would later be celebrated by fans and the press can be traced to a small house on Chesterfield Avenue in a neighborhood called Northgate.

Paul Fidrych was of Polish heritage, one generation removed from immigration from the old country through Ellis Island. As with many children of parents who appreciated the opportunity America presented, Paul knew the value of hard work. It was a value he would later pass to his children by example. Growing up in Worcester, the second largest city in Massachusetts, Paul was big, outgoing, and loved sports, particularly baseball and football. A standout football player in high school, he dreamed of playing the game professionally. One day, while swimming with friends, he misjudged the depth of the water as he jumped from a bridge, resulting in a leg and hip injury that ended his football career. He was still good enough in baseball to play for hometown Worcester College, however.

While in college, Paul met and fell in love with Virginia Madsen, a petite woman who shared his outgoing personality and zest for life. There was one problem, which was not insignificant in those days: he was Catholic and she was Protestant. She didn't want to convert, and he respected her opinion. Virginia signed a document promising to raise her children in the Catholic Church. The signed document made the church happy, and the couple was married in the rectory. Virginia would later keep her word to the church, and although not attending herself, she would adopt certain Catholic customs such as the rosary beads she would nervously destroy on a routine basis while watching her son play baseball.

Upon graduation from college, Paul took a job teaching at a junior high school in Worcester, where the couple lived in a small apartment. Paul and Virginia had a daughter, Paula, in 1952. A son, named Mark Steven Fidrych, was born two years later on August 14, 1954.

Soon after Mark was born, Paul and Virginia moved their family to nearby Northboro, a quiet town of less than ten thousand located about fifty miles west of Boston. Although settlers in the area date back to the mid-1600s, Northboro was still fairly undeveloped and was considered to be out in the country, containing only a single blinking light. Northboro was right on the old Post Road, later called Route 20, which led early settlers from Boston to western Massachusetts. Paul and Virginia bought a house in the new Northgate section of Northboro. Situated on land that only a few years earlier had been a potato farm, Northgate was a new type of development—similar to many developments that had sprung up across the country in the postwar years, modeled after the more famous Levittown in New York—a mass-produced, planned suburb. The same simple, easy-to-build floor plans allowed the neighborhoods to be constructed quickly and at lower cost. They offered workers and veterans a chance to own their own land and house—a place to raise their baby boomers. The houses in Northgate were all the same—called Capes, short for Cape Cods. The Capes were compact two-story houses with wooden shutters and a characteristic steep, perfectly pitched roof that would give the inhabitants a headache if they stood up too quickly away from the exact center of the upstairs room. The houses were close together with small unfenced yards. Paul and Virginia's Cape cost the grand sum of $9,000.

The town of Northboro held a hardworking, generally well-educated, middle-class population. Northgate was a homogeneous community in which no one was really much better off than anyone else. Everyone had everything they needed—maybe not every-thing they wanted, but everything they needed. All the kids in the neighborhood were equal. The homogeneous houses of Northgate held homogeneous families: two-parent families with the father working and the mother tending to the house and kids. Being a new community, almost every house had kids. There were lots of kids. Households with six or eight kids were not uncommon. The fathers made modifications to their Capes to wedge more living space into the attics and cellars for their growing families. North-gate was a tight-knit community in which the young inhabitants would remain close far into their adult years and retain a sense of belonging even after they had moved away. It was the kind of com-munity in which everyone knew everyone else; the type where kids knew they could never get away with anything because someone else's mom would surely see them, and when they did, they would surely call their mom, and there would surely be heck to pay when they got home. People left their doors unlocked and there was little thought of crime. The parents regularly got together for cards or golf or bowling. Northgate was not a place for loners. There was always someone to play with. It was baby boomer paradise; classic postwar American suburbia—a great place to grow up.

The Fidryches' Cape grew crowded as Paula and Mark were followed by Carol, four years after Mark, and finally Lorie, six years after Carol. It soon became apparent that young Mark was an ac-tive child. The world was full of mystery and exciting things, and the happy little guy seemed determined to explore them all. He had a likeable personality—always smiling, always having fun, but he was active. Very active. Years later, his mother would tell reporters about the time he got lost in a department store when he was three and they found him playing in the display window. Then there was the time he poured Comet cleanser all over her maple coffee table and rubbed it in. "He was in the cupboard all the time," she would tell them.

Active little boys receive a rude welcome when they arrive in elementary school and are suddenly thrust into a world dominated by women telling them to sit still and be quiet. Sitting still and being quiet were not exactly Mark's strong points, but he tried. Mark always wanted to please people. He wanted to do well in school and make his parents happy, but for some reason, he just couldn't. Listening to tales of Mark's activity level from family and former teachers, an observer could safely conclude that nowadays Mark would certainly be labeled as having attention deficit disorder. In 1960, there were no labels—only bad-conduct grades in school. Conduct grades became the bane of Mark's existence at Fannie Proctor Elementary School. Good little boys got plusses in conduct. Minuses meant there was a problem. Mark got more than his share of minuses the first few years. "My father was always going, 'What's the minus for?'" Mark would later explain. "And the teachers were saying, 'It's like this, Mr. Fidrych, he likes throwing Chiclets, he likes throwing raisins, he likes talking in class.'"

Mark struggled mightily in school—reading seemed impossible. The letters appeared to be a jumble to his active eyes. Mark repeated first grade. Then he repeated second grade. He sadly watched as his friends moved two grades ahead of him. Already tall for his age, Mark towered over his new classmates, making it impossible not to stand out. "I stopped raising my hand in class," Mark later said. "I wanted to disappear." Paul, the schoolteacher, was determined to help his son and got tutors for him over the summers to work with his reading, but it was something Mark would struggle with for years. The accepted medical definition of dyslexia is a difficulty in reading comprehension in an otherwise normally intelligent child. By this definition, Mark most likely had dyslexia, which is often mistakenly thought to involve reversing letters and words. In the early sixties, schools were not equipped to give special help to children with reading disabilities—the kids were passed on and forced to make do the best they could. And that's what Mark Fidrych did; he did the best he could. "Later in life, you say, 'Maybe it will come eventually,'" Mark said sadly in 2000 while discussing his reading problems. "But it never really did."

Mark's reputation as a behavioral handful grew in the teachers' lounge at Proctor. "Teachers always seemed to know about me even before I got there," Mark said. "Sometimes they would get me in their class and say, 'You're not as bad as I heard.' " But teachers realized that Mark was not mean-spirited, just active. Teachers couldn't help but like Mark because of his irrepressible personality and the fact that he kept them laughing. Things just seemed to happen to Mark. Like the time on the playground when he was bouncing an acorn off the sidewalk. It took an unexpected bounce and landed in the cup of a passing teacher—splashing coffee all over her clothes. Mark was the type of student a teacher would never forget; the type of student a teacher liked, but liked even better the next year when he was in someone else's class.

Fortunately for Mark, there was another world besides school; another world not ruled by people telling you to be quiet and sit still; a world where you could be as active as you wanted—the world outside. A large gang of neighborhood kids Mark's age played together constantly during their childhood and adolescent years. Back then, kids played outside all the time. Computers? Video games? Hadn't been invented yet. Television? Only three channels, and besides, Mom wouldn't let you back in the house during the day and most moms had a rule against TV before dinnertime. Winters were spent sledding down any number of great hills in the neighborhood—the big one behind Proctor Elementary School was a particular favorite—and having snowball fights. Summers were a time of constant play outside; they would leave the house after breakfast and not come home until dinner. They spent a lot of time in the nearby woods, playing army and building forts. There were kickball games in the streets, cops and robbers games on bikes, and hide-and-seek games around half-built houses. There was a standing mom rule in the neighborhood that kids had to be home by the time the streetlights came on, but otherwise, it was free range.

Because of the times and the community in which they lived, Mark and his friends enjoyed a sense of freedom that modern children and parents would be unable to fathom. School was within walking distance. The small downtown commercial area of Northboro and the baseball fields were easy bike rides from the neighborhood. Every kid had a bike and they roamed the area in packs.

Saturdays they would ride to Sawyer's Bowladrome in town and hang out all morning. When it was really hot, there was the community pool, and, years later, Northboro residents would remember the ritual of always checking the coin return slot on the pay phone at the pool (a common practice among all the kids, but one that years later would cause second looks when performed by a major league baseball player). When kids felt mischievous, they might ring door bells and run off.

While enjoying these other pursuits, for the boys, it was mostly sports that dominated their time. They enjoyed whatever particular sport was in season, but baseball was clearly the favorite—everybody played baseball. Nothing else held such a hallowed place in the hearts of kids of that era as baseball. Perhaps the contemporary philosopher Foghorn Leghorn said it best at the time, voicing what most kids felt: "There's something kind of eee-yew about a kid that's never played baseball."

Often the gang would play baseball in the school yard, but when that became too crowded, they built their own field. Mark, about ten at the time, and his friends borrowed tools from their fathers, cleared an empty field near his house, and laid out a diamond. They made base paths, a mound, and even a backstop. The outfield end of the field stopped at a neighbor's fence—the perfect distance for a home run (although sometimes the lady beyond the fence refused to give the home run balls back). "It was a neighborhood project for kids," says Jim Jablonski, Mark's next-door neighbor on Chesterfield Avenue. "We would work on the field half the day and play baseball the other half."

The field backed up to the house of Ray Dumas. Ray's kids, Ray and Kevin were part of Mark's group. Mr. Dumas was a lifetime baseball lover. He had played semipro ball when younger and still played a mean game of softball. Dumas helped the kids construct the backstop on their field. He was also an umpire who worked area games, Little League through Legion, for over thirty-five years. He had a front-row view of young Mark's progress on the baseball field over the years. "He was always a happy kid," says Dumas. "He was always into something. A very good ballplayer even when he was little, he always had a strong arm. The kids would play baseball out there in the field every day in the summers. If there weren't enough kids to have a real game, they would play hot box or some other type of baseball game." Perhaps surprising to modern parents, their games raged gloriously without interference from adults—the kids policed their own games and made their own rules.

Paul Fidrych was also a baseball lover. He was determined to give his son every chance he never had. Paul spent hours with young Mark, teaching him the finer points of the game in endless backyard sessions—catching him, hitting him grounders, encouraging the active child to stay focused while playing baseball. "His dad was always out in the yard with him," says Jablonski. "Not just playing catch, but Mark pitching to him. That's where he developed his control. There wasn't a fence, and if Mark threw a pitch his dad couldn't catch, he had to go get it. So that was a good incentive to have good control." Unlike the classroom, Mark could still move and be hyperactive on the baseball field as long as he could focus on the task at hand. There was no one on the baseball field telling him to be still and be quiet. Mark fell in love with sports, particularly baseball.

Paul Fidrych was always there, a partner in Mark's baseball development. He coached many of Mark's teams in Little League and Babe Ruth League. "He knew a lot about baseball; he was a good coach. Very competitive but a nice guy," says Kevin Dumas.

"He was a tough guy as a coach, a disciplinarian, demanding but not overly so," says Dan Coakley, another member of their group. "He expected a lot, communicated well. Not afraid to tell you the way it was. He was also a nice guy. I respected Paul Fidrych."

While they were living in the middle of Red Sox Nation, Mark, unlike his father and neighbors, was not particularly a rabid fan of the Red Sox. Actually Mark wasn't really a fan of professional baseball at all. Because reading was such hard work, he didn't spend his time reading *Sports Illustrated* and the *Sporting News* like his father. He was too active to sit still and watch a game on television.

He was too busy playing himself to be bothered with others playing the game elsewhere. Even in his teens, the only Red Sox players Mark knew about were Carl Yastrzemski (you couldn't live in Massachusetts and not know about Yaz) and George Scott (because he heard he drove a cool car). Playing baseball was the thing; not reading about it or watching it—playing it was where the true fun was for Mark.

In the sixties, baseball was the only sport deemed important enough by adults in the area to have organized leagues for kids. Northboro had a great Little League program with well-maintained fields and lots of parental support. The Opening Day festivities and parade down Main Street were a highlight for the whole town each year. Absolutely nothing in the world was more grown-up looking, more cool, more of a sign of being an unqualified success in the world than the thick wool Little League uniform with the team name in script across the chest, the baggy pants, and the crumpled hat—especially when it was being worn by your big brother. Every kid in town looked forward to the day when he was old enough to play Little League baseball. The Northboro Little League was a community endeavor. Adults without any kids playing often watched the games or even coached. Kids showed up when they weren't playing—to watch their buddies play and to see everyone else. There were no travel teams in those days to siphon off the best talent—everyone played in town. The games were unapologetically competitive. At the end of the year, the best players were picked to compete on the All-Star teams—the pride of Northboro taking on the best of neighboring towns.

Kids soon learned, without being told, who the best players in the league were. Everyone knew who was leading the league in home runs. They knew which pitchers they hoped to avoid and which ones they hoped they would face. Paul Fidrych's boy had the reputation as the former. He was a hard thrower. "I played on the same team with Mark in the Minor League as a nine- and ten-year-old," says Mark's friend Paul Beals. "We won the championship one year. Mark pitched or played shortstop. He was a good athlete. When he pitched, it was an easy day for me at first base.

Usually in a six-inning game, of the eighteen outs, probably thirteen or fourteen would be strikeouts. He was good. Does anybody really think they'll make the pros at that time? That is something that happens to other people. But Mark was good."

"But he wasn't really identified as that much better than everyone else at a young age," says Jim Jablonski. "He was an All-Star, but there were a lot of really good baseball players in that neighborhood. That's all we did most of the time, and there were a lot of guys who were good."

"I joked with him that he needed to work on his home run trot," continues Jablonski. "Once he hit a grand slam, and he jumped up and down more than he ran around the bases."

"Not too many people got hits off Mark," says his catcher, David Miles. "He didn't have great control then—does anybody at nine? He'd either strike everybody out or walk them or hit them. He was pretty high-strung. I don't remember him talking to the ball, but he had similar mannerisms."

Ah yes, the mannerisms. The antics. They were there all right. Mark's hyperactivity manifested itself on the mound at the earliest age. Even as a nine-year-old, Mark's mound behavior was full of movement. Tall for his age and gangly, he was a peculiar sight on the mound. "He was always moving," says Beals. "Maybe it was nervous energy, but he was just a fidgety guy." Smoothing the mound with his hands, talking (whether to himself or the ball)—it was all there as a kid. But the other kids didn't make a big deal about it. That was just Mark being Mark. Besides, when someone is striking out most of the other team, he can do about anything he wants before throwing the ball. The little boy who could not sit still in class was remarkably focused on the baseball field. It was almost as if he realized at that young age that by doing the same things, incorporating them into a routine, and constantly reminding himself of what needed to be done (by talking to himself), he could keep himself zeroed in; a response to the encouragement of his father who, well aware of his son's activity level, continually urged him on with the mantra, "Focus, Mark."

Mr. Dumas, who was a good friend of Paul Fidrych, recalls

that it was Paul who taught Mark to smooth the mound. "His father always told him to be comfortable on the mound; he'd tell him, 'Make sure the mound is just right.' He didn't want him stepping in the other pitcher's hole. He'd say, 'Make your own hole.'"

The Fidrych house held a close family with lots of laughter, parents who were involved with their children, and an endless assortment of animals, birds, and domestic rodents. Mark's favorite pet was a dalmatian named Domino. The three sisters remember watching Saturday morning cartoons while sitting on the couch with their brother and Sunday family dinners—one o'clock sharp, no excuse for missing it. There were a lot of family traditions such as the annual Easter egg battle. Each person hard-boiled an egg and colored it. Then they tapped the other person's egg on the end. The last egg to crack was the winner. The sisters warmly recall fishing trips and family vacations; four kids packed into a station wagon driving to places like Niagra Falls.

Youngest sister Lorie learned at an early age to keep a wary eye as she moved through the house—an attack of noogies could come from her big brother at any time. "But I always managed to get him back," she says. "I would spray him down with perfume when he was getting ready for a date or pour chocolate syrup on him when he was in the shower.

"What you saw out on the mound in the majors—that was just him," continues Lorie. "If you ever came over for dinner—it was talk, talk, talk, constant energy and movement. That's how he was."

Mark was close to his parents and would remain so through adulthood. While during the sixties it was not uncommon for fathers and sons to have great conflicts as their opinions and outlooks on the world grew in divergent directions, there was apparently little of that in the Fidrych household. Paul had a profound effect on his growing son. "Mark and Dad were always in the backyard playing," says Paula. "My dad was the one who saw the potential in Mark. Mark was a good guy, but academically he was not a scholar. My dad said, 'That's okay, because you have a gift for baseball.'"

Paul was also an excellent candlepin bowler and passed on that skill to Mark, who won a regional television bowling competition in his early teens.

While Mark shared sports and work with his father, he had a different kind of closeness with his mother. Virginia was short, thin, very outgoing, and hyper like her son. She was frequently exasperated by Mark's actions but could not stay mad at him. "She felt 'Marky' couldn't do anything wrong," says Paula. "I think he was probably the favorite. He was the only boy in the family. She would always fix him special dishes and cakes. Mark always sent her roses on her birthday when he got older."

It is important in understanding his personality to know that Mark's parents filled him with old-school values and a strong work ethic but did not discourage him from expressing his individuality. And Mark Fidrych possessed a plethora of individuality just waiting to be expressed.

But things just seemed to happen to Mark. Once, on a vacation, he was teasing his sister by pretending to throw her shoes— brand-new Stride Rites—out the back window. One shoe slipped and he accidently threw it out. The terrified kids waited about ten miles before mustering up the courage to tell the parents what had happened. It was chalked up to the growing legend of Mark.

"We did give our parents some headaches," says Paula. "It was innocent fun." Like the time Paula and Mark asked their parents if they could convert their bedroom into a haunted house for Halloween. "They said, 'Sure,'" says Paula. "We were going to charge our friends twenty-five cents to go through it. Mark put a butcher knife in the headboard of the bed, and we poured ketchup all over the white sheets. When we brought our parents up, I thought they were going to die.

"Things just always seemed to happen to Mark," adds Paula.

There was the time when Mark was five and he and Paula were rushing down the stairs to the basement. "Mark said, 'I can fly,'" remembers Paula. "I said, 'You can't fly.' But he wouldn't believe me. So I pushed him." Unfortunately, Mark found out that his big sister was right, he couldn't fly. He fell down and broke his leg.

Then there was the time a little later when some friends came to the door as the family was eating. Mark was so excited to go play that he forgot to put down his fork before he bolted through the door. He tripped on the step, fell down, and the fork punctured the skin under his eye. "The sharp end of the fork actually curved under his eyeball," explains Paula. "My mother went out there, and when he turned around the fork looked like it was sticking out of his eye. You could hear her screaming all over the neighborhood."

Once when Paul had a large fire of burning trash at a construction site, Mark was having fun rolling down a nearby hill. He misjudged the landing and rolled through the fire, burning his face. "We were always going to the hospital," laughs Carol. "Our childhood was full of scratches and bandages, mostly on Mark."

While most of the scratches and bandages were on Mark, family and friends received their share of scrapes and scares in Mark's adventures. Once while at the lake fishing, Mark got bored and decided to wait in the family Oldsmobile. The car mysteriously slipped out of gear. It rolled down the hill into the lake with Paul chasing after it. Fortunately, the car came to a stop in the shallow water.

Then, there was the time in their early teens when friend Dan Coakley was teaching Mark to play golf in Dan's backyard. "I've got a seven-stitch scar in my head from that golf lesson," laughs Dan. "I showed him how to swing a few times, then he goes, 'Okay, I got it, I got it.' Then he swung the club and hit me in the head. I was bleeding all over the place. Mark was really upset. He ran into my house yelling, 'Mrs. Coakley, I've killed Dan.'"

When Mark was a little older he bought a minibike. He proudly put his mother on and showed her how to start it. Unfortunately, she gunned it and took off before he had a chance to tell her other details—like how to stop. Mark chased his terrified mother as she zigzagged, screaming, all over the yard and across the street, finally catching her up against a neighbor's garage. Good times. Good times.

Paula will never forget her first car. "It was an old Volkswagen," she says. "I got it for five hundred dollars when I was eighteen (1970). Mark had just got his license, and he begged and begged for me to let him take the car out with his friends. I knew better, but I finally said, 'Okay.' When he came back, the whole side of the car was damaged. I asked him what happened, and he said, 'Well, we were driving it on the ice and I think I took the corner too fast.' They had been out sliding on the ice for fun. My dad told him he had to fix it up. Mark felt real bad about it. He said, 'I'll fix it up for you so good you won't even recognize it, I promise.' Well, he was right. When Mark and his friends brought it back, I didn't recognize it. They had taken out the backseat and put in an American flag backseat. They had changed the horn so that when you pushed the button it went *aaoooooga*. They gave me a go-kart steering wheel and painted the fenders different colors. We still laughed over that car whenever we would get together thirty years later."

There was rarely any sitting around in the Fidrych household. When not playing sports or going to the hospital, Mark had work to do. He learned the old-fashioned New England respect for money and frugality from his father: if you want something, earn it; don't expect something for nothing and don't waste your money once you get it. Paul Fidrych worked a second job pouring concrete and often took Mark with him. There were also trips to the junkyard for scrap metal to earn extra money. Mark worked regularly growing up. First, there was a paper route; waking up early and strapping on the canvas bag full of papers, then riding his bike through the neighborhood and showing off his arm. The hardest part of that job was collection day—knocking on doors to get the payment and recording it in the little spiral notebook, dealing with the same deadbeats each time who always seemed to be out of money on collection days and had to be hounded. Mark later bagged groceries to supplement his income. In the summers, there was money to be made caddying at the Juniper Hills Golf Course, which was a short bike ride from the Fidrych house.

When Mark was fourteen, his father helped him get a job at the gas station of a friend. Mark had always enjoyed tinkering with engines—lawnmowers, cars, motorcycles—anything with a motor. He loved working at the garage. He saved up the money from this first real job and bought his own motorcycle. A few years later, he went to work at Pierce Oil and Gas in the middle of Northboro because the bearded midtwenties Dave Pierce offered to pay him $2.25 an hour and didn't care whether or not he got his hair cut. Dave Pierce became a mentor of sorts to Mark, teaching him how to fix motorcycles and work on engines. Mark threw as much energy into his work at the gas station as he did on the baseball field. "Mark was one of the hardest-working people I ever met in my life," says high school friend Brad Ostiguy. "When he worked at the gas station, he would sprint out to your car, clean all the windows, check the oil—he was just full of energy and full of life in everything he did."

It was this idyllic childhood that set the foundation for Mark Fidrych: a combination of Norman Rockwell and *Leave It to Beaver*, with a dash of Huck Finn tossed in; the good part of Huck Finn—the good-natured, adventurous, inquisitive kid much more comfortable with the freedom of the great outdoors than in the classroom. No matter where life would take Mark in the future, Northboro would always be home, and he would always plan to return.

Mark was a good athlete in all sports as he got older. Taller than most kids, he was wiry and gangly, but surprisingly coordinated. He played on a town youth football team in seventh and eighth grade called the Northboro Steelers. The Steelers were undefeated in his second season. Mark was a receiver and defensive end and showed the traits that were becoming characteristic of him—enthusiasm and emotion. Friends and teammates recall that he played all out until the whistle blew. In his last game Mark caught a touchdown pass—his first one. Few witnesses remember the score of the game, but everyone remembers the emotion Mark showed as he broke into tears after the catch.

By the time Mark reached Babe Ruth League as a thirteen-year-old, he was an accomplished pitcher and definitely one of the best in the area. Fred LeClaire was the All-Star coach for the Northboro Babe Ruth League. "Mark was great in Babe Ruth League," he recalls. "No one could touch him. He was overpowering. He was a good, coachable kid too. Paid attention when you would teach him stuff. But he didn't really need much teaching by then. His dad had taught him everything he needed. He was very close to his dad. Mark was always laughing and liked to have fun, but he was respectful of his elders. I remember one game in the All-Star tournament, we were playing a good team and needed to win. Mark walked the first three batters. The only problem he ever had was that he was so good, sometimes he would drift off. I went out there and reminded him how important the game was. So then he struck out the next three batters. He just blew them away."

Mark Fidrych grew up during an era of great social change, but the kids in his circle of friends didn't seem too concerned with the outside world. The one concession to the changing attitudes involved their hair. Mark wore his in a crew cut throughout the midsixties; however, in junior high he began to let his hair grow out as was becoming the fashion. As he did, a funny thing happened. "It came in curly," says Paula. "He had this huge head of the most gorgeous curls I'd ever seen. I was so jealous. I wanted to go to the hairdresser and get mine curled like that. He would just run his hand through it—that's all he needed to do to comb it." Paula didn't know it at the time, but in a few years, those gorgeous curls would become part of the most famous head of hair in the country.

Mark showed up at Algonquin Regional High School in the fall of 1970. Talk to anyone who knew Mark Fidrych in high school and the phrase "never a dull moment" appears, as if by magic, within thirty seconds. In the classroom he was still very active. He drove a few teachers nuts, but he was nice about it. "He was so friendly and had such a fun-loving personality you just had to like him," says Robert Boberg, his ninth-grade English teacher. "But you were constantly saying, 'Mark, will you PLEASE sit down.'"

"Mark was in my tenth-grade biology class," recalls science teacher and baseball coach Jack Wallace. "He was active in class, but he would work at it. He was pretty cooperative. And he was a good kid. Once Mark was scrambling down the hall and the chemistry teacher happened to step out into the hall at the wrong time. Mark just flattened her. It was an accident. He was very apologetic. She was okay, but he helped her up and kept apologizing until the next class took place. He was very sincere about it. We talked about it later and, being a teacher first, I was impressed that he apologized and helped her. It kind of defined his character. Most of the teachers liked him. He was active, but was polite to adults."

Most kids at Algonquin knew Mark Fidrych—tall, lanky, all arms and legs, with a big personality—he stood out. If you had to put him in a group, it would have been the jocks, but he was friendly with everyone. There was no hint of a pampered arrogant athlete. "Back then, Mark was exactly the same as you later saw with the Tigers," says high school friend and baseball teammate Jeff Henningson. "Always a character. Lots of energy. It wasn't an act, it was just Mark."

Mark was known for being a little wild, a little eccentric, definitely extroverted, and a fun-loving guy. He was also known as a guy who would befriend anyone, regardless of social status. He would not only talk to new kids in school, but would show them around and maybe give them a ride home. He is remembered by freshman baseball players for being nice to them and making them feel like a part of the team when he was an upperclassman. "Mark had absolutely no prejudices," says Paula. "He would talk to and make friends with anyone."

Diane Bonnell will never forget her first day at Algonquin. Rushing into a class wearing the short skirt and sandals of the time, she tripped and slid into the front of the room. She was saved from embarrassment when a tall curly-haired kid in the front row jumped up, spread his arms wide with his palms facing the ground, and yelled, "Safe!"

"I remember once in school, I was sick and missed a few days," says Dan Coakley. "Mark came over and hung around with me. It was the kind of thing that was unusual for someone that age to think about doing for a friend. But that's the way he was. He always thought about other people."

Mark was immediately recognized as a very good athlete in

all sports in high school. Back then, before the era of year-round specialization, the best athletes played two or three sports in school. "He was a very good basketball player," says Brad Ostiguy, who played both baseball and basketball with Mark. "He would never give up. He would just keeping fighting and fighting for rebounds. The basketball coach, Phil Phillips, and the baseball coach, Jack Wallace, were both very tough and demanding. You either accepted that and played harder, or you couldn't take it. Mark was an extremely hardworking guy. He didn't have any trouble with the coaches. He kept us laughing, but not around Coach Wallace."

Confident in his abilities, Mark also allowed himself to dream. "He always said from the time I met him when we were fourteen that he was going to pitch in the major leagues," says Ostiguy.

"I can remember when we were sophomores, Mark saying, 'Someday I'm going to be a bonus baby,'" says Coakley. "We laughed at him. But his father knew he had talent. He was well taught. Mark was very good, but never the kind of athlete who had the golden spoon. He worked hard."

As with most similarly sized towns, activities for high-school-aged kids included hanging out, driving around, and goofing off—mostly hanging out. In Northboro, the favorite place to hang out was a field down a long dirt road back in the woods. It was called by everyone, imaginatively enough, "The Field." At The Field, kids gathered around bonfires, sat on the hoods of their cars, cranked up the stereos in their cars, and let the good times roll—a pre-Internet style of social networking.

While Mark distinguished himself as one of the best high school pitchers in the area as a sophomore at Algonquin, American Legion ball is where he really built a reputation. The high school baseball seasons in Massachusetts were fairly short—it's hard to play baseball when snow is on the ground. Most of the best baseball was played in American Legion. Back then, every town had a man like Ted Rolfe. He worked for the state employment agency, but he lived for baseball. Rolfe had played semipro baseball in the area years earlier after graduating from Boston University, and then he had turned to coaching kids. A thin guy, kind of hyper, always chewing gum, always talking, he had a passion for the game and passed it on to his players. A good teacher who enjoyed interacting with his players, he had fun practices, but he got his point across and stressed fundamentals. He was a fiery competitor and could be combative to umpires guilty of being nearsighted. Rolfe was in his midforties when Mark played for him, in the midst of a three-decade career of managing American Legion programs in Northboro and nearby Marlboro.

The Legion team in Northboro drew kids from surrounding towns. Only the best local players got to be on the team. In fact, some years there were only one or two guys from Northboro. Mark made the Legion team the first year he tried out as a fifteen-year-old, but, as one of the youngest players on the team, he was a seldom-used shortstop. According to legend, the first time Rolfe saw Mark pitch the next year, he asked him, "Why didn't you tell me you were a pitcher?"

"You didn't ask," was the reply.

The next two years, Mark was the ace of the pitching staff. "Mark was very unique—there was nobody like him," says Legion teammate David Veinot, who also faced him during the school year while playing for Marlboro. "He was very competitive. He was a good guy to have on your team, but no one wanted to bat off him when he pitched batting practice. He was definitely a standout in the league."

The first game Mark pitched in Legion ball, on June 19, 1972, against Fitchburg, he threw a no-hitter while walking only two and striking out fourteen. "He was a real good pitcher then, right from the start," Rolfe said in 1976. "Unlike that first game, he was never the super strikeout pitcher, though he was very fast. But he always had the game under control. He did all the things he does now to concentrate. He'd go through a whole season of talking to the ball, but we didn't think anything of it. He was a free spirit. He did what he wanted, but he never caused any trouble." Mark was also noted at the time for his zeal in rushing to congratulate team-mates after good plays, even if they were in the outfield.

Mark didn't give up an earned run in the 1972 Legion season until July 4. The nearby *Enterprise-Sun* of Marlboro noted that year that "Coach Ted Rolfe's Northborough Legion baseball team has a lot to offer, but if you like to watch good pitching, Mark Fidrych is the name to watch for on these sunny days."

During the school year, Mark was the ace of the Algonquin staff. Jack Wallace was the baseball coach at the time. A young, dedicated teacher and coach, he first met Mark as the assistant football coach Mark's freshman year and got on him about too much socializing with players on the other football teams before and after games. On the baseball field, Jack Wallace ran a tight ship. He tolerated no goofing off and had no qualms about getting in someone's face to make a point. "Those were tough years to be a coach because there was a lot of stuff going on," says Wallace. "Attitudes were changing, a lot of kids were rebelling. You worried about discipline. And Massachusetts' eighteen-year-old drinking age at the time certainly didn't help any.

"Mark was a little different," Wallace continues. "Before I got to know him, just seeing him around school, I worried about how he would respond to the structure of a team and rules. But he never caused any problems. He was a great guy to have on a team. Back then, the kids from Northgate were really tough, competitive kids. If you got three or four of them on your team, you knew you were going to have a good team."

As with every authority figure of the time, hair was constantly an issue with Mr. Wallace. Mark's long curly coif was no exception. "Of course, everybody had a little trouble over their hair in those days, and Mark's was a little longer than most guys' hair," says Ostiguy, "but he always cut it just enough to keep the coaches happy."

After the first game of the 1973 high school season, the *Enterprise-Sun* reported, "Mark Fidrych, a junior righthander, showed why he is rated one of the best pitchers in the area Friday as he struck out 13 for the Algonquin High School Tomahawks in their 7–2 opening season encounter against Wayland." In his second game, Mark struck out seventeen in a 4–0 win over Westboro. It would take more than fifty-three innings for Mark to give up an earned run that season, but Algonquin struggled hitting, and Mark compiled a 4–3 record despite an ERA of .029—just two earned runs in sixty-two innings. One of the losses was by one run in a game in which his third baseman made three errors in one inning. In another loss he struck out twelve and gave up only one hit but was hurt by seven errors. Mark developed arm trouble the last part of the year that was severe enough to keep him from pitching in the high school postseason tournament.

Fortunately, Mark's arm healed quickly once the Legion schedule began that summer. "Any lingering doubts that the fans may have had about the tall right-hander's complete recovery from arm trouble were soundly crushed Saturday afternoon," the *Enterprise-Sun* announced July 9. "Fidrych was overpowering as he led Northboro to a revenge 2–0 win over Westboro." A week later Mark told a reporter that he thought trying to throw curveballs caused all his arm trouble and that he had stopped throwing them. "I throw the knuckler about twenty times a game, otherwise I stick with my fastball," he said.

One of the most memorable games of Mark's Legion career came in a matchup against Grafton Hill's Stan Saleski. Saleski, who went on to play minor league baseball and later became a scout for the Yankees, pitched twelve innings of no-hit ball. In the game that was still being talked about thirty years later, Mark matched him with twelve no-hit innings of his own. Saleski walked in the ninth inning, advanced on errors, but then was thrown out at the plate. Northboro scratched across a run to make Mark the winner in the thirteenth inning. "There were some games in Legion where Mark was just dominant," says Veinot. "He had a lot of good games."

It was during Legion ball that Mark first received an avian nickname. That's right, . . . the Mad Stork. "Once when Mark was pitching, there was an argument at the plate," recalls Veinot. "Mark didn't start it, but he came storming off the mound, all arms and legs everywhere. We called him the Mad Stork after that." The Mad Stork nickname only lasted the rest of that season and never seemed to catch on as well as another bird-inspired one would a few years later.

After Mark's junior year at Algonquin, he faced a critical decision regarding his last year of high school. Because he had repeated the two years in elementary school, he was now nineteen years old and would be ineligible to play in the Massachusetts High School Athletic Association public school league. Paul Fidrych felt it was worth the risk of going to a private school for his senior year. There he would be able to compete in sports against a higher level of competition and hopefully attract the attention of a scout or receive an offer of a college scholarship.

Fortunately, there was just the place they needed in nearby Worcester. With its impressive nineteenth-century architecture and beautiful tree-lined campus, Worcester Academy had a long and distinguished history. First opened in 1834, and boasting eight different former Harvard football captains among its alumni, the academy was proud of both its academics and athletics as it viewed sports to be an essential part of a good education. It was a partial residential-commuter school; some students lived on campus in dorms, but most, like Mark, drove from home every day. Many of the top athletes were postgrad students, working on their grades and games in preparation for college. Almost every student there planned on going to college. It was an all-male school when Mark arrived in the fall of 1973—females would not be allowed until 1975. Students were required to wear coats and ties to classes, but Mark, like a lot of other students, wore the same tie every day, no matter how filthy it became—a sort of early seventies show of disdain for the rules; a silent way of getting back at The Man.

Tom Blackburn coached both baseball and basketball and was the athletic director at Worcester Academy. He had played basketball (1955) and baseball (1956) on Duke teams that made the NCAA tournament. An excellent pitcher, he had thrown a no-hitter for Duke; however, an arm injury ended his professional aspirations and he returned to Massachusetts to teach and coach.

Blackburn had a good baseball mind and was especially a good coach for pitchers. He was very old-school, a stern disciplinarian; tough but fair. A master of The Look, he had steely eyes that would stop a wayward player in his tracks—he didn't need to yell.

Mark played both basketball and baseball at Worcester. In basketball, he was the sixth man, a hustler who made an immediate impact on the game when he entered. "He was good in that role," says Blackburn. "The game seemed to speed up when he came in. He was a real good basketball player."

But baseball was Mark's main focus. The arm trouble of the previous year was completely behind him and was never a factor at Worcester. Blackburn had watched Mark pitch in Legion ball and knew what he was getting. "He always had great control," says Blackburn. "He could throw it knee-high nine out of ten times right where he wanted it."

Mark stood out among his teammates, both with his personality and work ethic. "He was the hardest-working guy I ever saw," says Tom Zocco, a fellow baseball player at Worcester Academy. "We ran a lot together. I was a wrestler so I had to. We ran a lot of sprints. Mark liked to run as part of his training for baseball—most people didn't do that back then. Some of the other people looked at us like we were crazy, but he trained hard."

The early worries over grades were largely a thing of the past as Mark seemed to accept the fact that he was not going to be a scholar. "His main focus was to be a major league pitcher," says Blackburn. "You could tell by his actions and work ethic that he wanted to be a good player. He was strictly focusing on it then. That was unusual for that age. He was a different kind of player. He had a whole different style to him. But he was so humble about it that it attracted a lot of people to him. People wanted to see him succeed."

"Mark kept us laughing," says Zocco. "He was always joking, telling funny stories, pulling pranks. Sometimes Blackburn didn't like the laughing, but I think he probably let Mark get away with a little more because he knew what a competitor he was. Mark hated to lose."

Worcester played a tough schedule—a mix of other similar academies and small colleges as well as junior varsity teams from major universities such as the University of Massachusetts, Dartmouth, and Brown. Mark was the mainstay of the pitching staff—usually saved for the best teams. He actually had a losing record on the mound that year, but was hardly to blame, sometimes suffering from a lack of help or just the tough competition. One game, he threw a three-hitter against Dartmouth's JV team, giving up only three infield hits—no one hit a ball out of the infield—but lost.

"Mark was very supportive of his teammates even when they didn't play well," says Zocco. "And he was very genuine about that. He might yell at you in a competitive manner, but he was always supportive. You couldn't get mad at him. Even today, after fifty years, I've met a lot of people, but he's probably the most genuine person I've ever met—he was that way in school."

"Every pitch meant something to him," says Blackburn. "He was a competitor. When he was on the mound, he was total concentration. He was talking to himself all the time—that's how he kept himself in the game. He also did the thing with the mound. The first thing he would do was put down his glove and move the dirt around and pat it to get it where he wanted it. And he never let up in a game. Once he was pitching against Brown and we were winning by five or six runs in the later part of the game and a runner got to third base. The run wasn't really critical, but Mark worked and struck the batter out. He ran off the mound—he always ran on and off the field—and sat down next to me and said out loud, 'No way he was going to score.' Every run meant something to him."

Throughout Mark's high school years Paul Fidrych was always there. By all accounts, Paul was supportive, encouraging, and thoroughly involved with Mark's high school baseball career. He never missed a game. According to Paula and Carol, he made note of everything Mark did and discussed it with him after the game, even though Mark may not have felt like discussing it at the time, but he didn't seem to cross the line and take away the fun of the game. Unlike the parents of some star players, Paul never interfered with the coaches—he was content to watch and let the coaches do their job.

Mark had originally hoped to catch the attention of a college coach while at Worcester Academy, and he was disappointed that no college coach felt he was worthy of an offer. His scores on the SAT were not very good, and he had trouble getting accepted to

any college. Mark found one himself, a two-year engineering program at Highlands University in New Mexico. But Paul Fidrych
was not too keen on Highlands University. Late in the year, Blackburn spoke on Mark's behalf to an acquaintance who coached
baseball at Old Dominion in Virginia. He agreed to take Mark, but
not on scholarship.

As far as professional baseball, there was little reason to be
hopeful. The nearby Red Sox did not seem impressed with Mark.
The Red Sox scout for the area talked to him a few times, but didn't
show any real interest. "But there were quite a few scouts around.
They knew about him," says Blackburn, even if he didn't know
about them.

Unaware of the interest of any scouts, Mark figured his baseball career was over when the Worcester season concluded. He
continued his job at the gas station and also worked for a construction company, making three bucks an hour. He happily threw
himself into this work that appeared to be his destiny.

The Detroit Tigers hadn't really been in the picture at all.
Mark often later said the Tiger scout only saw him throw one pitch.
He had been playing in the outfield in the game the Tiger scout
saw and was called in to get out of the inning—which he did with
one pitch. It must have been one very good pitch to have impressed
the scout that much. In reality, Joe Cusick, the Tigers' New England scout, had talked to others who liked Mark's pitching ability,
and, unknown to Mark or Paul, he had been following Mark as
early as his sophomore year at Algonquin—sending back glowing
reports to the front office in Detroit. Cusick was impressed with
Mark's competitiveness and his body development. On one official
scouting report Cusick wrote, "This boy can play" and suggested,
"Draft for high class A." Cusick ranked Mark seventh among all
the prospects he scouted in his area. When it came time for the
1974 draft the Tigers selected Mark in the tenth round, the 232nd
player chosen.

Since there was no expectation of being selected, Mark didn't
pay any attention to the baseball draft and didn't even know when
it took place. He initially didn't know what to think when a friend

roared up to the gas station with the news that Mark had been drafted. In 1974, in the era of Vietnam, being told you were drafted was not exactly a good thing. But this was the baseball draft, his friend explained. Then Mark's father drove up in his car and repeated the news. "Hey, tell them you're not working here anymore," his father told him. Mark decided to work the rest of the day, still not sure about this draft business. "The whole family was just shocked when he got drafted," Carol later said.

Cusick called that night and arranged to meet the Fidryches at their house the next day. Negotiations did not take long—about long enough for Cusick to get a foot inside the door. "I met him at the door with the pen in my hand," Mark later said, actions that would have mortified a modern agent. Mark signed for a bonus of $3,000. He then packed his bags and set off for Lakeland, Florida, to meet up with the Tigers rookie league team. Paul Fidrych's son was now a professional baseball player.

2

Bristol

The Bristol Tigers were playing an early season game when Mark Fidrych took the field for his first professional appearance. The kid had looked good throwing from the practice mound, but you never know how a young player is going to do until he is actually in a game. Sometimes there are surprises. From the bench, Joe Lewis, the Tigers' hard-boiled, old-school manager, looked out at the mound and then growled, "What the hell is he doing out there?"

Jeff Hogan, Lewis' new twenty-six-year-old assistant, answered cautiously, "Well, he's patting down the mound . . . wait . . . yeah, that's what he's doing."

"Grod," Joe yelled to John Grodzicki, the roving pitching instructor, seeking a second opinion, "what the hell is he doing out there?"

"He's patting down the mound Joe," the seasoned pitching coach answered rapidly and with assurance.

The young pitcher began to circle the mound quickly, all the while moving his lips, visibly talking. "Christ, Hogan," Joe yelled, "what the hell is he doing now?"

"I think he's talking to the ball . . . uh, Joe . . . yeah, that's what he's doing," Hogan said.

"Jesus Christ, Hogan, we got another one," Joe grumbled.

Mark Fidrych had joined the other members of the Tigers' Bristol Rookie League team in Lakeland, Florida, in June of 1974 for a week of training before heading north to start the season. Bristol was a short-season Class A team—the bottom rung of the ladder. Hoot Evers, director of the Tiger farm system, was in Lakeland to look over the prospects, along with pitching instructor John Grodzicki, Bristol manager Joe Lewis, and his assistant Jeff Hogan. They all knew about several of the rookies and were eager to see them in action; high draft picks such as athletic shortstop Stephen Viefhaus and third baseman Lance Parrish. The muscular Parrish, who would soon be moved to catcher, had been the Tigers' number one pick in the draft. A great football player, Parrish had been headed to UCLA as a quarterback before the Tigers paid him a large bonus to stick with baseball. No one was eager to see Mark Fidrych in Lakeland. It had not taken a large bonus to persuade Mark Fidrych to forego college.

"No one in the organization had a clue about how good Mark was coming in," says Hogan. "Back then, scouting wasn't what it is today. Mark was a low-round pick. Detroit really didn't have any idea what they were getting."

Mark made an impression the first day. His constant energy and noise were impossible to miss. And he wasn't sure exactly which position he was there to play—he wanted to play them all. "After the pitchers had thrown a little, Mark came up and said, 'Coach, I want to go work out with the outfielders because I'm really a good hitter. I've always played outfield when I'm not pitching,'" Hogan recalls. "And Joe said, 'Mark, you were signed as a pitcher. You're in professional ball now. You're only a pitcher.' And Mark looks over and goes, 'I know, but I can hit better than those guys.' And we had some really good hitters that year. A few of them had good major league careers. We had to convince him that he was only there to be a pitcher."

Later, the pitchers broke up for pitching fielding practice, in which the pitcher throws, the coach hits a grounder to the right side, and the pitcher covers first base. "I looked and there were arms and legs going everywhere," says Hogan. "The curly hair was shooting out from under his hat, he was running like crazy, flapping his arms, squawking, and I looked at him and said, 'He looks like Big Bird.' Then I said, 'He's The Bird.' And he was called The Bird from that moment on."

"Besides, *Fidrych* is too hard to say," Hogan told Mark.

All baseball players have nicknames. It's kind of a male-bonding thing—and it certainly makes it easier to deal with long, hard-to-pronounce last names. While the majority of nicknames are derived from a highly scientific process (step one: take the first syllable of the last name; step two: add "ie"), sometimes circumstances or fate dictate more memorable nicknames. The other players quickly picked up on The Bird. "Everybody called him Bird after that," says pitcher Bob Sykes. "It made sense. He looked like Big Bird, and, of course, the way he acted, it fit him perfectly." Mark would be known as Bird throughout the minors, but it was just a name; no one would make a big deal over it until he hit the majors.

Mark was different in other ways also. While most of the players had good spikes and equipment, Mark had an old pair of white cleats and a beat-up Spalding glove that he called his Spag special. When informed that he couldn't wear white cleats in the Tigers organization, Mark was at a loss as to how to pay for new ones. Sometimes, things have a way of working out. As Mark later said, using his unique glass-is-half-full philosophy, "I lucked out. The week we were there, some little kids broke into the locker room. They stole the equipment! They stole my glove and spikes! So I got new ones—I lucked out."

"Also, he called everybody coach," says Hogan. "In pro ball, you call people by their first name, but he kept calling us coach. Joe would say, 'Mark, it's Joe, not coach. You're not in school anymore.' But we were always 'coach' the whole year to Mark."

The Bristol Tigers were a collection of eighteen- to twenty-one-year-olds right out of high school or college. They were members of the Appalachian League—a rookie league tucked into the mountains of West Virginia, Virginia and eastern Tennessee. Thirty-four players took the field for Bristol at one time or another in 1974. Mark, like the other players in the league, was unaware of the statistics of the time that showed that, of all baseball players signed to contracts, only 2.8 percent ever made it to play in a single major league game. He only knew that there were a lot of players on the team and a lot at every level above—good-looking players who had all been stars in their hometowns. Even though they were teammates, there was an unspoken competition among the players as they were all hoping to work their way up to the pinnacle of the organization. A look at the rosters from that year reveals that most teams in the league had only one or two players who eventually made it to the majors. Future Brave star Dale Murphy of Kingsport, Terry Puhl of the Covington Astros, and Butch Wynegar of the Elizabethton Twins would go on to prominent major league careers. Bristol had four players who would make the majors: outfielder Tim Corcoran, who hit .370 in 1974, catcher Lance Parrish, who hit .213 (mainly because no one would throw him a fastball and it took him a while to learn to hit the curve), pitcher Bob Sykes, and Mark Fidrych. Most of the players in the league were destined to spend a few years in the low minors and then move on to other jobs.

The man to whom the Tiger brass trusted their prized draft picks was forty-three-year-old Joe Lewis. An All-American pitcher for Duke in the early 1950s, he had led them to the College World Series twice. Signed by the Tigers, he built a reputation as a gritty, hard-nosed player with no fear. He soon hurt his arm, however, and lost his great fastball. He pitched in the minors from 1953 to 1958, rising to Triple A, but no further, and fashioning a 36–44 minor league pitching record. Thereafter, it became his life's work to train others to make it further than he had.

Joe Lewis was a hard-drinking, chain-smoking, square-jawed tough guy with piercing eyes. Seeing him in a bar, you would give him plenty of space—the kind of guy nobody would want to step out into the alley with. Serious and gruff, with a drill-sergeant voice and an icy gaze that could make strong men step back, he could be very intimidating—especially to young players away from home for the first time. He was the perfect manager for first-year professionals and he loved his work. "Joe had the kind of personality needed for a manager of rookie ball so these young players wouldn't walk all over you," said Alan Trammell, who played in Bristol in 1976. "If you were around him or wanted to play ball for him, you behaved. Joe wanted dedication to the game."

"Joe was a tough, driving taskmaster with the exterior of a man that had learned to whisper in a steel mill," said Hogan. "As tough as Joe was, the young players all knew he cared about them and their futures."

Lewis was also vice principal and head baseball coach at Durfee High School in Fall River, Massachusetts, during the school year. Since the Rookie League started in June, after the draft, this was a good fit for his schedule. He used his experience to help the young players. Radiating a confidence that he absolutely knew what he was doing at all times, he commanded respect. He rarely had personality clashes with players because no one dared question him. He was known for his baseball knowledge, fairness to players, and brutal honesty. He did not hesitate to let players know when he was dissatisfied with their efforts; "horseshit" was his favorite expression on those occasions. He was old-school in every sense of the phrase—he tolerated no showboating or hot-dogging and was a fanatic about fundamentals. While he was generally a no-nonsense guy, he had a dry sense of humor and was known to pull a clubhouse prank or two—he always got away with them because he was the least likely culprit.

Joe Lewis was first and foremost an organization man. He was intensely loyal to the Tigers but was always a little apprehensive that he wasn't doing a good enough job to impress those at the top. He understood that, above all, it was his purpose to get guys ready to move up the baseball ladder. He was determined that no one under his tutelage would fail, and he hated to see wasted talent.

At the first practice, Lewis had a speech he liked to use to welcome the players into the ranks of professional baseball. He

would tell the kids that they were not with their mommas or high
school coaches anymore. If they worked hard, some would go on
in the organization. He impressed upon them the importance of
dedication and work to make it in professional baseball. On his
first day with the 1974 team Joe Lewis didn't know that he was
looking at the best minor league team he would ever manage.

Assistant coach Jeff Hogan had been a standout at Florida
State in the late sixties in both baseball and basketball, becoming a
member of the 1,000-point club on the hardwood while playing
with future Celtic great Dave Cowens. A shortstop in baseball, he
was drafted by the Tigers and played several years in their farm
system before deciding to go back for his graduate degree. The Tigers called and asked him to help out in the minors during the summer while he was finishing grad school. A relatively young coach,
the outgoing, amiable Hogan was in his late twenties in 1974, which
helped him connect with the young players on the team. He would
later move to Tallahasee and fashion a legendary high school baseball coaching career.

John Grodzicki was the roving pitching instructor for the Tigers' farm system. It was his job to keep tabs on all the pitching
prospects. He had come up through the Cardinals system in the
1940s—a big kid with a smoking fastball. Cardinal brass, including
Branch Rickey, figured he had a good big-league career ahead of
him, but World War II interrupted his plans. He had hurt his leg in
a parachute jump in Germany and was never able to reach the majors when he returned. When asked about it years later, he always
shrugged it off: "A lot of guys came out of the war in worse shape
than I did."

The fifty-something-year-old Grodzicki seemed much older
than his years, although he could still throw batting practice to the
minor leaguers and make them look bad with his changeup. He
was hard-nosed but had an easy, down-to-earth way about him
when helping the young pitchers, especially when dealing with
their confidence and keeping them from getting down on themselves. He offered help but didn't force it. If a young pitcher resisted
or mouthed off, he would just say, "You don't want my help, then

forget it. Do it your way." He seemed to answer every problem with his favorite saying, "Rome wasn't built in a day," meaning, well, meaning whatever the pitcher wanted it to mean. Mark Fidrych took it to mean that he needed to keep working and slowly make progress. Also, Mark took it to mean that when you have a bad day, that Rome wasn't torn down in a day either—so don't worry about the bad game. Just come back the next day ready to play again. Grodzicki's second favorite saying was, "You put your uniform on," as in, "You did terrible today, but at least you put your uniform on—just drop it and worry about tomorrow." It was good stuff for the fragile psyches of young pitchers.

Grodzicki watched each of the pitchers throw in mound sessions the first few days at Lakeland. He was impressed with what he saw in Mark Fidrych. It was obvious Fidrych had excellent control for a young pitcher and good stuff—his ball really moved. Grodzicki did make one suggestion after a short time, however. Mark had a knuckleball of which he was very proud. He had used it a lot in high school and Legion ball—often throwing it with full counts. Grodzicki told Mark to lose the knuckleball and develop a changeup. Incredulously Mark asked, "What do you mean? That pitch helped get me here."

Grodzicki answered, "They're gonna kill it. Take my word for it. It don't do nothing. Back there it did something, because those guys don't know how to hit the ball."

While disappointed to give up his prized possession, Mark took the advice. He later said, "So I just said, 'All right' and threw it out."

This ability to take advice and to not get down on himself would play a major role in Mark's rapid progress through the minors. "Mark really latched on to Grod from day one," says fellow rookie pitcher Bob Sykes. "They had opposite personalities, but they really bonded well. Grod had a huge influence on Mark. Mark really loved him. Grod had a good ability to break down guys and figure out what was best. The big thing with him was the mental approach. I saw some guys with big bonuses come through who just blew Grod off and didn't listen, and some of them didn't make it. But Mark really took everything he said to heart." Later, Grodzicki would frequently drop by the players' trailer to talk and fix up a batch of his famous golapki, a cabbage dish stuffed with ground beef, peppers, and whatever else he felt like throwing in at the time. "We would eat those things until we got sick," says Sykes, "but it was really good. And it was great that he took the time to hang out with us and show interest. He made us feel like we belonged."

As the Bristol Tigers began their schedule, it was soon obvious they were the class of the Appalachian League. Fidrych, an unheralded, low-round pick, was originally slated for middle relief duty. Like almost all the rookies on the team, Mark had been a starter in high school and Legion, but he didn't complain when told he would be a reliever. "I said, 'Fine, I've got a job. They want me to relief, I'll try reliefin'.' "

In one of Mark's first games, he was inserted in the bottom of the ninth with a small lead and proceeded to walk the bases loaded. Joe Lewis marched to the mound. Bristol police officer Charlie Roark, who also worked the field as security, later recalled the scene: "Now, you can hear everything they are saying on the mound. Mark was begging for Joe to let him stay in the game. Mark is begging like hell and everybody can hear him. Joe let him stay in. Mark threw three straight strikeouts after that."

Unfortunately for the eager young Bird, the Tigers were so strong that there was little call for a middle "reliefer" throughout the early part of the season. The starting pitching, particularly Sykes, who would compile a remarkable 11–0 record with an ERA of 1.04, rarely needed help. The team's staff was filled with promising pitchers waiting their chance to prove themselves. Mark later said, "My buddy, Melvin Ray, was sitting in the dugout with me, telling me not to get depressed. He says, 'I've been around for two years, and I'm still here. You'll get your chance. But you got to change the way you think. You see that starter up there right now? . . . Well, you better be sitting here right now praying that he flubs up.' And I says, 'I can't do that. We're a team.' And he says, 'But Mark, if he doesn't flub up, you'll never get up there. Don't think of it as bad, because when he flubs up and you get out there, don't you think I'll be sitting here praying that you flub up so I can get out there and show my talent?'"

Grodzicki visited a few weeks into the season and asked Mark how things were going. "I don't even know what a game looks like," Mark replied glumly. Not long after, however, closer Alley-cat Johnson began struggling, and Mark was made the full-time closer. He would keep that job the rest of the season and be named to the All-Star team. In twenty-three games for Bristol, Mark compiled a 3–0 record with an ERA of 2.38 and forty strikeouts in thirty-four innings. "Mark pitched great for us that year," says Hogan. "He was really a competitor. He hated to even give up one run. I remember he cried the first time he gave up a run; you would have thought he lost the World Series. But the big thing was his control—he could throw that thing through a keyhole and he was consistent. He was always down around the knees. He threw very few pitches where people were going to tee off on it. He really worked the corners, he changed speeds, and he never went to sleep and just laid one in there. There was a purpose on every single pitch. And he had so much action on the ball, he just overwhelmed the guys in the Rookie League.

"All that stuff on the field—he did it the first time I saw him in Bristol the same as the last time I saw him in the big leagues," continues Hogan. "But it wasn't an act. That was just him. He was just genuine and excited to be in pro ball. One time an outfielder made a good play and Mark sprinted off the mound, ran out to the outfield, and shook the guy's hand. He was just excited the guy caught the ball. You could tell it wasn't an act."

Regardless of his behavior between pitches, it was obvious that Mark had the talent and mental ability to go far. "Bird was the fiercest competitor I ever saw," says Sykes. "He may have looked like a clown out there sometimes, but he was an unbelievably fierce competitor. He hated to lose."

"He talked like the devil to the ball and to everyone else," Joe Lewis told a reporter in 1976. "He was just intense. And he really worked hard. He was so reliable I started using him all the time." Lewis had a special signal for when he wanted Mark to warm up in the bullpen. Since the minor league parks didn't have phone hookups between the dugout and the bullpen, Lewis would stand up on the top step of the dugout and flap his arms like a bird. That was the message for The Bird to get busy.

Life as a Rookie League baseball player was not easy. Lewis had infamous morning workouts in which he drilled fundamentals almost every day when the club was at home. The players would work out several hours, drive or hitchhike home for lunch and a short rest, then return for the game, often not getting back home until late at night. There were games every day. The cramped ancient parks had poorly maintained infields strewn with rocks. The Bristol field was tended by a local who had a hound that often left small presents on the field, which unlucky players later discovered. The fans, often drunk and abusive, crowded around the dugout (and sometimes tried to get in to pick up bats and practice their swings). The humidity and mosquitoes in the mountain night air were sometimes unbearable. Players, on their own for laundry, often wore personal items for several days, which gave the small moldy clubhouse a particularly singular odor. The only semblance of air-conditioning in the steamy clubhouse was a small portable fan next to the manager's cubicle. It was not difficult to eat all of the $3.50 daily meal money in one setting and have nothing left for the rest of the day. The players mostly ate what they were able to fix on their small budget with their small kitchen know-how, with a group often gathering in one trailer for a pot of someone's specialty. Added to the culture shock for Mark was the fact that the locals spoke a brand of English that was not entirely the same language as that practiced in Massachusetts.

Road trips in the Appalachian League were an adventure: bumpy rides on a rickety bus with cracked windows, sucking down exhaust fumes in the back. The towns were small mountain communities—Marion, Pulaski, and Covington, Virginia, along with Bluefield, West Virginia, and the larger Tennessee towns of Bristol, Kingsport, and Johnson City. Travel along winding two-lane roads through the mountains was agonizingly slow. And if they got behind a coal truck, it was even slower. One harrowing trip, the brakes went out on the bus as it was coming off the mountain into Pulaski. The bus driver yelled to the players, "Hold on, you guys! We don't have any brakes." As the players sat in terrified silence, the bus careened through the town with the driver honking his horn and pulling on the emergency brake, which didn't help. The bus made a sharp turn to avoid a brick wall—feeling as if it was coming up on two wheels—knocked down several signs, and narrowly missed a couple of cars before finally coming to a stop. The rattled bus driver's shirt was soaked with sweat. One side of the bus was smashed up. Manager Lewis turned in his seat, looked back at his shaken players, and said, "All right, you guys, go mess around and come back in an hour for the game." Ah, life in the minors.

Although the lifestyle appeared tough to outsiders, it was heaven to the players. They were young, playing baseball, and getting paid to do it—five hundred dollars a month in Mark's case. "Getting this paycheck I never thought I'd get," said Mark. What could be better?

"It was exciting playing professional baseball," says Sykes. "It was all baseball, all the time. It was a neat way of life for us at that age." Along with the other players, Mark generally had fun at Bristol, enjoying the freedom of being on his own. As in high school, he kept everyone loose and laughing. There were lots of practical jokes, such as pouring water from the second floor of a motel onto a hapless teammate's head as he attempted to talk to a girl. And then there would be the waiting for the inevitable payback. Mark got fined a few times. Once some of the guys bet him five dollars he wouldn't run around the motel in his underwear. "We fined him more than five bucks for that," says Hogan. "But he was still happy and figured he made money on the deal because the guys gave him the five dollars."

Mark later said, "I remember Alleycat Johnson telling me, 'You know, Mark, when you're on that mound, you're a master, a scientist. But when you walk off it, you're crazy; no one knows what you'll do. You've got a million-dollar arm and a ten-cent mind.'"

Mark initially shared a cramped trailer with three other players in the Jim Dandy Trailer Park on the outskirts of Bristol—not exactly the high-rent section of town. The trailer park was several miles from the field, and they all piled in with the two players who had cars to get to and from work.

Since Mark didn't have a car in Bristol, the transportation options were limited, and, since there was little money anyway, he rarely went into town. The players spent a lot of time in each other's trailers, listening to music and drinking beer. There were initially three trailers in a row occupied by ballplayers. The loud music late at night apparently irritated some of their higher-class neighbors, and one night they returned from a road trip to find that their trailers had been broken into. Nothing was stolen, but it had been a message: "Keep the noise down because we can get into your trailer anytime we want."

Thereafter, some of the other players were scared into moving to safer surroundings, and Mark moved in with Bob Sykes. He and Sykes struck up a close friendship; Mark would later be the best man at Sykes' wedding before the 1977 season. Bob and Mark had no other trouble with their neighbors because they were much quieter.

There was not a lot to do between games. "Mark wasn't really a big bar hopper," says Sykes. As far as girls, Mark stated in his autobiography that he didn't date much at Bristol: "The chicks that were around, they didn't like me because I was too open . . . the ones I met were neat chicks . . . but you just met 'em and you never goofed around with 'em that year. Because I was involved with a chick at home." Mark had a girlfriend back in Northboro he had dated for some time before leaving for pro baseball. He didn't go out with any girls in Bristol because, "I was still goin' with her. And I had in my mind, I said, I ain't goin' out with no chick." He was disappointed when she broke up with him by mail late in the season. "She gave me a Dear John letter. And just said, 'Hey, y'know—you must be foolin' around.' And here I *wasn't* foolin' around." Mark was learning the hard way the dangers and pains of trying to maintain a long-distance relationship at that age. He later told a friend that he would never marry until he was completely finished with baseball.

For the most part, the players relied on each other—forming a brotherhood and camaraderie as strong as any college fraternity. "We played a whole lot of cards with the other guys in our trailers," says Sykes. "I bought a BB gun and we used it to target-shoot cans." While the atmosphere off the field was generally boring, sometimes excitement found them.

"The trailer park was built on the side of a mountain, out in the middle of nowhere," continues Sykes. "At the bottom of the hill there was a fence and beyond that kind of a small cliff. One night, about two in the morning, we heard a huge crash. We went out and there was a car wreck, the brakes had gone out, and it had gone through the fence and over the cliff. We ran down there and the car was on its side. It was smoking and gas was everywhere. It looked ready to blow at any minute. We heard some crying from in the car. Bird climbed right through a window and into the car. It was dark, and I can remember him in there saying, 'I can't see anything, but I can feel one.' He grabbed an arm and pulled a kid out. Then he went back in and pulled another kid out." Sykes pauses. "I'm getting choked up just thinking about it," he continues. "It never entered his mind that it was dangerous. He didn't even hesitate before he jumped in that car." The two kids were carried up to their trailer where an ambulance soon arrived and took them safely to the hospital.

It is insightful that Mark only mentioned this episode once in all his future interviews—in the *Rolling Stone* article. In that, he made no mention of his own heroics, but rather just talked about the kids and the parents in the car. Sykes worked years as a deputy sheriff after baseball and must have seen some bad things over that time. It is obvious from his emotional reaction while recounting the episode thirty-six years later that it was a rather unusual act of courage for a nineteen-year-old. And then, the next day at the park, it was business as usual for Mark; no big deal.

Despite the occasional off-field adventure, Lewis and Hogan did a good job of keeping the guys focused on baseball. The old-school Lewis was adamant in his belief that the players needed strict discipline on and off the field at that stage of their careers. Perhaps remembering his own boisterous behavior at that age,

Lewis was always suspicious of the youngsters. Frequently Lewis and Hogan would use the good cop–bad cop routine with the gravelly voiced, serious Lewis playing the tough—a routine that worked perfectly on the teenagers. Lewis had a curfew for players and frequently had bed checks. For the players, the bed checks were nerve-wracking, even for the good boys—midnight and the manager is knocking on your door—but Lewis enjoyed them. "Joe's favorite thing was to get a few beers under his belt, and out of nowhere he'd say, 'Let's go check the rooms,'" said a former assistant. Sometimes, they would backfire, however. In one famous bed check in the early 1970s, Lewis had discovered three women in a player's room. He hit the ceiling, kicked the women out with a torrent of profanity, and fined the player. He later discovered that the player, who had recently left Catholic seminary to join the team, was being visited by three nuns who were friends from his previous life—a story that other players might have tried on their managers but in this case was actually true.

Once in 1974, there was a late-night card game in the players' motel room. Mark was lying on a bed watching the game but not playing because the stakes were too high for his frugal tastes ("They were betting *dollars*."). Lewis heard the noise and pounded on the door. As some of the players scrambled out the back window of the room to avoid capture, Mark rolled over and pretended to be asleep. Lewis exploded when he found not only players up late, but his ancient trainer, Bob Birnbaum, in the room also playing cards, and he cursed the trainer all the way down the hall back to his room.

There was one memorable night in which Fidrych was the recipient of Lewis' anger, and it resulted in Mark believing that his baseball career was coming to a premature end on the night of his twentieth birthday, August 14, 1974. "I got a call at the motel I stayed in—it was Joe," says Hogan. "He said, 'Can you come pick me up? I got a call from the trailer park. The Bird has a big party going on up there and they're making a lot of noise.' It was Mark's birthday and I guess they were getting pretty loud." Mark had recently pitched a lot, and Lewis had given him two days off. The other players threw a surprise birthday party back at the Jim Dandy.

The landlord of the trailer park had called Lewis, so at 1:30 AM, Hogan picked up the manager and they headed to the trailer park. As the wives of both coaches had just gotten into town for a visit, neither was in a good mood to be rousted at that hour. "On the way over, Joe says in his gravelly voice, 'Now look, whatever happens, you've got my back, because I'm going to go in there and rattle some cages.' By the time we got there, it was pretty much broken up except for Bird and Bobby Sykes, who were rooming together at the time. So we go in there with Joe acting tough. Obviously, Mark had been drinking." Mark tried to look casual leaning against a wall, but his hand slipped and he almost fell down. "One of the first things out of his mouth was, 'Hey Joe, you guys want a beer? I got a Heineken here.'"

Mark later admitted, "I thought, well, I'll offer him a beer. Maybe he'll like me."

"Now Joe, who would normally drink a beer at the drop of a hat, just flipped out when Bird said that," continues Hogan.

"Sit your ass down," Lewis shouted. "Just look at yourself."

"Mark immediately starts confessing to everything," says Hogan, "and Lewis really laid into them. He gave them the best dressing down of two professional athletes I had ever seen. He really had them going. He finished up saying, 'You guys need to pack your gear and get on a bus tomorrow. You're out of here.' Now, by this time, these are the two best pitching prospects in the Detroit organization so I knew that Joe wasn't going to send them home, but they didn't. Fidrych starts crying that his dad's going to kill him. 'I can't go home. What am I going to tell my dad?'"

"Lewis really let us have it," says Sykes. "He made us think that we were finished; he acted like we were kicked off the team. We were scared. I think he may have even acted like he would have plane tickets for us the next day. We worried all night. When we got to the park the next day, we went in and apologized to Lewis and asked, 'Is there anything we can do to get back on the team?' He said, 'Go get in your uniforms, just don't let it ever happen again.' We were so thankful. But it was a good lesson."

The Bristol Tigers ran away with the 1974 Appalachian League

pennant with a 52-and-17 record. They clinched the championship two weeks before the end of the season. The closest team was
ten and a half games back. Late in the season, there was talk in the
Tiger organization of moving Mark up to Clinton. Lewis squashed
that idea and kept him in Bristol. After the season, Lewis explained
to Mark that it was better to remain in Bristol because he may not
have gotten as much playing time in Clinton. Mark agreed and appreciated the fact that Lewis seemed to be looking out for his best
interests.

Mark had performed well at Bristol, but was not yet regarded
as a sure-thing major leaguer. It was still too early. "It was neat
later to be able to say I helped coach Mark Fidrych in the Rookie
League," says Hogan. "He had done real well for us, but when I left
there, I had no idea he was going to be that big of a deal."

"We had five pitchers on that team who we considered major
league prospects," said Tiger executive Bill Lajoie in 1976. "Mark
was one of them, but he didn't look that much more outstanding
than any of the others."

After the season, Mark, along with Bob Sykes, reported to
Dunedin for the Florida Instructional League, which ran from late
September to mid-November. The best prospects at several levels of
the organization were invited to participate there. They were the
players the organization felt had the best chances of becoming
major leaguers. There were also several young players from the big
club who needed to work on something, so it was pretty fast competition. Mark made nineteen appearances in Dunedin, all in relief, and again pitched well.

Mark returned to Northboro for the off-season, satisfied after
a successful first year of professional baseball. That winter, he had
only one thought on his mind: he couldn't wait for spring.

3

Lakeland, Montgomery, and Evansville

Frank MacCormack was hanging out in the rec room at Fetzer Hall in Lakeland, Florida. Fetzer Hall, home to all Tiger minor leaguers in spring training, was a renovated ex-military barracks on the property of a World War I airfield that had been converted into Tiger Town. The twenty-one-year-old MacCormack was feeling good about himself. The hard-throwing pitcher was fresh off an impressive season at Class A Lakeland and figured to start the 1975 season no lower than AA. As he played Ping-Pong, he couldn't help but notice another player, a guy he had seen around a few times but didn't know. The guy was playing pool—rather loudly. The guy was Mark Fidrych. "I thought he was nuts," says MacCormack. "He was trying to do all these crazy trick shots, talking nonstop, just saying anything." MacCormack, a cocky, street-smart wise guy from New Jersey, became annoyed listening to the nonsense and tossed a few snide comments and thinly veiled insults in Mark's direction. Mark endured the taunts for a while but finally dropped his pool stick and approached MacCormack, wondering who this guy was who was hassling him before he even knew him. The two pitchers were separated and cooler heads prevailed fortunately.

Later, after this crude introduction, the two got to know each other and became friends. "I ended up rooming with him on and off for the next two years, in Evansville and even in Detroit after I got called up," says MacCormack. "He was a character right from the start. He wasn't shy—he had no pretentions about himself. He walked around and said what he felt, whatever came into his head. He didn't think about the repercussions of anything he said—I mean that in an innocent sort of way. After getting to know him, we became good friends, really good friends." He pauses. "He was still nuts though."

Not being allowed to bring a car to camp, Mark had gotten his buddies to drive him down from Massachusetts for his first spring training at Tiger Town in 1975. Mark, Wayne Hey, Bob Murphy, and Bill McAfee—neighborhood friends since early childhood—all piled into a small car packed with Mark's gear. The plan was for the other three to head to the new Disney World park in Orlando after dropping off Mark. They pulled up to the Tigers' headquarters and Mark unloaded his stuff from the trunk. The four small-town boys looked at all the professional baseball players entering, feeling like little kids with their noses pressed against a candy store window as they recognized players they had previously seen on television. Suddenly feeling out of place in the presence of the major leaguers, the three friends told Mark, "You've got to go in there. We're leaving."

Mark was slated to start the 1975 season with the Class A Lakeland Tigers along with a lot of his Bristol teammates. It was one step up the ladder. There were about 150 minor league players in camp, all competing for the same spots. The reality that there were a finite number of jobs available faced them every day. All the players had hopes, aspirations, and signed contracts, but they all knew they had to prove themselves—they could be released any day. In the dorm and on the field, they met and mingled with their future teammates and competitors-for-jobs. While some players were reserved and cautious, preferring to keep their cards close to their chest, others were not. Mark Fidrych, particularly, was not. Outgoing, talkative, uninhibited as always, he was not hard to notice.

The players spent much free time at Zimmerman's Bar, about a half an hour away, laughing over beers and playing pinball, one of Mark's favorite activities. Zimmerman's was a small bar—not much bigger than a diner. Players went there after games and practice; often the place would be filled with nothing but players and a few writers. The owner liked baseball players and made them comfortable. The trick for the players was to be back in the dorm by the 11:30 curfew—not an easy task for those without cars. They had to either bum rides back with older players or writers or use their thumb. If no one picked them up hitchhiking, they walked the whole way. The doors to the dorm were locked at 11:30—anyone not present at that time got fined when they showed up and begged to get in. Mark and his roommate learned a way around that, however. They unscrewed the bolts on the window to their first-floor room and were able to sneak back in when the need arose.

Being caught outside the locked dorm was only one of the hazards wayward players faced. "One night I was driving back to camp," recalled Hoot Evers in 1976, "and I saw this strange figure hitchhiking on the road. He had no shirt on, just cut-off jeans and tennis shoes that had to be at least ten years old. And his body was baked sun red. He had been on the beach all afternoon and was trying to get back to camp before curfew." Recognizing Mark, the director of Tiger player development picked him up. Mark was not exactly happy to be found in that condition by Evers. "Of all the luck," he said when he got into the car. "All the cars that go by and I gotta get picked up by my boss."

Patrick Zier was a young sports reporter for the *Lakeland Ledger* in 1975. Sometimes referred to as the hippie sportswriter, Zier had long hair and a beard—the kind of look that would have gotten him thrown out of most clubhouses only a few years earlier. "When are you going to get a haircut?" Jim Campbell would joke with him when he saw him at the baseball field in Lakeland. Zier would answer back to the bald general manager: "When you get a wig." Because of his casual appearance and attitude, and the fact that he was closer in age, Zier was able to get to know the players better than the older reporters. He often hung out with them at

Zimmerman's and enjoyed their company away from the park. He sometimes bought a case of beer for the clubhouse when the team won a big series. Players learned that he could be trusted—something said off the record was kept just that. Zier was able to get a bird's-eye view of Mark Fidrych from the beginning—before events would turn him into a media sensation—and watch him progress over the ensuing years each time he returned to Lakeland. "Mark was pretty much a normal guy back then," Zier says. "He was a typical kid, just more exuberant and hyper. But otherwise he liked to fool around with the guys, just like any of the other players. He really wasn't that much different. I would have never called him a flake. I think a lot of that flake stuff got blown out of proportion by the writers later; not the Detroit writers who got to know him, but the out-of-town guys who were just looking for a good story. Mark was very open; he didn't hold anything back. He was never reserved. He always said whatever he felt, and occasionally that got him into trouble. Sometimes things got misinterpreted.

"When you were in Lakeland back then," Zier continues, "you were a nobody. There were no agents, there wasn't anybody who had big bonuses back then. Nobody was making any money. They were just regular young guys. They did what regular young guys will do. But you could tell Mark could pitch in 1975. I think everybody at that time knew he had one of the best arms in the system. And he did a lot of the same things on the mound that he did later. He was very exuberant on the field. People didn't make as big a deal about it here—maybe because the crowds were so small. I think he fed off the crowds—as they got bigger, he could feel the energy. He was very genuine, he wasn't crazy. He really wanted to get good at baseball. He knew it was the only thing he could do that set him apart."

For all his fun off the field, Mark knew when it was time to work. He had a serious side and a very strong determination to succeed. Zier later recalled one night when he gave Mark a ride home. Mark talked candidly about himself, and "unlike most people, he knew his strengths and weaknesses and was willing to face up to them. He was not real smart, he said. He couldn't go to college and make something of himself. Baseball was like college for him, he said. 'And I'm going to make it to the big leagues, you watch, because I know if I don't, I'm nothing.' "

The 1975 Lakeland Tigers were managed by a fifty-six-year-old lifer named Stubby Overmire. Stubby pitched in the majors from 1943 to 1952 with the Tigers, Browns, and Yankees, then managed in the minors from 1954 to 1975. Overmire was well liked but somewhat lax in his rules. He didn't hold the reins as tight as some in the organization felt that he should have, reasoning that if a player was old enough to sign a pro contract he was old enough to run his own life. Stubby's genial nature made discipline distasteful. Although he applied discipline when necessary, players had to get pretty far out of line to agitate Stubby, and he had few rules. Naturally, there were those who took advantage of this.

"In some ways, perhaps, Stubby wasn't cut out to be a manager in the low minors," wrote Patrick Zier in 1977. "He was just too nice a guy." He knew baseball, however, and was quick to spot exceptional talent. It gave him great satisfaction when his guys moved up to the next level. He loved calling a player in and telling him to pack his bags for Montgomery. When it was time for the bad news that the player was going the other direction, however, Stubby might brood about it for days. "Stubby understood what it was to want to be a major leaguer," Zier wrote. "He understood the sacrifices the individuals on his team made. He knew what it was to work and devote your life to something, and he understood the frustration of being told all that was for nothing."

Conditions at Lakeland were better than at Bristol—a step up. Nicer buses. Nicer hotels. Nicer towns to visit. But it was still low-level minor league baseball with the players not making much money. Always on the lookout for cheap accommodations, Mark rented a cramped old trailer a few miles from the Tigers' home of Joker Marchant Stadium. Teammates joked that he lived in a hot dog stand, but, in reality, most hot dog stands may have been a little more spacious—and better smelling. Still without a car, Mark was dependent on others to get around, but overall life was good.

The players were fortunate that the people of Lakeland were

very supportive of Tiger baseball. A number of businessmen regularly met with players and enjoyed their company. "My father owned several businesses in Lakeland and he loved baseball," says Diane Horn Whitaker, who was nineteen years old in 1975. "He always invited players over to our house. They would just hang out and play pool. Sometimes we would have cookouts or take them skiing; just stuff for them to have fun. Of course, Dad paid for a lot of things because they didn't have any money back then. We were big baseball fans, so we had a lot of fun with the guys. Mark was part of a group that would hang out with us a lot. He was very down to earth. He was just a really nice guy, always happy. Definitely not extravagant; he had very simple tastes. He always wore this plaid shirt—I thought it was the only shirt he had.

"But he was humble and appreciated everything he had," she continues. "He was very serious about baseball. He always said he was going to make it to the majors. And after he did, stardom didn't change him when he came back to Lakeland each year for spring training."

Paul Fidrych could not have been more proud of how his son was doing playing professional baseball. Paul's schedule as a teacher allowed him time off during the summer to see quite a few of Mark's games. "We went everywhere—Bristol, Lakeland, Evansville," says Lorie Fidrych. "When we drove down to visit him at Lakeland, we stayed with Mark in the little trailer and I had to sleep on the floor. I didn't like it because there were a lot of cockroaches in the floor, and there were alligators everywhere. But Mark didn't care too much about how his apartment was—he didn't spend much time there. He always seemed happy when we came down to see him. We would go down to the bullpen and sometimes get to go out on the field. That was impressive to me because I was little. My parents were so proud of him."

"Mark had a really neat relationship with his family," says Bob Sykes. "His parents and sisters came to see him quite a bit— even when we were in Dunedin in the fall league. You could tell they were very close." Mark couldn't wait to call home after every good outing on the mound.

At Lakeland, Mark became a starting pitcher again. "We think he has an outstanding arm," Hoot Evers told Zier early in the season. "We wanted to see what he could do as a starter."

"I had always been a starter in high school," added Mark, "but after I signed they told me I was going to be a reliever, so I relieved. I just do what they tell me. I figure they know what they're doing."

Stubby Overmire was impressed with Mark's intensity and desire. "When we first got him he'd come into the dugout after the first inning and go right over to the john and throw up," he said in 1976. "I'd ask him if he was all right, and he'd say, 'Sure. I always do that.' He was liable to say any damn thing that came into his mind. But his concentration was incredible. When he was on the mound, he didn't know anyone else was in the park."

Not knowing anyone else was in the park, Mark was prone to strange actions on the mound. Mike Coombs was a catcher at Lakeland along with Lance Parrish. "The Bird did basically the same things at Lakeland that he does with Detroit," Coombs said in 1977. "But you didn't notice it as much because you just figured he was crazy. He walked around in those high-top white sneakers, cut-off shorts, and a Perry Como sweater and was just a crazy guy. . . . I enjoyed catching him."

Patrick Zier called him "Fidgety Fidrych" in the *Lakeland Ledger* and wrote of Mark's mound behavior in early 1975: "Mark Fidrych is a nervous person, you know, one of those kind of people that hates to be still. He moves around a lot and he also has a fast-ball that moves."

Opposing manager Rac Slider of the St. Petersburg Cardinals noted, "He may talk to himself on the mound, but he's a good pitcher."

One game, Mark pitched a complete game in a 5–2 win, despite getting sick in the dugout three times between innings. "I drank too much cold water," he explained to Zier after the game.

Mark began the season well by winning his first three starts. Then he lost five in a row. Most of the losses were due to a lack of run support, errors, and an infuriating string of cheap hits—bloops over infielders' heads and seeing-eye bleeders. The losing streak bewildered Mark, who asked Overmire what he was doing wrong. Stubby explained that he was completing his games and throwing well, just not getting any hitting support. He told Mark that he still had confidence in him and to just keep throwing the way he was.

In late July, Mark was met by the manager when he arrived at the park. Stubby told him, "Give your uniform to Bronson." Bronson was the Lakeland equipment manager. There was only one reason to give him your uniform: because you wouldn't be needing it anymore. With a 5–9 record, Mark's first thought was, "I'm gone." Overmire, seeing his shocked face, quickly added the good news, "You're going up to Double A."

Hoot Evers later told Mark they hoped that moving to a winning environment would improve things for him. "I was down at Lakeland," Mark later said. "Everyone was. I think they sent me to Montgomery to improve my morale." They also knew that Mark was throwing well and not being hit hard despite his losing record and ERA of 3.77. Four of his losses had been by one run. They knew Mark Fidrych was a rising star in the system.

The Montgomery Rebels were a good team and were leading the Southern League when Mark arrived. Montgomery was managed by Les Moss, who was the polar opposite of the easygoing Overmire. The first thing he said when he greeted Mark was, "You gotta get a haircut." When Mark showed up at the park the next day, fresh off a cheap hack job on his hair, Moss was unimpressed. "I thought I told you to get a haircut?"

Mark answered, "I did."

"Yeah, I know," replied Moss. "Only next time I tell you to get a haircut, go get a good one."

Moss ran a tight ship. If someone didn't show up on time, everybody got fined ten dollars. Miss a sign—ten dollars. Get picked off—ten dollars. There were lots of ways for a player to lose money. New guys were quickly taught the facts of the system by the other players upon arrival. To keep up morale, Moss held a lottery on pay day every two weeks and picked three names to divide up the pot of fines.

Mark was beginning to learn that one had to adjust to the

changes of minor league life on the fly. He quickly found himself an apartment in Montgomery. He was upset that he had recently paid a month's rent in advance on his Lakeland hot-dog stand, which was now lost. He paid a month's rent for his new apartment, $125, then left with the team for a fifteen-day road trip.

With the Rebels, it was back to the bullpen for Mark. He quickly impressed the right people by pitching very well. Mark noticed an improvement in the infield play behind him—especially with double plays on ground balls. For a low-ball pitcher, that was a big help. He pitched in seven games and had a 2–0 record.

August 16, before he even had time to enjoy his new apartment in Montgomery, Mark was promoted again, this time to Triple-A Evansville. In Detroit, the season was going poorly—the Tigers were in last place. Their relief ace, John Hiller, had been hurt along with several other pitchers, and the Tigers had sought pitching help from Evansville. This opened some spots. Tiger general manager Jim Campbell had followed Montgomery for several days to watch Mark and a few others pitch and had liked what he saw.

Another step up. Nicer hotels, they flew for away games, and meal money was now ten dollars a day. Mark lost another half-month's rent (and the fifty dollar deposit) as he vacated his apartment to head to Evansville, but on the bright side, his pay, which had increased to $800 at Double A, was now bumped up to $1,200 a month in Evansville—pretty good money for a twenty-year-old who only a year earlier was working at a gas station. Mark got the news of the promotion while the Rebels were playing in Orlando and flew directly to join the Evansville team on the road in Wichita, arriving with only the clothes he had taken with him on the road trip. The rest of his clothes were still in Montgomery and had to be shipped later.

The Evansville Triplets were a hot team. Managed by former Tiger Fred Hatfield, another competitive tough guy, they had started the season near the bottom of the standings, losing ten straight and nineteen out of twenty-three during one stretch in May. After getting reinforcements in the form of number one draft pick first baseman Jason Thompson and several good pitchers who moved up from Montgomery, including Mark Lemongello and Frank MacCormack, they turned their season around. They had won sixteen of the previous twenty-two games and were in first place when Mark Fidrych was called up. He made an immediate impression on the Triplets, arriving at the field as the game was just starting. "Mark jumped out of the taxi all wound up," says catcher Bruce Kimm. "He thought he was going to pitch that day. I told him to relax, that he was pitching the next day." Kimm, who would become Mark's private catcher in Detroit the next year, had seen him briefly in spring training but had not met him. "I had never seen anything like him," Kimm continues. "The next night was his first start in Triple A. It was really something. The first inning, our shortstop Chuck Scrivener made a play—a pretty good play, but not a great play—a play we had seen him make a lot. Mark went over and shook his hand, right in the middle of the inning. We razzed him a little bit about it back in the dugout, and he said, 'Well, they don't make plays like that in A or Double-A ball.' That was sort of neat because nobody had ever done that before."

Mark, a starter again, quickly became the ace of the staff, going 4–1 with a 1.59 ERA in six games to finish up the season. "He stood out even in Evansville," says pitching coach Fred Gladding. "He had good command of the strike zone and he was such a great competitor. He didn't like to lose. He was very easy to coach. He would listen to you and do what you suggested. But I didn't have to make many changes with him. The first time I saw that stuff that he did on the mound, I went, 'Wow, what is this?' But then you realized that he did the same thing every time and it was just his way of concentrating."

"Mark was already good when he got to Evansville," says Kimm. "And he pretty much did the same stuff at Evansville in 1975 that he did at Detroit in 1976. We had a little fence in front of the dugout. Instead of going around it like everybody else, he would jump over the top of it. He never walked—he sprinted from the dugout to the mound and back. He was just an excitable guy. When he pitched, you could feel the crowd getting into it."

The crowd. Fans responded to Mark in Evansville just like

they would the next year in Detroit. "Even in Evansville the fans were crazy about him," says Gladding. "He talked to everybody, signed autographs, posed for pictures, would do anything they asked. He interacted with the fans like you'd never seen anybody do. And he looked liked he enjoyed talking to them. You could tell he enjoyed them as much as they enjoyed him." There was just something about the guy: magnetism, charisma, something. But whatever it was, fans loved it.

Mark Peerman was nine years old when his parents first took him to see Mark Fidrych pitch at Bosse Field in Evansville. "The thing I remember after all these years is the show he put on, all the stuff he did," says Peerman, now forty-five. "I was hooked instantly. He was so unique, no one else did anything like he did. Also, the way he applauded his teammates was special. He would shout and point at them and shake his fist at them when they made a play. I think it came across to the fans how sincere he was. The fans really appreciated his effort. Everyone loved him." And Mark loved to interact with fans, especially kids.

"One game we got there real early and went down by the dugout," Peerman continues. "He came over and talked to us. I had on a T-shirt that I had used a marker on to make a homemade jersey, to look like what the Triplets wore. Mark noticed it and said he liked it. He was just great. He posed with us for a picture and gave us an autographed ball. I still have the ball."

Mark moved into an apartment with pitchers Lemongello, Mac-Cormack, Ed Glynn and Dennis DeBarr. The five teammates spent a lot of time together away from the park. "It was crazy hanging out with him," says MacCormack. "He had so much energy. It seemed like he never paid attention. He was constantly talking, doing things, bouncing around. His thoughts would change every second. You'd go nuts trying to keep up with him. You couldn't keep up with him. He acted like a scatterbrain, but then he'd get on the field and you never saw such concentration on the mound. He could just block out everything—an unbelievable ability to focus. We thought he was some sort of savant for pitching."

Pitcher Steve Grilli was also at Evansville and would play

with Mark later for several years. "Mark was the same that year as he was the rest of his life," says Grilli. "He was a free spirit, but very genuine. Kind of a blue-collar type guy. He always enjoyed whatever he was doing. He didn't really get caught up in a lot of other stuff; he was just playing baseball, something he enjoyed doing. He had a lot of the same mannerisms, but the coaches didn't make a big deal about them in Evansville—it was just something he did. He was just being himself and nobody told him to stop."

In nine starts at Evansville, including the playoffs, Mark only lost two games: 2–1 and 1–0. On August 27, the Triplets were in position to clinch the divisional title against Omaha. Mark was scheduled to start. Before the game, he told manager Hatfield to go ahead and order a case of champagne. Hatfield replied that if Mark didn't win, he would smash all the bottles over Mark's head. Mark won 2–1, and the champagne bottles were opened and enjoyed, not broken over his head.

In the American Association playoffs against Denver, Mark took the mound with the Triplets leading the best-of-seven series three games to two. In a game notable for the contributions of future major league managers, shortstop Tony LaRussa got Denver on the board first, scoring a run with an infield ground out. After giving up two runs in the fifth, Mark slammed the door and pitched seven scoreless innings as the Triplets tied the game and sent it into extra innings. Infielder Jerry Manual hit a two-out home run in the twelfth inning to give the Triplets the win. Mark finished the twelve-inning game with an eight-hitter and the victory. After getting the last out, Mark raced to the plate and gave catcher Gene Lamont a big hug, then ran out to center field where Art James had just made the last catch and gave him a big hug also. One line in the minor league section of the back pages of the *Sporting News* gave observant major league fans a hint of things to come when it stated, "A pitcher who talks to himself on the mound, Fidrych followed his division-clincher against Omaha by twice beating Denver in the playoffs."

After Evansville went on to win the Junior World Series crown, there was talk of promoting several pitchers, particularly

Lemongello, MacCormack, and Fidrych. "Everybody is talking about those pitchers, everybody," Tiger manager Ralph Houk told a reporter. The team decided against moving Mark up though. He would have to be content with two promotions in 1975. Houk later explained, "If we had been in a pennant race, we might have brought him up. But that would have meant we would have had to put him on the roster and protect him in the draft, and there was no need for us to do that."

It had been a fantastic year for Mark Fidrych—vaulting from Single A to Triple A in less than four months. He had rapidly become a mature pitcher; his numbers had gotten better at each step up, against tougher competition. Two factors played a role: (1) the fielding play around him improved drastically as Mark moved up the ladder, and (2) with the excellent defensive catcher Kimm behind the plate, he could throw his slider in the dirt with confidence. All the low balls that were beat into the ground became outs—double plays with men on base. As Mark later said about Evansville, "I threw the ball and just said . . . they're gonna make the plays . . . going for a double play. . . . They get you out of it. Just like that! You know how much that takes off your mind?" Mark's control got better at each step up in the minor leagues also. He struck out fewer batters, walked much fewer, and threw fewer pitches to get guys out. Mark gave credit to Tiger pitcher Vern Ruhle for teaching him, while they were together in winter ball after the 1974 season, to let the infielders help him and not to try to strike everyone out. In Bristol and Lakeland, Mark walked one batter every two and a half innings. In Montgomery and Evansville, he walked about one every five.

After the season, Mark had five days to go home and then reported to the Florida Instructional League as he had in 1974. This time, however, he went as a man who had proven himself to be a definite major league prospect. Grodzicki told him not to worry about his record but to work on his change-up as much as possible in Florida. Even so, Mark posted a 4–2 record and led the Tigers to the Northern Division title. The schedule was much more relaxing in Florida and the players had time to enjoy the amenities and the ocean. "Me and Mark went fishing a lot," says pitcher Dave Rozema. "One day, Mark goes, 'I'm tired of catching this small stuff, I'm going for a shark.' And he put a huge chunk of meat on the line. It hadn't been in the water long before something big grabbed it and took off. We couldn't get it in, it broke the line. Mark was just rolling laughing."

After the fall season concluded, Mark went back to Northboro for the winter, fresh off playing for three first-place teams in a row. Relaxing and hanging out with his friends, he didn't realize that it would be the last time he would ever be plain-old Fid from Northboro—he was about to hook his line on one of the biggest great-white media sharks of all time.

4

Detroit

Part of the Bird legend that would grow later that summer held that Mark Fidrych was an unknown who won a job with the Tigers in 1976 based on a strong spring performance; he had been in the major league camp only to provide an extra arm for throwing batting practice to the veterans until the roster pitchers got in shape, but he had somehow worked his way onto the team. This is an obvious embellishment, the old "rookie from nowhere makes good" story. Mark Fidrych was definitely known when he showed up in Lakeland in March of 1976.

The Tigers' general manager, Jim Campbell, certainly knew about him. He had watched him pitch in Montgomery and Evansville and he knew what the Tigers possessed in this excitable, talkative pitcher. Campbell had rejected offers for him all winter from other teams who had been interested after watching him in the Junior World Series.

Ralph Houk certainly knew about him. He had watched him pitch at Dunedin in the Fall Instructional League and had been impressed. He had recognized the confidence, the unusual control, the movement on the ball. Ralph Houk had seen enough major league pitchers to know that this kid had it. And he had also heard the glowing reports from Fred Gladding.

Gladding, who had been promoted and would be the Tigers' pitching coach in 1976, had been thoroughly impressed watching Mark pitch for the Evansville Triplets at the end of the 1975 season. Evansville had several very good pitchers that year, but Gladding knew who the prize of the bunch was. He was confident Mark was ready to make an immediate impact on the major leagues. "I knew he (Mark Fidrych) would be good before we even started that spring," he says. "There was no doubt in my mind that he could do it." Gladding became the prophet of The Bird. He told anyone who would listen about the kid.

Gladding told Houk. "Ralph Houk asked me about him, and I said, 'This kid can pitch as good as anybody on our staff right now. Ignore all that stuff he does, he just gets people out.' "

Gladding told the other Tiger players. "Fred Gladding was telling us that they had a guy who talked to the baseball, but he could really pitch," says second baseman Gary Sutherland. "Of course, we were going, 'Yea, you're crazy. Nobody does that.' "

Gladding told his former teammates. "When we played the Tigers that spring, Fred was talking to me before the game, and he said, 'Watch this kid. He's just unbelievable. Not only is he good, he'll put on a show for you.' " says Jack Billingham, who had been Gladding's roommate while playing for the Astros and was pitching for the Reds in 1976. "Fred told me he was something special, that he was going to make an impact."

In truth, Houk and Campbell were already sold on Fidrych before spring training began. "Very few pitchers make a staff in spring training," said Houk. "We were definitely counting on him as one of our starters when we went to spring training."

"We certainly intended to keep him," Houk said later in 1976. "Unless something happened like an injury, or he was just awful. . . . But there was no reason to put him on the major league roster during the winter. We didn't have to protect him. He had options left, so why put him on the roster? If he had gotten hurt or something, then we would have wasted one of his options." Houk kept everyone, including Mark, in suspense until the end of camp, however.

So Mark Fidrych was definitely not an unknown in camp in 1976. People knew about him. They had heard about him. But the stories didn't do justice. This was something you just had to see for yourself.

Officially a nonroster invitee to the Tigers camp, Mark was oblivious to the expectations of Houk, Gladding, and Campbell. As far as he knew, he *was* an unknown in camp only there to throw batting practice to the veterans until the roster pitchers got their arms warmed up. He was given number 62—not exactly a number to give a rookie hopes of sticking around. As in 1975, he lived in Fetzer Hall, the dorm at the minor league camp, with the other minor league prospects, while the major leaguers enjoyed nicer accommodations in the nearby Holiday Inn. Along with the other minor league prospects, Mark ate in the farm chow hall and played Ping-Pong and pool in the farm rec room. But this year he had access to the major league clubhouse and was on the field with the major leaguers.

The kid from Northboro was amazed at the bounty of riches available to major leaguers. "I walked into that big league clubhouse in Lakeland and went, 'Wow! Free orange juice! Free chewing gum! Free chewing tobacco! I don't even chew tobacco, but I think I'm gonna start,'" Mark recalled in 2001. "I was in heaven. Five pairs of spikes, gloves a dime a dozen, big league uniforms with our names on the back. Audry, our minor league secretary, gave me writing paper with the Detroit emblem stamped on it so I could write letters home. It made me feel like a big shot."

Luckily for Mark, there were some openings available on the Tiger pitching staff—it was a staff that had faired poorly in 1975. The ace was Joe Coleman, a twenty-nine-year-old who had won twenty-three games for the Tigers in 1973 but had fallen to 10–18 in 1975. Dave Roberts was a proven major league starter acquired from the Astros in the off-season. Vern Ruhle was coming off a fine rookie season with the Tigers in which he had gone 11–12. Ray Bare and twenty-seven-year-old Lerrin LaGrow, a Tiger since 1970, were tentatively expected to round out the rotation. All the impressive young pitchers from the 1975 American Association pennant winner in Evansville were in camp competing for major league jobs. They were all aware that, coming off a bad season in a rebuilding year, the Tigers were expected to go north with a young, untested team.

Veterans usually don't pay much attention to the crowds of rookie hopefuls in training camp—after so many years, they have seen them come and go. A lot of arms are needed early in the spring for batting practice—most of those are soon gone. The official roster had forty men on it at the beginning of camp, but only twenty-five would make the team, so fifteen *roster* players would eventually be cut—that didn't bode well for all the nonroster players milling around the field with high numbers on their backs. But it was hard not to pay at least some attention to Mark Fidrych. He unwittingly forced people to take notice. "The big thing I remember is that his tennis shoes were torn apart and he wore raggedy T-shirts and cut-off shorts all the time," says veteran John Hiller. "Usually we don't dress up much at spring training, but his clothes were a little worse than most. And he had that big head of curly hair. By 1976, that was kind of the beginning of long hair in baseball, but that curly hair really stood out. And, of course, he was full of energy."

"He was a kind of eccentric, excitable, fun-loving guy," says Sutherland. "We saw that before we saw him pitch, just running around in camp." Mark was not one to quietly sit in the background—it was not his nature. He was constantly chattering. He would literally say anything that popped into his head. He was constantly on the go, doing something—doing anything. "What people saw on the field, that's just the way he was twenty-four hours a day," says Sutherland. "It was all real stuff."

Initially, veterans were a little hesitant and curious about some of Mark's mannerisms. Some questioned his seeming innocence and awe at his surroundings. "This kid is from Boston?" thought catcher Bill Freehan. "Shouldn't he be more sophisticated?" But it was impossible not to enjoy being around him; he just seemed to always have fun. "Because of his enthusiasm, he kind of grew on people," says Houk. "With his personality, all you could do was like him."

Detroit writers, getting a close look at Mark for the first time, began to sense that he was special, and not just as a pitcher. Four days into camp, Dan Ewald fired one of the first shots of The Bird legend back to Detroit in a *Detroit News* article entitled, "Rare Bird: Tiger Rookie Pitcher Fidrych Livens Up Camp." Ewald gave readers an accurate preview of what to expect from Mark that summer, telling them, "Detroit fans are going to love him. Not just because he's the brightest young pitching prospect in the entire system. But because Fidrych is one of those colorful personalities who makes watching baseball true entertainment." Ewald quoted Jim Campbell as saying, "I hope some of the other players don't try to change his habits because this guy is really something to see." Ralph Houk added, "He never sits still. He works so fast that he may have been the first player in history to throw twenty-five minutes of batting practice in fifteen minutes." Ewald informed Detroit fans that Mark was called The Bird and revealed that "Fidrych's best act is to talk to the ball after each pitch." And, in a statement that would later make him seem like a soothsayer, Ewald concluded with, "It's only a matter of time before he puts on his act in Tiger Stadium. The fans will simply love it."

Each spring, fans up north receive breathy missives such as this over rookies. Each year, most of the subjects of these reports are quickly forgotten once the regular season starts as major league pitchers get their curveballs working and hitters get in shape. Most fans take these reports with a grain of salt—aware of the inevitability of rookie burnouts.

But Mark's live arm and control were definitely impressing the people in Lakeland who made the decisions. While not correcting the reporters who wrote that Mark probably would not make the team, Ralph Houk knew better. The more he saw of Mark, the more he was convinced that Gladding's reports were right on target. "I thought he was ready for the majors," says Houk. "A lot of people were surprised when I kept him that spring. Initially, I don't think some of the other people on our staff thought we'd keep him, but I certainly did. When we had meetings I said, 'As far as I'm concerned, I think he can make our ball club and pitch for us right now.'"

The Tiger players were also taking note of his talent. As the spring went on they realized that Mark could help the team in 1976. "We had to hit off him in batting practice and in intrasquad games," says Sutherland. "When we saw him pitch, we realized how good this guy was. He was an exceptional talent. We could see that he had what it took. Of course, you never know how a rookie is going to react to the pressure until he is on the mound in a real game."

Mark made his first start against major league hitters on March 26, facing the Cardinals in Lakeland. As would be expected, the Cardinal players were greatly amused by Mark's activities on the mound and offered loud comments from their dugout while he went through his soon-to-be-famous routine. After he pitched three scoreless innings against them, however, they could not help but be impressed with his pitching.

Reporters were amazed that this small-town guy with less than two years of minor league service did not seem to be awed by famous opponents. In fact, he rarely knew the names of any of his opponents. "He didn't really know a lot of the guys he played against," says Frank MacCormack. "Sometimes that helps. You don't get nervous if you don't know how good these guys are. To him, they were just players and he just went right at everybody." Once in spring training, Mark was sitting outside the clubhouse with minor league pitcher Dave Rozema when a Tiger scout thought he would give the kids a thrill and introduce them to one of his important friends who happened to be visiting. After the scout made the introductions and hands were shaken, the two men walked away. Mark turned to Rozema and asked, "Who was that guy anyway?" It had been the Yankees' Billy Martin, probably the best-known manager in the majors at the time.

Mark watched his friends and teammates from the previous year's Evansville team get sent back down little by little. On March

28, the Tigers assigned Bruce Kimm, shortstop Mark Wagner, and Frank MacCormack to the Evansville roster along with three other rookies. That left thirty-one players in camp—six more needed to be cut before they headed north. That day, Mark started against the Boston Red Sox. It was the biggest game of his life to that point— a Northboro kid taking on the mighty Sox. Television crews were there from Boston. Mark knew that his friends and classmates back home would be watching the game. A large number of New Englanders were there in person as the Joker Marchant Stadium stands filled fast. Attendance was announced as 4,031—only forty-four seats empty.

Mark had been surprised thirty-six hours earlier when he was told that he would be starting the game. He was obviously more keyed up than usual, going against what was essentially his home-town team. Teammates advised him to relax and told him to treat it as any exhibition game, but that did little to help. In an event that would later be retold by numerous reporters and added to Bird lore, Mark was warming up in the bullpen, just beyond the first-base bleachers, when he remembered that he had forgotten his protective cup. He ran into the clubhouse and returned with it. Then, on the bullpen mound, in full view of the stands, oblivious to the rest of the stadium, he pulled his uniform pants down and inserted the cup in his athletic supporter. Now fully protected, he resumed warming up for the game.

Bernie Carbo opened the game with a single for the Red Sox. Mark nervously paced the mound, talked to himself, gestured with his hands almost frantically to get the ball lower, and then proceeded to retire the next three batters in order and sprinted to the dugout. He pitched a scoreless second, but struggled for two additional innings before leaving in the fourth. He was hit hard, although three infield errors hurt his cause. He gave up eight runs and eight hits, with the big blow being a three-run double by Carl Yastrzemski.

Mark's friends at home were disappointed in the game. "I was watching that preseason game while I was at college," says Legion teammate David Veinot. "After Yaz got that big hit off

Mark, I thought, 'Oh no. There's no way he's going to make it now.' "

Although Mark obviously wished for better results, he did not appear too depressed to reporters in the clubhouse after the game, remembering that Rome was not built in a day and that he had at least put his uniform on. And, in what would become a Fidrych trademark, he specifically refused to blame his teammates for their errors. "Hey, I'll clue you," he said, "these guys behind me are the best I'll ever have behind me. . . . The trouble tonight was that the Red Sox were hitting the baseball." Opponents were taking notice of Mark's activity on the mound as well as his pitching. The *Lakeland Ledger*'s Bill Clark noted that Red Sox catcher Carlton Fisk chuckled to him after the game over Mark's "tendency to be hyperactive on the mound." Sox coach Don Zimmer commented that he had never seen anything like him in all his twenty-eight years of baseball.

While Mark's friends and family were discouraged in his performance against Boston, Ralph Houk was not. He told reporters the poor showing "might have done him good because he hadn't been hit in so long he probably didn't know it could happen." Houk added, "There's something about this Fidrych you have to like. He's a battler. He was just trying too hard, I think."

Mark bounced back, and in his next start held the defending world champion Cincinnati Reds hitless over three innings. On April 2, the Tigers unloaded one of their projected starting pitchers, Lerrin LaGrow, to the Cardinals for $30,000 and the ubiquitous player to be named later. It was reported in the papers that Houk was trying to decide on whether to start the season with nine or ten pitchers on the roster. According to reporters, the apparent tenth pitcher still in camp, sitting on the bubble, was a lanky, curly haired twenty-one-year-old with a unique nickname.

The final cut was made on April 6. Mark found himself sitting in the major league clubhouse when Houk gathered the team for a talk. Afterward, Mark went into the manager's office and got the official news. Once Houk told him he was now a Tiger, Mark had a hard time keeping still waiting for Houk to stop talking so he could bolt from the room and tell the world. *Detroit News* columnist Jerry Green later wrote that he saw Mark come running out of Houk's office, squawking and flapping his arms. He sprinted to the clubhouse phone and called home collect. "Mom, Dad," Green said he heard in a voice that carried across the clubhouse, "I made it."

Mark told his father, "Thanks for all the work you did with me, 'cause it happened. It's gonna be in the papers tomorrow. You're gonna see it in the *Telegram-Gazette*: Mark Fidrych of Northboro is going to the big leagues."

"It's not every day a kid makes it," Mark beamed to Green after he hung up. "I tell you, man, it's the rush of my life. I'll never have a high like it. I went to stand up and I shook so much I couldn't stand." He later told Dan Ewald, "If they want me to be batboy all season, I will . . . I'll do whatever they want—anything. Never in my wildest imagination did I think I had a chance at making the team. When I was told, I started to sweat. I'm not on earth now. I may never come down."

Mark soon came down when he learned that along with the great achievement came great sacrifice—specifically, he had to dress like a big leaguer now. He was informed that his ensemble of T-shirts and cut-off jeans would not do. Mark Fidrych owned exactly one suit—a green one he had bought for a wedding a few years earlier—hardly suitable for major league travel. Jim Campbell called Mark into his office and told him, "I'm sending you to a friend of mine who'll set you up with suits and ties." Campbell handed him the address of a fine clothing store in Lakeland. Campbell and his secretary, along with Audrey, the minor league secretary, eagerly awaited Mark's return to see what the famously casual-dressing pitcher would pick out. They were disappointed, however, when Mark returned empty handed. He had suffered sticker shock at the store.

Irritated, Campbell told Mark, "Get in the car, we're going back to the store." Mark replied, "I gotta tell ya, Mr. Campbell, it's a little overpriced." When Campbell suggested that Mark use some of his signing bonus to buy the clothes, Mark informed him that the bonus was gone. It had only been $3,000; most of it went to pay off his tuition from Worcester Academy and the rest went for a stereo system. Campbell then escorted his prized rookie pitcher back to the store and told him to pick out anything he wanted—it was on the Tigers; sort of an extra bonus for making the team so soon. Mark delightedly hurried over to the nicer racks this time. "So I got three leisure suits, a brown London Fog coat, belts, socks, and shoes," Mark later said. "Underwear was the only thing I didn't need." They returned to Tiger Town and treated the two secretaries to a fashion show.

At this point it is important to pause and understand the times in which Mark Fidrych arrived in the major leagues in order to fully appreciate the impact he was to have on the nation, the game of baseball, and the city of Detroit. The United States was a country in flux as it prepared to celebrate its bicentennial in 1976. The turbulent years of the sixties had passed but were still fresh on everyone's minds. The rebellion of the country's youth against the establishment, manifested in their music, fashion, hair, and attitudes in general, had been met with resentment and backlash from the older generation. Society had been divided along battle lines of appearance (crew cuts vs. long-hairs), fashion (suits vs. jeans), or age (over thirty vs. under thirty). In the early seventies, however, a nervous feeling of détente was established between the generations.

By 1976 Americans had come to realize that there were much more important things than appearance as they were anxious to forget Vietnam, long gas lines, runaway inflation, political scandals, and economic depression. Many of the conservative perceptions seemed to belong to ancient history as the pendulum not only swung, it became completely unhinged. Cries over impending moral decay faded as radical ideas of the sixties gained wider acceptance and were mainstreamed. The midseventies became a time when the funky could coexist side by side with the dorky, and thirty years later, looking at pictures, it could be difficult to tell which was which. Fashion grew to outlandish proportions: lapels and ties became wider, collars larger, colors louder. Boundaries for hairstyles became blurred. Frequently teachers had longer hair than students, and it seemed everyone under sixty wore their hair over their ears and had facial hair. Americans became more tolerant of expressions of individuality. It was not uncommon to see such a paradoxical sight as a fifty-year-old conservative ex-military high school teacher sitting in church on a Sunday morning with hair over his ears, sporting a mustache and wearing a lime green leisure suit—anything was fair game. This was important because there was no longer an automatic angry rejection by adults of anyone with long or unusual hair.

Sports heroes of the seventies had progressed from the quiet humble dignity of Bart Starr and Johnny Unitas to the brash, look-at-me antics of Joe Namath and Muhammad Ali. Reggie Jackson and other sluggers now stood at home plate admiring their home runs before beginning their trot—actions that only a few years earlier would have earned them a one-way ticket to the seat of their pants via chin music.

In the entertainment world, the ideal hero was being redefined as well. The straight-laced, crew-cut, platitude-wielding Joe Friday was replaced by the bushy-haired, .357 Magnum–toting Harry Callahan as the antihero became popular. Results and not rules were the important thing, and the greatest crime of all was hypocrisy.

While this great social attitude change was taking over the country in the seventies, the game of baseball was in trouble. Attendance had flatlined or was declining for most teams. The NFL was overtaking baseball as the national pastime. Ratings for *Monday Night Football* were much better than *Monday Night Baseball*. People complained that baseball games lasted too long and were too boring for television. The game's greatest stars, such as Willie Mays, Hank Aaron, Mickey Mantle, Al Kaline, and Harmon Killebrew, were either retired or nearing retirement, and there was a desperate need for new stars to fill the void.

Many franchises were barely getting by. Even the mighty New York Yankees were in financial peril. In 1972, the Columbia Broadcasting System (CBS), which had bought the team in 1964 for

$13.2 million, sold it to a partnership led by forty-two-year-old George Steinbrenner at the bargain-basement price of $10 million—the most prestigious franchise in baseball history had *lost* $3.2 million in value over eight years.

For years, baseball owners had operated under the reserve clause, which had tied players to the team that signed them for life, and had ruled the game with impunity. Players had essentially no negotiating power. In 1967, about half of all major league baseball players earned less than $17,000 per year. That year, a labor lawyer named Marvin Miller was hired by the Baseball Players Association to negotiate with owners on the Basic Agreement, the general contract covering all collective working conditions. The players gradually made economic progress, but it was not without a very public and particularly nasty fight. In March 1972, the players held the first strike in baseball history, wiping out part of spring training and causing the cancellation of games at the beginning of the season. The strike lasted thirteen days before the two sides reached an agreement.

In 1973, with the players seeking additional improvements to retirement benefits and an increase in minimum salaries, the owners voted to delay spring training—locking out the players. After three weeks of contentious and public debate the owners agreed to salary arbitration and an increase in the minimum salary from $13,500 to $15,000. The owners, realizing their power was slipping away, braced for more assaults and vowed to hold the line.

About this time, agents began showing up on the baseball scene in ever-increasing numbers. With agents representing them, baseball players were no longer pushovers in negotiations with owners. Holdouts and signings became bigger news. Salaries escalated.

The most significant tremor in the force of the grand old game was felt when the reserve clause was finally struck down. After the 1974 season, Catfish Hunter, the best pitcher on the world champion Oakland A's, charged that owner Charlie Finley had breached his contract by failing to meet the deadline to pay $50,000 to a life insurance fund. It would turn out to be the most expensive $50,000 an owner ever saved. An arbitrator declared Hunter a free agent.

After a feeding frenzy of bidding by owners, Hunter signed a five-year contract with the Yankees for $3.75 million, which was three times the salary of any other major league baseball player and nearly half the amount Steinbrenner had paid for the whole franchise a few years earlier.

In January of 1976 a federal judge upheld a ruling by an arbitrator who had declared pitchers Andy Messersmith and Dave Mc-Nally free agents because they had played the 1975 season without a signed contract. This ruling was the final blow to owners—it opened the way for the flood of free agents. A large number of the game's biggest stars announced their intention to become free agents after the 1976 season. The size of future salaries was limited only by the imagination.

In February, the owners, still stinging from the ruling on free agency, announced they would not open their training camps until a new labor contract had been signed. Commissioner Bowie Kuhn, not wanting to see another work stoppage, stepped in and ordered the owners to open the camps, and each complied within a few days. Kuhn would himself become embroiled in legal drama during the season when he was personally hit with a nasty lawsuit filed by Charlie Finley after he blocked Finley from selling three of his best players.

The net effect of all these events was that, much more than ever before, baseball news was being monopolized by talk of salaries, labor problems, and lawsuits—money was seemingly more important now than batting averages and win-loss percentages. Baseball fans grew sick of both greedy owners and greedy players. Fans soon decided they didn't care which side was right as long as they would just shut up and play ball. Fans longed for the bygone era—which had never really existed—in which players loved the game so much they would have played for nothing.

In Detroit, the Tigers had also been experiencing troubles. Professional baseball in Detroit predates Henry Ford's assembly lines, and the blue-collar inhabitants of the city have long held fanatical affection for their team. The Tigers were a very good, conservative organization, and it started at the top. Owner John Fetzer, a disciplined, private, self-made man who had built a radio and television broadcasting empire, bought part ownership of the Tigers in 1956 and became full owner in 1961. He passionately believed that the Tigers belonged to the citizens of Detroit. Soon after taking over the team, he changed the name of the stadium at the corner of Michigan and Trumbull from Briggs Stadium (named for the previous owners) to Tiger Stadium. He believed the club's most valuable asset was a productive farm system. He was a silent, hands-off owner, rarely setting foot in the clubhouse or mingling with players, and he wisely preferred to let the professionals run the team.

The professional whom Fetzer trusted more than any other was Jim Campbell. Fifty-two years old in 1976, Campbell was a portly, round-faced, cigar-smoking workaholic. Bald except for some closely cropped sprouts above his ears, he had dark bushy eyebrows and an amiable smile. He was honest and, like his boss, very conservative. He could be stubborn and demanding with employees, but was universally well liked. It was not uncommon for players to drop in to see him and shoot the breeze before going to work. Campbell had started in the Tiger organization in 1949 following his graduation from Ohio State. His first job was as business manager of the club's Thomasville, Georgia, team in Class D, the deepest cellar of the minors. The day he reported for work, the Thomasville ballpark burned down. Rather than becoming discouraged by this event, Campbell figured baseball work could only go up from there, and it did. He gradually worked his way up the ladder with a variety of front-office jobs and was named general manager of the Tigers in 1962.

Campbell was intensely loyal to both John Fetzer and his money. Like all general managers, he kept a tight rein on player salaries. In 1968, Tiger pitcher Mickey Lolich earned $30,000. After helping the Tigers to the championship by winning three World Series games, he understandably expected a slight raise for the next year. And that's exactly what he got—a slight raise to $40,000. That same year, Campbell refused to negotiate with agent Bob Woolf, who had been hired by pitcher Earl Wilson. Therefore, during the contract discussion, Wilson frequently excused himself to go to the bathroom and called Woolf from a phone down the hall. The Tigers had never granted a multiyear contract until Campbell begrudgingly agreed to a three-year deal with new Tiger Rusty Staub before the 1976 season. That deal made Staub, an established All-Star obtained from the Mets, the highest-paid Tiger of all time at $105,000 a year. Campbell was determined not to enter the arms race of escalating salaries and the free agent buying frenzy that other general managers and owners, like so many lemmings running off a cliff, were eagerly joining. The Tigers would not sign a major free agent until 1984. While strictly watching the bottom line of the business, Campbell and the Tiger organization were also committed to being as loyal as possible to players and treating them as family. Willie Horton, Mickey Lolich, Mickey Stanley, Bill Freehan, Gates Brown, and John Hiller were all given special days, saluted, and given engraved clocks to commemorate ten or more years with the team.

The Tigers had been very good in the not-so-distant past. They had lost the pennant on the last day of the season in 1967 and then won it all in 1968 behind Denny McLain's thirty-one wins. They won the division under fiery manager Billy Martin in 1972, coming within one agonizing run of beating the A's in the playoffs, but it was a team on the edge of decline as the organization had waited too long to start reloading. The youth movement brought on difficult times. After Martin had worn out his welcome in 1973, Campbell brought in Ralph Houk to preside over the rebuilding effort. With the cupboard bare, the Tigers came in last place in both 1974 and 1975. The 1975 team, with a record of 57–102, was the worst in the majors, the second worst team in Detroit history, and lost nineteen games in a row at one point. All-time Tiger favorite Al Kaline had hung up his spikes in 1974, and pitching ace Mickey Lolich had been traded after the 1975 season. There was a need for a new fan favorite in Detroit.

The city of Detroit itself had followed the Tigers' fortunes. Detroit had been shocked, along with the rest of the country, by the long gas lines and rising prices forced by the oil-producing countries of the Middle East. Detroit car makers had been slow in responding with small, gas-efficient cars, and as a result, the entire city was in a depression. Jobs evaporated. Eventually over one-third of the local auto workers were laid off. The murder rate skyrocketed, crime and drug abuse were rampant, and Detroit earned the reputation as the most dangerous city in the nation.

Crime and the fear of crime caused a mass exodus to the suburbs. There were several highly publicized incidents of wild gangs attacking concertgoers and others downtown. In 1975, the Tigers' attendance came close to dropping below a million for the first time in years. Fires were frequently visible from the stadium. Fans were tired of losing and were afraid to venture downtown to games at Tiger Stadium. The risk of being murdered in the murder capital of the country was worth it if the team was winning, but nobody wanted to get killed going to see a last-place team. As with the Tigers, the other sports in town gave fans little to feel good about as the Lions, Pistons, and Red Wings were all awful. The city's inhabitants were desperate for something or someone to cheer for.

It was against this backdrop of national change and local despair that a tall, curly headed twenty-one-year-old rookie pitcher packed his bags and prepared to head north with the Detroit Tigers baseball team to begin the 1976 season.

As a young baseball player, Mark Fidrych had landed in an ideal situation. Despite their poor outlook for the season, the Tigers had a good team atmosphere because of the leadership from the older players who had experienced success. Also, Mark could not have picked a better manager to break in under than Ralph Houk. The fifty-six-year-old Houk had been in professional baseball for thirty-eight years. Originally coming up through the Yankees' system as a catcher, he had the misfortune of arriving at roughly the same time as Yogi Berra. The light-hitting Houk spent most of his eight years as a Yankee sitting in the bullpen, waiting to warm up relievers. But he put that time to good use by studying the game and discussing situations and pitching with the bullpen pitchers. While not getting on the field much, Ralph impressed everyone in the organization with his knowledge and leadership qualities.

Houk had interrupted his young career to become an Army Ranger during World War II. As a lieutenant, he had landed at Omaha Beach shortly after D-Day and fought his way across Europe, once having a bullet pass through part of his helmet, narrowly missing his skull. He spent an uncomfortable December in a small Belgium town called Bastogne in 1944. There, during the Battle of the Bulge, he had distinguished himself, eventually earned a promotion to major, and won the Silver Star, Purple Heart, and Bronze Star.

After the war, Houk worked his way up the baseball ranks, succeeded Casey Stengel as manager of the Yankees, and led them to World Series titles in 1961 and 1962 and the American League pennant in 1963. After a short stint as general manager, he returned to the field to manage the Yankees through 1973, leaving as George Steinbrenner was taking control. Houk's friend Jim Campbell had talked him into moving to Detroit to preside over the rebuilding effort in 1974.

Although he had a feared, explosive temper, the powerfully built Houk rarely showed it by the midseventies. He had a friendly personality and a characteristic infectious chuckle, but no one questioned the rule of "the Major." He was the rare man who commanded—and received—respect from other men merely with his presence. When he said to do something, it was done. Houk didn't consider himself to be a superstrategist and did not overmanage. He treated his players as adults and trusted them to do what was best. He was patient with young players and universally viewed as a players' manager. His years as a backup catcher had taught him how to handle pitchers as well as how to keep role players happy. Red Sox pitcher Bruce Hurst later recalled that, as a rookie, he was struggling and entered Houk's office to plead for patience. Houk told him, "Kid, I don't care if you get another out the rest of the year. You're getting the ball every five days, so get the hell out of my office."

Dave Rozema, who made the Tigers as a twenty-year-old rookie pitcher in 1977, says, "Ralph told me, 'You just give me 100 percent. I don't care what your record is, you're my pitcher. So relax and do your best.' When a manager says that, you feel his sincerity and confidence and you can go out and have a good year." Mark Fidrych got a similar speech at the beginning of the 1976 season, along with advice to avoid wasting too much energy on booze and women.

Ralph Houk believed in letting pitchers pitch. The classic example of this was his management of Whitey Ford with the Yankees. The Hall of Fame left-hander had been frustrated by Casey Stengel's handling in the fifties. Stengel frequently skipped Ford in the rotation and limited his innings during the regular season. Some felt that Yankee management also had a hand in this because they disliked having pitchers reach the magical number of twenty wins in a season, which would have made them overvalue themselves and expect something unreasonable, like a raise. Ford rarely threw more than 200 innings a season and he averaged just fourteen wins per year in his last four seasons with Stengel. When Houk took over the Yankees in 1961, he made it clear that he would not baby the pitchers. Ford flourished, throwing 283 innings and winning twenty-five games in 1961. He followed that with 257 and seventeen in 1962 and 269 and twenty-four in 1963.

Houk, aware of the trials that await any rookie, asked veteran John Hiller to take the locker next to Mark's in the clubhouse. Hiller, the relief ace of the staff, was a low-key, classy, stable guy who Houk knew would look after Mark. The thirty-three-year-old Hiller had been with the Tigers since 1965. He had made a miraculous comeback to the majors after suffering a heart attack in 1971. By 1976, still an excellent pitcher, he was one of the elder statesmen and leaders of the Tigers. Similarly, Houk assigned veteran pitcher Joe Coleman to be Mark's roommate on the road.

Over the years, Mark frequently gave the Tiger veterans credit for making him feel like part of the team right from the start. In addition to Hiller and Coleman, Willie Horton, Mickey Stanley, Bill Freehan (holdovers from the 1968 World Series champs), and Rusty Staub were especially helpful to the rookie. Horton, the muscular outfielder from inner-city Detroit, was one of the most prominent voices in the clubhouse. He traditionally hosted a barbecue in the parking lot of the Holiday Inn near the end of spring training. He had driven over to the minor league dorm to personally escort Mark to the 1976 cookout. Early in the season, Horton told reporters that Mark Fidrych was "definitely a moll digger." He explained that was Horton-speak meaning "everyday people, one of the boys." Horton went on to explain his role with helping the young players on the team: "These kids are just coming along, just getting started, and I want to help them. I want them to learn to live on and off the field. You have to be together if you're going to win. . . . You've got to make the kids feel good."

On the trip into Cleveland for Opening Day, Hiller, Staub, Coleman, and Dave Roberts took Mark out for dinner at a nice restaurant. They talked to Mark and told him what to expect from the coming year. When the dinner was over, the veterans picked up the tab. They told him that in the future, "Just treat a rookie the way we treated you just now."

"That was something that the Tigers did in those days," says Hiller. While rookies had a very hard time breaking into some teams, Tiger tradition dating back to the midsixties made life somewhat easier for them. "If you went out somewhere with a few veterans, they would pick up your tab. Nobody was making any money then. It was just something veterans did, especially the first part of the year. The veterans also helped teach the rookies things about life in the big leagues."

There were lots of things Mark needed to learn about life in the big leagues, but his youthful exuberance and sense of humor disarmed most people. On one of the first bus trips with the squad in the spring, the veterans had been amused when Mark boarded the team bus carrying a quart of milk and a sandwich in a paper bag. He was informed that major league players receive enough meal money that they don't need to brown-bag it. The veterans, along with reporters, also laughed at Mark's habit of constantly sticking his finger in the coin return slot of every pay phone he passed—hoping to score a dime or nickel absentmindedly left by the previous user. Mark later told a reporter that early in camp he smeared tobacco juice on the front of his uniform so his major league teammates would think he chewed. He reportedly later got sick after chewing tobacco and thereafter stuck with what would become a Bird trademark: a huge wad of bubble gum, blowing enormous bubbles in the dugout.

Once early in the regular season, Mark went out to get some new clothes shortly before the bus was leaving for the park. He came back wearing his new clothes and got on the bus. Teammates noticed that his clothes still had the tags on them, but nobody said anything to him about it. After the game, they went out to dinner and he still had the tags on. "Why didn't anybody tell me?" he asked his teammates when he finally noticed. "It's more fun this way," one replied laughing.

During an April trip to California, Mark went out with a few teammates to a bar, but discovered he had forgotten to bring his identification. No problem. When carded by the bartender, Mark borrowed shortstop Tom Veryzer's ID. The bartender skeptically eyed the card for the 6-1, 185 Veryzer while looking over Mark's curly hair and 6-3, 170-pound frame. "What did you say your name was?" he asked. "I'm Mark Fidrych. I play for the Detroit Tigers," Mark proudly told the man. The bartender laughed and went ahead and served him.

After an early season loss before Mark had pitched in a game, he flew into the clubhouse to get to the postgame spread for something to eat. That night, shortstop Tom Veryzer told him, "Ralph told me that he didn't want to make any scene about it, but when you lose, walk to the lunch. . . . Don't act happy." Veryzer let Mark worry over the manager's disapproval for a while before he finally told him that Houk hadn't said anything. "But *I'm* telling you. Because when you ran by me, you almost knocked me over." Don't act happy when the team loses.

With the help of teammates, Mark found a small apartment in the Detroit blue-collar suburb of Southgate. Nothing fancy—there was no guarantee how long he would remain in Detroit; the possibility of a sudden demotion to Evansville was a constant concern for the untried rookie. Several teammates lived nearby and they could carpool to work to save on gas. While worrying over how he could afford to pay his bills in the city, Mark decided to forego luxuries such as a telephone or a television.

As they settled into Detroit, when it was time to go out, teammates introduced Mark to the Detroit institution of the Lindell AC. A Detroit landmark since the late 1950s and located near Tiger Stadium, the Lindell was one of the first sports bars in the country (the *AC* stood for *athletic club*). It was sort of a midwestern low-brow counterpart to New York's Toots Shor's. The Lindell was the kind of establishment that does not exist anymore—relegated to the twentieth century, to a time when famous athletes and ordinary people could, and did, eat and drink side by side. It was the type of place that, after a Tiger game, a man might take his twelve-year-old son and have a few beers while the kid munched a burger. If they got lucky, they might see any number of real baseball players hanging around in their natural environment—they might even have a few words with them and come away with some autographs if they were polite and not too pushy and the players weren't too involved in other pursuits. Owned by the Butsicaris brothers, the Lindell had a long and illustrious history. It had allegedly been the establishment in which Lion star Alex Karras had been alleged by NFL Commissioner Pete Rozelle to have allegedly placed bets that led to his year-long suspension in 1963. Later Karras was involved in a much-celebrated brawl there with flamboyant wrestler Dick the Bruiser. After a late-season game in 1969, Billy Martin, visiting manager of the division-leading Minnesota Twins, had been knocking back a few in the Lindell when he became involved in a serious intellectual disagreement with his best pitcher, Dave Boswell. Martin and Boswell politely decided to continue their academic discussion in the alley, whereupon Martin allegedly broke Boswell's jaw with a well-placed right fist.

The Lindell was the favorite postgame hangout for both Tigers and visiting players, as it was only a short walk, or stumble, to the hotel most frequently used by other teams. Over the years, athletes had donated numerous items to the brothers, and by the seventies, the walls resembled a museum. There was a bat autographed by Mickey Mantle, memorabilia from Billy Martin and Whitey Ford, along with numerous other jerseys and balls and gloves. Wayne Walker, a longtime Lion linebacker, even had a, uh, necessary piece of athletic apparel bronzed and placed on the wall. Such was the atmosphere and history of the Lindell AC.

Coming out of spring training, Ralph Houk's plan was to work Mark into the lineup carefully. He didn't want to throw him to the wolves and risk damaging his confidence. He was aware of his age and the fact that he had shot through the minors so quickly. Houk had told Mark that it would be better to go north with the big club and just sit and observe than to be pitching regularly in the minors. The lighter schedule early in the year allowed Houk to go with a four-man veteran pitching rotation the first month, but Mark worked regularly in front of coaches on the sidelines. He otherwise spent his time yakking constantly and cheering his teammates exuberantly from the bench; so exuberantly, in fact, that early in the season, Houk asked Mark to move down to the far end of the bench during games to save the manager's ears and sanity. Mark yelled from the bench like everyone used to in Little League games. Teammates almost expected him to break into a chorus of "Pitcher's bad, catcher's worse, who's that monkey sitting on first?"

"When he wasn't pitching, he supported the team from the bench like you've never seen or heard anybody do," says Sutherland. "Most pitchers are fairly subdued in the games they're not pitching, but Mark was running up and down the bench, telling this guy 'good hit' and that guy 'great play' and saying 'hang in there' when somebody made a mistake. The most refreshing part is that it wasn't a put-on. He really cared how the team was doing when he wasn't playing—this was his team now and he was supporting it."

Even though the Tigers got off to a poor start and he could have been tempted to try a new arm, Houk stuck to his plan. Mark made his major league debut on April 20, entering as a reliever in the ninth inning in Oakland in front of 3,000 fans. With the score tied and a runner on third, Mark threw two pitches to Don Baylor. The second one was lined into left field for a hit and the game was over. Since the runner was the responsibility of the preceding pitcher, Mark was not charged with the loss, but that didn't lessen the sting of being unsuccessful his first time out. The game was otherwise remarkable for the fact that starting catcher Milt May broke his ankle. Rookie Bruce Kimm would be called up from Evansville to take his place.

April 22, Mark pitched against the Reds in an exhibition in Cincinnati. Each year back then, the Tigers and Reds played a home-and-away set of exhibitions early in the year to benefit amateur baseball teams in Michigan and Ohio. This was the perfect opportunity for a young pitcher to work against major leaguers without too much pressure.

On May 5, Mark saw his second major league action, mopping up the ninth inning against the Twins in an 8–2 Tiger loss. This time, despite some control problems, he worked a scoreless inning after giving up two hits.

May 10, Mark pitched five innings and was the winner in the exhibition game against the Reds, despite giving up five runs. He was hit pretty hard by the world champs. "If the rookie righthander was talking to the ball, as he says he does, the ball wasn't listening," wrote Hal Schram of the *Detroit Free Press*.

In Ralph Houk's view, everything was coming along on schedule. While part of the Bird Legend later stated that Mark only got a chance to start because his roommate, Joe Coleman, got sick, this is not true. Houk had been planning to start Mark all along. He now had two brief relief appearances and two exhibition games against major league hitters under his belt. Houk felt he was ready.

The major league starting debut of Mark Fidrych came in Detroit on May 15 against the Indians. The day started out overcast with a threat of rain; a dark and dreary day. As he nervously watched the weather, Mark was afraid of another planned start being washed away. A week earlier he had been scheduled to start a game, but a rainout had caused a shuffling of the rotation, and his family, which had excitedly driven from Massachusetts, had returned home disappointed. This time, with the worrisome weather report, Mark had not invited his family to come for the game, fearful of another disappointment. He drove his small Dodge Colt through light traffic up to the corner of Michigan and Trumbull several hours before game time. Tiger Stadium was empty as he parked and entered the clubhouse. It drizzled on and off, and the game was delayed for an agonizing hour, but it finally cleared enough to play ball. Mark took the mound in Tiger Stadium in front of 14,583 fans who had shown up faithfully to watch a 12–11 Tiger team take on the Indians. A few of the more observant fans may have been aware that the rookie who had been the subject of a couple of amusing articles was going to make his first start, but most were not. "Anybody know this guy? When did they call him up?" both fans and Cleveland players asked each other about the tall skinny pitcher with the difficult-to-pronounce last name. It is doubtful that either expected much. There was no hint that the dismal Detroit summer was about to experience a colossal turn-around.

Ralph Houk picked Bruce Kimm to be the catcher. "You know him better than anybody," Houk told the twenty-four-year-old Kimm, thinking that having a familiar hand behind the plate would provide comfort to the rookie pitcher. An excellent defensive catcher with a strong arm and a very good handler of pitchers, Kimm had labored seven years in the minor league systems of the Angels, White Sox, and Tigers. He had been relegated to the bench behind veteran catchers John Wockenfuss and Bill Freehan since being called up. As he warmed up before the game, Kimm had no way of knowing the part he would soon play in baseball lore.

"Going into the game, we were going to go with his strengths," says Kimm, speaking of Mark Fidrych's first start. "We weren't going to worry about the scouting report on the other team. I knew he had a well-above-average fastball; a running sinker he could put where he wanted, on either corner. He also had a very good slider—two outstanding pitches and great control. We were just going to go right at them. Before the game, Mark was the same as always. If he was nervous that first game, he didn't show it."

Any last-minute advice from his pitching coach before the rookie took the mound? "I just gave him the ball and told him to go out and pitch," says Gladding.

Mark breezed through the first inning. Initially, the Indian players were focused on Mark's pitches and how he was throwing. "Like any time you face someone you haven't seen before, guys would come back to the dugout and talk about what he had," says Doug Howard, the Indian first baseman that game. "Everyone wants to know how fast he seems, what his curveball is like, how the ball is moving." It was evident pretty quickly that this kid had some serious stuff.

The Tigers staked Mark to a lead with a run in the bottom of the first on a Willie Horton sacrifice fly. The fans, along with the players in both dugouts, began to notice some unusual activities on the mound, but Mark was working so fast there was little time to appreciate anything other than the fact that the innings were flying by. After each pitch, he would grab the return throw from Kimm, immediately get on the mound, and prepare to throw; feet together, bent forward at the hip, with the ball held in his glove in front of his face while he peered in at the plate. His lips were constantly moving while he held the ball in front of him. He then went into a smooth, fluid, long-armed motion and unleashed his surprisingly quick fastball, which dove as it reached the batter. His slider was even better—sharply breaking about a foot right at the plate. This kid was not nervously nibbling, he was going directly at the hitters—good old-fashioned "here it is, try to hit it." But nothing was in a spot where it could be hit hard—everything was on the corners, mostly at the knees.

Mark was in perpetual motion on the field. He went to a knee and groomed the mound with his left hand when he found it not to his liking. He refused to let the grounds crew get onto the mound one inning—preferring to do it himself. He actually grabbed a handful of sand from their wheelbarrow, carried it back to the mound, and patted it in place. Several times he stood on the mound facing the plate and held out the ball in his right hand with his elbow bent—appearing like a dart player aiming for a bull's-eye. He frequently windmilled his arm to keep it loose. He fidgeted and nervously paced around the mound after each pitch that was not to his liking, motioning downward with both hands while talking to himself—telling himself to keep the ball down. He openly applauded teammates after everything other than a routine play. He was constantly twitching, chewing bubble gum, and tugging on the bill of his cap. He sprinted on and off the field between innings. The fans began to get into the game as they watched this unusual act on the mound.

"We thought he was crazy," says Howard. "Some guys thought he was being a jerk, just doing it to be a wise guy. You don't know about the guy, you wonder what he's doing. But it's also fun to see somebody who loves the game and acts like he enjoys it."

The Tiger players were also amused at Mark's behavior. Due to the spring routine of split squads and days off, some of the Tiger veterans hadn't seen him pitch in the spring training games. Also, with the real major league game pressure, Mark was much more focused and oblivious to the rest of the stadium—and much more animated than he had been in Florida. "We were sitting there thinking, 'What in the world is going on out there,'" says catcher John Wockenfuss.

The game was televised by the Tigers' local affiliate with longtime announcer George Kell in the booth along with Tiger legend Al Kaline. After a few innings, Kell turned to Kaline and, in his characteristic slow Arkansas drawl, said, "You know Al, that guy is kind of goofy out there."

All across the region, fans watching on television or listening to the radio realized something special was happening. Michael Happy, who would grow up to write for the *Detroit News*, was playing basketball with his brother in the yard. His father came out and told them, "Get in here, kids. There's a guy throwing for the Tigers who talks to the ball." They went in and watched the sight that had enraptured their father—and witnessed a game they would never forget.

The Indians could not muster a base runner until Alan Ashby walked on a 3–1 pitch with two outs in the fifth inning. The first Indian hit did not come until the seventh when Buddy Bell singled under third baseman Aurelio Rodriguez's glove. After another single, Bell scored on Rico Carty's ground-out to make the score 2–1.

Rather than unravel under the pressure, Mark retired the next seven batters in a row to hold on to the win—a two-hitter in his first major league start. He ecstatically romped over the field, shaking the hands of all his teammates. That was unusual in itself for a regular season game. "That was never really done before then," says Hiller. "Nowadays, players shake hands and stuff on the field— Mark really started that. Back then, you would wait until you got into the dugout."

The Tiger faithful left the park impressed by the rookie, but there was otherwise little fanfare. They perhaps made a mental note as they filed out to make sure to listen to his next game, and maybe even to try to find out how to pronounce his last name, but there was no recognition of the explosion that was to come.

After the game, the reporters who flocked to the Tiger clubhouse found that this indeed was no ordinary rookie. There were none of the usual shy, self-conscious rookie mumblings coming from Mark Fidrych. There was no need for reporters to work hard to pry loose a usable quote. Actually, the problem was you couldn't shut the guy up. "I'll never get over this," Mark gushed while hopping around his locker, barely able to be still long enough for an interview. "Besides joining the club, this is the biggest thrill of my life. I can't believe it. But hey, I only struck out five batters. The other guys did all the rest of the work. I did one-third of the work and they did two-thirds." When asked if he actually talked to the ball on the mound, he initially denied it, then confessed, "I really don't know what I do out there."

The reporters found the wide-eyed, happy-to-be-here youth refreshing. "You know what's really neat about being in the big leagues?" he asked. "It's going and seeing all those good fields, especially the stadiums. In high school I played on fields that had weeds in the infield. And in the minors I saw some fields that were kept up and some that weren't. Here they cut the weeds. It's neat to see fields that were kept up like that." How many other major leaguers had they interviewed who were thrilled to find weedless fields?

In the visiting clubhouse, thirty-six-year-old slugger Rico Carty, who had been on an 11-for-15 streak entering the game, was not happy about being blanked by the rookie. "The first time I got up, he pointed the ball at me, and I said to myself, 'What the hell is he doing and saying?'" Carty said. It had an unsettling effect on the Indians' best hitter, who thought the rookie was trying to hypnotize him. "My mind was more on what he was doing than concentrating on my hitting. In the dugout everyone kept saying, 'Let's get that guy, let's get him.' But we were too concerned about that and didn't pay attention to our hitting." He added, "How can you hit when you're laughing?"

Indian outfielder John Lowenstein said that the next time they faced Fidrych he was going to call time and ask the umpire to inspect the ball. Then he would grab the ball and hold it to his ear to try to listen to what The Bird had told it.

The home-plate umpire for the game, Marty Springstead, said after the game that if his colleague, Dale Ford, hadn't warned him about Fidrych's strange behavior, he might have kicked him out of the game. "It was lucky Ford told me about him because I would have thought he was yelling at me when he started all the talking on the mound. Ford had him in the minors and he was going to run him, too. But the kid's manager came out and told Ford, 'He's not yelling at you.' When an umpire sees a guy out there talking like that, you think he's cursing you. But this kid is different."

The next day's *Detroit Free Press* had a picture of Mark bent over grooming the mound and another of him aiming the ball. A wire report to papers across the country began, "Mark Fidrych, an eccentric right-hander who talks to the ball between pitches . . ." People were beginning to suspect that strange things were happening in Detroit. Strange things indeed.

When asked about the game the next day, Houk told Patrick Zier, "He was just like you know him down there. He was up and down, talking to the ball, you know Mark. This was the way we had it planned all along. We've been working with him on the side, trying to get him calmed down and used to being up here. We wanted to make sure he was settled down before he pitched. One thing that helped him a lot was that Bruce Kimm caught him. Kimm has caught him before and knows how to work with him." Kimm would be Mark's personal catcher the rest of the season.

The good outing earned Mark another start; this time, it was against the defending American League champs, the Red Sox in Boston. With the game being only forty minutes from Northboro, it seemed as though the entire town migrated to Fenway to watch. Northboro residents ran into hometown acquaintances in the restrooms and aisles at the stadium. It was a thrill for Mark's friends and former teammates to see him on the famous field. "It gave me goose bumps coming into Fenway Park and seeing the sign for the starting pitchers: Fidrych vs. Tiant," says David Veinot.

"We went down near the rail and yelled at him, 'Hey Fiddie, come over here,'" says Paul Beals. "He came over on the field near the rail and started talking to us." Seeing their friend on a major league field, wearing a major league uniform, seemed surreal. "We were all wondering, 'How good is he going to do against the Red Sox?' This kid from Northboro was pitching against the Red Sox. It was great because just a few years ago, he had been hanging out with us. Nobody else knew who this kid was. We were thinking, 'Just don't get blown out or embarrass yourself.'"

Ralph Houk was a little worried that the hometown hoopla would affect Mark, especially since he had been treated so rudely by the Red Sox hitters in Florida two months earlier. But Mark seemed impervious to the nerves everyone else was feeling. "He was talking to all of us just like it was before a Babe Ruth League game," says Kevin Dumas. "But that was when it really hit us— there is a guy who played with you in Little League and Babe Ruth League and now he's on the field at Fenway in a uniform pitching."

Before the game Mark told a local reporter, "It's really nice having all these people here to see me. But I think it's gonna be fun. They don't make me nervous. In fact, just thinking about them gets me up even more for the game."

With his family and friends watching, Mark pitched another excellent game. Working fast, going right after the batters, and painting the corners as he had against the Indians, he held the Red Sox in check most of the game. In the fourth inning, Carlton Fisk walked. Yaz came to the plate and went with an outside pitch, hitting it high into the screen behind the Green Monster in left. "Mark was so keyed up, it looked like he chased Yaz around the bases," says Fred LeClaire, his Babe Ruth coach who attended the game with the Fidrych family. After the home run, the rookie pitcher maintained his composure and the Red Sox got only one hit, a single, over the next four innings as Mark completed the game. Unfortunately, the Tigers were unable to score off Luis Tiant, and Mark was tagged with the loss, 2–0. The loss dropped the Tigers to 14–19, one game behind Milwaukee in the cellar of the AL East.

After the game, Mark talked to his parents outside the visitors' clubhouse and told them, "You'd better not go in there," because the loss made six in a row and manager Houk was close to erupting, says Fred LeClaire. "Then Mark looked at me and said, 'Mr. L., I'll be right back, wait here.' He disappeared back through the door, and after a few minutes he came out and gave me a baseball signed by Luis Tiant and Carlton Fisk. Mark signed it also. That is still one of my most cherished possessions." The seventy-something-year-old lifelong Red Sox fan pauses, then adds, "You're making me choke up just thinking about it. That was such a thoughtful thing for him to do."

Later, Virginia Fidrych provided some laughs when she reportedly boarded the Tigers' chartered bus outside Fenway. Mark groaned, "Mom, you got to get off the bus."

Mark got to swing by Northboro for a quick visit before the team hit the road. He took time to stop by Proctor Elementary and talk to fifth graders, telling them he owed his success to his mother and father who encouraged and supported his efforts to become "one of a million" chosen to play in the major leagues.

Mark's next outing came six days later in Detroit against the Brewers. He got a special thrill when he faced Hank Aaron in the first inning with runners on first and second and two outs. The all-time home-run king, playing in his final season, was one baseball player Mark definitely knew. Aaron struck out swinging on an inside fastball. When Mark got back to the dugout he said, "Whoa, I struck out Hank Aaron!" Pretty heady stuff for a twenty-one-year-old baseball player.

Mark was not as sharp against the Brewers as he had been the previous two games, but he displayed a late-inning tenacity that would become characteristic over the course of the season. The Tiger team displayed a tendency for late-inning dramatics in order to win for the rookie, which would also become characteristic. They were down 3–1 going into the bottom of the ninth but rallied for two runs to send the game into extra innings. Mark set down the Brewers in the tenth, but gave up a run in the top of the eleventh. The Tigers then came back for two in the bottom of the eleventh for the win.

After the game, when asked about Mark Fidrych's "strange conduct" on the mound, Brewer slugger George Scott said, "I like it. That's confidence. A lot of people call it flaky and a lot of people call it looney, but I like it. His ball really moved. The ball exploded. I asked the man to check the ball one time because I thought he was throwing a spitter. This guy could be a goodie." Three good games in a row—word was starting to get around.

On June 5, Mark produced another eleven-inning complete game, his second in five days. This time, he beat the Rangers in Texas. A large crowd of 36,825 had shown up to see the Rangers' new acquisition, All-Star Bert Blyleven. They got more than their money's worth as both pitchers battled to the end. After falling behind 2–0 on three hits in the third inning, Mark shut the Rangers out on just three hits the rest of the game and retired the last ten batters. Meanwhile, the Tigers scored one in the sixth, one in the eighth, and, finally, one in the eleventh for the win.

Afterward, an elated Fidrych told reporters, "Far out. What else can I say? I don't know what to think. This is a rush."

"I liked the big crowd," he continued. "Look, man, they were booing me, weren't they? They don't boo you when you're losing. I knew they weren't booing Blyleven, so it had to be me. And maybe it psyched me up."

It was about this time that the machinery that formulated the Legend of the Bird started cranking things out. For the most part, three people were responsible for much of what would be repeated over the next few months and would spread across the country like so much southern kudzu: beat reporters Dan Ewald of the *Detroit News* and Jim Hawkins of the *Detroit Free Press* and *Detroit News* columnist Jerry Green. The thirty-two-year-old bushy-haired, side-burned Hawkins, who frequently wore the garishly loud outfits of the times, had experience in dealing with unusual Tiger pitchers. He had achieved a dubious distinction in 1970 when he was the recipient of a bucket of water in the Tiger clubhouse thrown by Denny McLain, which led to one of McLain's suspensions. Hawkins wrote a weekly update on the Tigers for the *Sporting News*, and Green was a contributor to *Baseball Digest* and *Sports Illustrated*, giving them both a national platform to spread the amusing, often embellished, reports of The Bird. Mark's natural sense of humor, impulsiveness, and naïve openness gave them plenty of fuel. With his obvious fan appeal and the fact that he was rapidly racking up wins, he was a newsman's dream. He never gave a bland cliché— he always had something good to say. He was easy copy. And with his background and unknown status before the year, all the elements were present for a great myth.

Initially, part of the drive for the myth-making process was due to good old-fashioned newspaper rivalry. The two major daily newspapers in Detroit had a long history of competition. Indeed, the only time peace existed between the two papers had been during the newspaper strike of 1968, when they cooperated for the general welfare. The leaders of both papers could see the possibilities in this new Detroit sports personality, and they were determined not to be outdone by their rivals in either column space or hyperbole.

Initially, the elder statesman of Detroit sportswriting, Joe Falls, remained above the fray in the competition over The Bird, taking a wait-and-see approach to this new phenomenon. Falls, forty-eight years old in 1976, had been writing about sports in Detroit since 1953. In addition to being the dean of Detroit sportswriting, he also wrote a prestigious weekly general column in the *Sporting News*. A large man with an ample gut, the enormous glasses of the times, and an equally enormous head of bushy hair that was on its way to becoming gray, Joe Falls was a serious man who wrote serious columns. His formal education had admittedly barely included high school. He had learned his craft on the job and took it, well, seriously. He loved the old players of his youth—loved Joe DiMaggio; loved Ted Williams—and he did not appreciate imposters on the baseball field who claimed to be stars but did not measure up to guys like Jolting Joe and Teddy Ballgame. Falls liked to play the roll of curmudgeon and did not hesitate to call out pretenders to the throne of the sports gods. In the early sixties, he had famously carried on a feud with Tiger star Rocky Colavito and even invented a stat, the "runs not batted in," in which he regularly charted men Colavito did not bat in, but should have—even as Colavito put up RBI totals that reached 140 in 1961. Falls proudly held a stated principle that he never socialized with the men he wrote about— thus preventing a temptation to go easy on them. It was a not-so-funny joke with Tiger players that if Falls ever wrote a good column about you, watch out, because the next one would bury you just to even things out. Joe Falls was not about to publicly acknowledge this new Bird guy yet and would come to be the lone journalist who felt it his duty to keep him in line.

On June 7, Ewald ran a column in the *News* entitled, "When Fidrych Talks, Baseball Listens." The same day, Hawkins countered in the *Free Press* with "Fidrych Is Not Flaky . . . It's the Rest of Us." The obvious winner of this journalistic sparing round was Hawkins. He detailed things that would come to be repeated numerous times over the ensuing months and used as standard Bird fare, such as the tobacco smearing and false ID incidents. He also wrote about the time over the winter in which Mark and some Northboro friends went out to a disco, laid down on their backs, and rolled around, calling their new dance the "Fried Egg." "My friends invented it," Mark said. "It was really neat to do. The people loved it. They clapped and thought it was great. But the bouncer asked us to leave. I guess he didn't think it was so funny." Hawkins noted that when he asked Mark for a funny story for the paper, Mark told him one of questionable color and phraseology. Hawkins told Mark, "I can't put that in the paper."

"Sure you can," Mark replied. "I don't care."

Ewald fought back on June 11 with "Having a Ball: 'Bird' Likes Lofty Perch." Ewald reported that "Tiger fans . . . are getting a genuine kick out of watching a player look as if he is having fun."

"Hey man," Mark said, "I can hear all the people yelling for me. It's neat." Ewald informed readers that when not pitching, Mark was still having fun, "sitting at the end of the dugout blowing giant bubbles and yelling at his teammates louder than anyone in the bleachers. In the clubhouse, he never stays in one place long enough to carry on a conversation of more than two sentences. He is perpetual motion."

"I've always been hyper," Mark added. "Whatever I do, I get a bang out of it."

Detroit fans were beginning to get a bang out of it also and eagerly joined in the fun. The Bird story was rescuing an otherwise bleak season for the Tigers—their record stood at 22–28 after fifty games. One letter writer to the *Free Press* in early June suggested that Tiger hitters start talking to their bats in order to hit better. Fans began showing up at Tiger Stadium in ever-increasing numbers to see this new pitcher, loudly enjoying themselves while doing so. Over the month of June, as Mark's record increased from 4–1, to 5–1, to 6–1, the attendance increased from 14,800, to 17,000, to 36,370. A gathering storm was taking place in Detroit—or maybe a gathering party.

Mark completed every game he started. The games were almost all close, and the last few innings, when the young pitcher should have been getting tired, it seemed as though he could smell the victory and turn up the intensity—week after week he protected tight leads without failing. The Tigers players, seemingly inspired, continued to score runs late to help pull out wins for him. Four of his first five wins came in the final at-bat. While not every game Mark pitched was great, he never had a bad one as he reeled off wins of 3–2, 4–3, 4–3, and 7–3.

There was something magnetic about this young pitcher that made everyone want to watch him—fans, opponents, and teammates alike. "After I got older, there weren't very many teammates that I would stop and watch pitch," says Hiller, who had a normal routine in the bullpen while awaiting the possibility of getting in. "But Mark was definitely one that we all stopped what we were doing to watch. Part was what he did, but also part was that he pitched so well."

Bruce Kimm later said that he would notice Tiger players getting as pumped up as the fans when Mark took the mound. "There was a buzz in the air," says Kimm.

"He was an easy pitcher for our players to play behind," said Houk, "because he never wasted any pitches, and, as you know, any pitcher who gets the first ball over and gets ahead of the hitters, usually the fielders play better behind him because they're always ready; they think the ball is going to be hit."

Mark was initially oblivious to the reaction of others to his performance on the mound. According to friends, he was shocked by his popularity and the uproar that grew after the first few games. He had been just trying to do his job—trying to get hitters out and help the team win—nothing more; a rookie who was just happy to be in the majors and trying to make sure he stayed there. He was amazed at the explosion of sentiment from the ever-growing cadre of fans. He did not understand that a chain reaction had already been initiated, one that would soon mushroom into unbelievable proportions.

On June 24, Mark faced the Red Sox in Fenway Park again. Once more a large contingent from Northboro helped fill the stadium. "I took my son, who was ten, to see him," says Robert Boberg, Mark's ninth-grade English teacher. "We were down along the right-field line, and we saw a big crowd, and it was Mark signing autographs. We must have been about fifty yards away, and he looked up and spotted me, and he yelled, 'Mr. Boberg!' Of course we felt like everybody in the whole park was looking at us now. So we walked up to where he was, and he goes, 'Mr. Boberg, what are you doing here?' Just like he couldn't understand that one of his old teachers would drive over just to watch him."

This time, Mark got more hitting support and beat the Red

Sox 6–3. Things looked shaky for the rookie when the Red Sox scored three times in the fourth, two on solo home runs by Fred Lynn and Yaz, who was quickly becoming Mark's nemesis. Mark settled down to shut out the Red Sox the rest of the way, however. In the Red Sox ninth things once again turned dicey. With two outs and one on, Tiger third baseman Aurelio Rodriguez dropped an easy pop fly that would have ended the game. That brought the tying run, the dangerous Rico Petrocelli, to the plate. Rather than go to pieces, Mark went over and patted Rodriguez on the back, then proceeded to strike Petrocelli out on three pitches.

"It looked like Rocket City," Mark told reporters after the game. "I had a sore neck from turning around and watching the ball fly over the fence. I didn't think I was going to make it. . . . Ralph (Houk) came out to the mound and said if I'd hold these guys, they'd get me some runs. And they did. They deserve all the credit."

Reporters spotted Mark's proud parents waiting outside the clubhouse. Virginia was fingering a broken string of rosary beads. "This is the third set of rosary beads that I've broken this year," she told them. "I get so nervous. I pull them and they break. . . . They're what give Mark his strength. I'm Protestant and my husband is Catholic. I brought Mark up Catholic. He wears a prayer medal around his neck and that gives him strength. But it's these beads, the beads and my prayers."

Paul told them, "He loves baseball so much he probably would play for nothing—but I guess we had better not tell Jim Campbell that."

After the game, Mark was able to stop by Northboro to spend the night with friends and family. When he arrived at The Cutoff, a popular bar, he was greeted by about 150 neighbors. "One of his friends balled him out for letting Yaz hit a homer," his father remarked to reporters. "He told Mark, 'I told you how to pitch to Yaz.'"

The win over the Red Sox improved Mark's record to 7–1 and dropped his ERA to 2.19. There was talk of Mark as a front-runner for Rookie of the Year and a possible spot on the All-Star team. His next start was scheduled to be on a Monday night, June 28, against the first-place Yankees in Detroit. Relaxing in Northboro with his family and friends after the Red Sox game, Mark didn't know it, but by next Tuesday his life would never be the same.

5

Birdmania

The *Monday Night Baseball* "Game of the Week" was started by NBC in 1966. While it did not become the staple that *Monday Night Football* eventually did, it was still quite popular in 1975 when ABC outbid NBC for the rights. Ratings had been slipping during the 1976 season, however, and there were complaints about the broadcasting team of Bob Prince, Warner Wolf, and Bob Uecker. Desperate to score some big ratings, the network had been advertising the June 28 matchup between the Eastern Division–leading Yankees and The Bird heavily.

Before the game Detroit fans could sense that something big was happening, and they wanted to be a part of it. Bill Freehan told reporters, "My phone started ringing at eight in the morning and didn't stop all day. Everyone wanted tickets to see The Bird pitch. I bought fifty-two tickets for friends and relatives." A buzz grew throughout Detroit during the day. The buzz made Jim Campbell happy. Well back in the standings, the fourth-place Tigers had not been drawing well, averaging barely 15,000 fans per home game. They would top that number for this game.

The day started out overcast, however, and there was some

doubt as to whether the game would be played. The weatherman had mentioned a very possible evening thunderstorm. With such a large crowd guaranteed, Jim Campbell would not allow it to rain—there was no way he would lose this gate. "Did you ever see baseball at three o'clock in the morning?" he asked Joe Falls. "We will play, I guarantee you that. If you've never seen a captive audience, you will see one this evening. We will have men with machine guns at all of the exit gates to keep everyone inside." He was joking. Maybe.

Huge numbers of enthusiastic fans began showing up early. There were three-mile backups on the expressways leading up to the park before the game. Ticket windows shut down almost an hour before the 8:40 PM start time. An estimated 10,000 fans were left in the streets without tickets. What was going on here? Just last year the Tigers lost 103 games, and now you couldn't get a ticket for a midseason game? Madness.

Mark Fidrych rode into Tiger Stadium with Tom Veryzer, who lived nearby. They arrived four hours before game time to see thousands of fans already congregated outside the gates. "Mark," Veryzer said, "these people aren't here to see Tommy Veryzer play shortstop."

In the enlisted barracks at Eglin Air Force Base in Florida, Jim Jablonski staked out the television in the dayroom a few hours before the game to make sure he could watch it. He had followed his childhood buddy's progress in the *Sporting News*, but this would be the first time he had a chance to see him in action, and he was determined not to let someone else turn to a different channel.

Back in Massachusetts, Mark's friends Kevin and Ray Dumas and Paul Beals, along with several others from Northboro, drove to Worcester to watch the game on a bigger screen in a bar that had cable and better reception. "It was amazing," says Kevin. "All of a sudden, you go from high school in Northboro, and then there he is on TV pitching against the Yankees. The bar was packed and noisy before the game even started. Everyone from the area was looking forward to seeing him."

Robert Boberg was sitting on his back porch in Northboro,

watching his former English pupil in the biggest game of his life. Earlier, Mr. Boberg's friend and fellow teacher, Jack Wallace, had noticed the surprising attention his former player was getting. "He said, 'Oh my God, they're calling Fiddy The Bird now,'" Boberg recalls.

On Chesterfield Avenue, the Fidryches were congregated around their small television set. Paul Fidrych smiled at his wife. "Virginia, this is national," he told her as he lit up a cigar for the start of the game. While appearing calm, he was every bit as nervous as his wife. "Normally, no one could talk to him while he was watching Mark pitch," says Paula. "He had to concentrate."

"He was very superstitious," adds Lorie. "If Mark was doing good, he would keep doing what he was doing. If Mark got into trouble, he would put out the cigar and cross his legs or something. Anything that would bring him luck."

Everyone in Northboro, it seems, was watching the game on television that night. One can almost envision deserted streets with signs on the windows of stores and restaurants reading, "Closed—watching the game."

ABC color commentator Warner Wolf, unfamiliar with Fidrych, was shocked when he arrived at Tiger Stadium that night. "As we got to the stadium, we go, 'Wait a minute. There's 50,000 people lined up around the block buying tickets. Is there another game or something?'" he recalled. "It's June 28, Yankees–Tigers, Monday night, who cares?" Fellow announcer Bob Uecker had seen The Bird pitch the eleven-inning complete game against the Brewers. He knew what was going on. He told Wolf before the game that he was in for a treat: "Warner, you got to see this kid. He's incredible."

"No one knew what he (Uecker) was talking about," Wolf said. "Most of the country hadn't even seen Fidrych yet."

During introductions, Wolf informed the television audience, "And on the mound is this young man by the name of Mark Feedrych [sic], and I guess there's a lot about him we don't understand." The camera panned through the sold-out crowd, which appeared to be more like that waiting for the ball to drop at Times

Square on New Year's Eve rather than a crowd waiting for a base-ball game. Wolf added, "Most of these people, in all fairness, are here to see Mark Feedrych pitch."

The fans themselves wasted no time in letting everyone know exactly why they were there—they cheered every move Mark made. They gave him a standing ovation when he hopped out of the dugout to warm up in the bullpen. They kept standing, waiting for his first toss, and when he threw it to Bill Freehan, they hollered even louder as if it was the greatest warm-up pitch they had ever seen. They yelled every time he threw the ball during warm-ups. They yelled when he sprinted to the mound after the national anthem. Youngsters moved through the aisles carrying Bird signs hastily drawn on bed sheets. Other signs littered the stands: "Go Get 'Em Bird," "Drop a Big One on Them Bird," "Give Them the Bird," and simply, "We Love You, Mark." Sporadic chants of "Go, Bird, Go" were started in the early innings.

The first Yankee batter, Mickey Rivers, grounded out on the second pitch, and Mark was on his way. The television audience was quickly mesmerized by the spectacle of this tall, skinny youngster as he stood on the mound in front of fifty thousand screaming fans, facing the venerable Yankees, seemingly in a world of his own as he went through a multitude of rapid twitches, cap tugs, and deep breaths after every pitch. In spite of all his hyperkinetic movements, he rarely left the mound between pitches and was working incredibly fast. Mark encountered no trouble in the first inning. He struck out Chris Chambliss looking for the third out and sprinted to the dugout.

As was the case with most teams when they faced The Bird for the first time, the Yankees initially seemed more concerned with what was taking place on the mound, but soon came to respect the way he was getting them out. "I've never seen anything quite like him," said Yankee outfielder Lou Piniella. "I sat on the top step of the dugout and laughed the whole time. But I know our hitters came back impressed. It wasn't all bull; there was some substance there."

"Fidrych was brilliant. Just brilliant," Rusty Staub later said of the game. "It was like an overmatch. He just had games when he didn't make a mistake, he just got you out. And people started realizing he was throwing hard." Twice the announcers mentioned that Mark had been timed at 93 miles per hour that night.

Mark seemed to be all Prince, Uecker, and Wolf were able to talk about on the air as they only occasionally interrupted their discussions of The Bird to inject minor details such as the batter, score, and inning. They showed him rearranging the dirt once in slow motion with a pat-by-pat commentary, and another time with a lengthy interview in which Mark explained, "I like to dig my own hole . . . if you look, you'll see other pitchers moving the dirt around, but they do it with their feet."

They told the audience about Aurelio Rodriguez dropping the potential third out at Boston in the previous game. "Feedrych [sic] patted him on the back, told him it was okay and that he would strike out the next batter, and he did."

They continually showed close-ups of Mark with his lips moving while holding the ball in front of him. "He's talking, telling the ball where he wants it to go," said Uecker. "That's got to bother the batter. . . . Look at that young guy talk to himself. If that ball starts talking back, he's in trouble. . . . If Fidrych continues this success you're going to have an awful lot of Little Leaguers doing the same thing."

The camera jumped from Mark talking to the ball to a fan in a yellow bird costume romping through the stands.

Later Uecker exclaimed, "He's tall, he's lean, he's got webbed feet."

Wolf: "Fidrych is working like he's trying to catch a train."

Uecker: "The more I watch this guy, I believe he's got it all."

Wolf: "I get a kick out of this guy."

Prince: "He's giving me duck bumps. And I've seen over 8,000 games."

Uecker: "I love this guy."

The actual game seemed secondary. After Elrod Hendricks homered for the Yankees in the second inning, Mark had little trouble. He kept going right at the hitters—getting ahead in the count, pounding the ball down in the strike zone. He did not walk a batter. Other than Hendricks, only two Yankees reached second base, and no one reached third all night. As the game proceeded, the fans were on their feet much of the time Mark was pitching, and the chants of "Go, Bird, Go" built to a crescendo.

At Eglin Air Force Base, the dayroom was initially empty other than Jablonski as airmen casually walked in and out. After a while, however, they were captured by the events on the small screen and sat down. The room gradually filled, and by the end of the game, there were no seats left—guys were sitting on armrests and on the floor watching. Jim beamed as he repeatedly told everyone, "That's my buddy there, we grew up together."

Paula Fidrych was watching the game with friends at college. "By the end of the game I had tears in my eyes, I was so proud," she says. In Worcester, Paul Beals and the Dumases joined the other patrons of the crowded, raucous bar cheering every pitch Fid made. In Northboro, Paul Fidrych lit another cigar and Virginia feverishly worked on her rosary beads. The game was going better than they could have dreamed. A few friends began showing up at their door. The Fidrych's small house would soon fill up as more friends and neighbors spontaneously dropped by.

Back in Tiger Stadium, Mark was in complete control. "In the seventh inning, we had a 4–1 lead and Mark was sitting next to me in the dugout while we were batting," says Gladding. "He looked at me and said, 'It's all over. They'll never touch me.' He was that confident." The crowd was in a frenzy as momentum built toward the end of the game.

"Look at Fidrych charge off that mound," said Uecker as Mark sprinted to the dugout amid thunderous cheers after the eighth inning.

"The fans are really getting a kick and reacting to Fidrych," said Wolf in a terrific understatement.

Mark took the mound for the ninth inning with Tiger Stadium rocking from 50,000 delerious fans. The cheers grew even louder when Chris Chambliss led off by striking out. The fans began chanting Mark's name. The next batter, Graig Nettles, quickly grounded out to second. With the fans on their feet, Oscar Gamble singled to center field, causing a slight delay in the celebration. Mark tugged at his cap, shrugged his shoulders, and franticly dug his foot in the dirt on the mound. He threw three straight balls to Elrod Hendricks, with the exceptional movement on the ball causing both fastballs and sliders to dive wickedly down and in to the left-handed batter. Mark walked in a few steps to take the return throw from Kimm, gesturing downward with his hands while talking to himself. The fans were ecstatic. Mark came back with two strikes, then Hendricks grounded out weakly to second, and the game was over; a 5–1 victory over the vaunted Yankees. The entire game had taken only one hour and fifty-one minutes—only slightly more time than a present-day manager uses to work through his myriad righty-lefty setup men and closers over the last three innings.

When it was over, the crowd in Detroit did not want the fun to end. Staub later recounted the scene: "I was the right-fielder. They made the last out of the game. I was coming all the way in, and it was more than just what you would normally see in a ballpark . . . the crowd was yelling, 'We want The Bird . . . We want The Bird.' I was one of the last players in the clubhouse. I went up to Fidrych, and he already had his uniform shirt off. He was excited and talking. I said, 'Mark, put your shirt back on.' He said, 'Are you crazy? The game's over.' I said, 'You have to put your shirt top back on, now, you're coming with me.' He finally realized I was serious. He said, 'What are we doing?' I said, 'Just trust me on this. I'll tell you when we get there.' I said, 'Put your shirt on, get your hat, and follow me.'

"I walked him down the runway, and I said to him, 'I want you to come to the end of this runway and listen. Can you hear those people?' And there were fifty thousand people, and this was fifteen minutes after the game. And they were yelling, 'We want The Bird.' I said, 'You're going to go out of the dugout, stand up on the field, and wave to the fans.' And he said, 'No way, I cannot do that.' I said, 'You're going to have to go out there and do this.'

"He said, 'You gotta come with me, you hit a home run.' I said, 'They're not saying, 'We want Rusty,' they're saying, 'We want The

Bird.' And you're going to give them The Bird. You're going to go out there, and I just want you to do one thing. Just like you have a clock. I want you to just tip your hat six times, as if you went around the clock, and at the end, just raise your hands and acknowledge the crowd, then you can come back.'

"It was electrifying for me to watch that happen to him," continued Staub. "It was more electrifying than if it happened to me, because I appreciated something that was new and great in the game that I hadn't seen in a while. I saw Koufax. When Vida Blue came up, he was pretty exciting. But nothing like this guy. There was nobody like Fidrych. I can only tell you that when he did that, the fans went crazy."

"In that one instant, he created something I never saw in baseball and have yet to see again," Staub added in 2002.

While fans sometimes had called a player back out after a milestone event or a big home run, it was unheard of for that to occur after a regular midseason game, especially after the players had gone to the clubhouse. "I don't think I can ever remember seeing a curtain call in baseball before that," says Kimm. "There's a good chance that game started the curtain call that you see in baseball now. Everybody on the bench thought it was fantastic. It was like a playoff atmosphere."

In the clubhouse later, Tom Veryzer told Mark, "Thanks. I may never get to play in a World Series, but that's what it must be like."

After the game in the noisy clubhouse, Mark wrote down *48,000* on a piece of paper he had hanging inside his locker. He had been keeping track of the attendance for his games. "They get your adrenalin flowing even more," he explained to reporters. "The people really get me up.

"I just kept telling myself, 'Just three more outs and the game is over . . . come on, just three more outs. Let it flow.' I kept saying over and over, 'Just let it flow . . . I gotta throw hard . . . I gotta throw hard.' I've got to do that, that's just my way to keep my mind on the game. If I don't, I relax, and my body seems to slow down. I've got to concentrate on every pitch."

He then added his usual plug for his teammates: "These guys are making me. If I was making myself, I'd be striking out everybody. If they don't play well behind me, I'm not even here."

Later, at his locker, Mark was asked by the New York press corps what he had to say in response to comments made by Yankee catcher Thurman Munson. Munson, an irascible, proud man in the midst of a season in which he would be named American League MVP, had sat out the game with an injury but had nonetheless called Fidrych "fly-by-night" and "a showboat" after the game. "Who's Thurman Munson?" Mark replied honestly. Hearing that, the New York reporters immediately bolted from the room, racing for a phone. Mark looked over to bullpen coach Jim Hegan, who was laughing so hard he could hardly stand up.

Hegan told him, "Mark, I know you. But those guys don't. I hate to tell you, but Thurman Munson may be the best catcher in the big leagues, and tomorrow, all the papers in New York will say 'Bird to Yankees: Thurman Who?'"

Mark Fidrych had come through. With so much riding on the game, for ABC, for the Detroit Tigers, for the city of Detroit, for baseball itself, Mark had come through. Television viewers at home knew they had just witnessed something special. It was a moment that would be frozen in time and never forgotten by those who witnessed it.

The next day, Mark "The Bird" Fidrych was a national star. "Did you see that guy last night?" was asked around watercoolers, in lunchrooms, and at workplaces across the country.

Baltimore Oriole first base coach Jim Frey later said, "Everywhere I went the next day, and I got a haircut and stopped at the hardware store and then went and got some groceries, I visited a friend of mine, and we had some people over to the house—all of them talked about one thing. I don't ever remember that happening before. I heard so many people talking about one baseball player."

First baseman Jason Thompson, who lived near Mark, told reporters that his phone rang off the hook the day after The

Game. Mark didn't have a phone in his apartment, usually using a pay phone in a supermarket down the street when needed. As a nearby source of a phone, Jason spent a good deal of his time Tuesday fetching Mark.

Virginia Fidrych told a local reporter that she didn't get to bed until 5:15 AM the night of the Yankee game. "People just kept calling or coming in," she said. "I kept cooking ham and eggs for people I'd never seen before."

Mrs. Ann Jablonski, Northboro police radio dispatcher, said Fidrych's game was "all the officers could talk about this morning . . . we're all very proud of him. He's putting Northboro and Worcester County on the map."

Everyone suddenly wanted to know more about The Bird. Seemingly every paper in the country dispatched someone to Detroit to find out about him. Where did he come from? What was he really like? Was it all just an act? Everyone wanted more of those funny quotes they heard about.

Tiger officials said that their phones had been ringing off the hook with fans calling wanting to know when Mark was scheduled to pitch next, reserving tickets, and trying to get in touch with Mark. Lew Matlin of the Tigers promotional office said that Mark received over 150 messages in the two days after the Yankee game. He told reporters that he and Hal Middlesworth took Mark off to the side for a thirty-minute talk to advise him on what to expect and how to handle the situation. But the truth was, they didn't know what to expect themselves; they couldn't know what to expect—there had never been anything like this demand for a particular player before.

Paul Fidrych, seeing what was happening, advised his son, "Don't get your head unscrewed." Tiger veterans also tried to give Mark advice on how to handle the media. "When I noticed all the attention he was getting, I tried to council him a little bit," says John Hiller. "Listen to the question and think a little before you answer and don't just blurt out the first thing that pops into your head. I also talked to him a little about how to carry himself in public, because everyone was going to be watching everything he did now. But he came from a good home, so he didn't have too much trouble. I don't think his parents had ever put him on a pedestal or made him feel he was more special than anyone else because he was a ballplayer, and so he didn't act that way. That helped his appeal."

And he certainly had appeal. Everyone loved The Bird. Mail began pouring in, everything from teenagers' marriage proposals to checks from people who thought he deserved more money. Teammates rigged up a gag telephone in his locker—the better to handle all his personal calls. The wire services began a practice they would continue the rest of the summer of routinely running pictures of The Bird: blowing enormous bubbles while watching a game, fielding ground balls between his legs in warm-ups, sitting in the dugout with his feet propped up, yelling from the bench while a nearby cameraman covered his ears, talking with fans, signing autographs, gesturing on the mound, laughing with teammates—in general just having a ball at the ballpark.

Articles about The Bird were printed in papers across the country that week. Most of them began by repeating many of the Bird stories of Hawkins and Ewald. Often, the articles were hastily thrown together with many mistakes regarding his family and hometown. Whatever was written became common knowledge, however, and was repeated by others whether it was accurate or embellished. Reporters were intent on building up the eccentric flaky angle and ignored statements to the contrary from Mark's teammates, such as Bruce Kimm who said, "He's not flaky," and Ralph Houk, who told them, "He's not quite as flaky as they say," and, "He's not nutty." The media as a whole recognized the great possibilities and piled on to make Mark into the greatest character baseball had seen in years. Dizzy Dean? Yogi Berra? Jimmy Piersall? Casey Stengel? Rank amateurs compared to The Bird. The giant snowball of The Bird myth was rolling downhill, picking up speed, unable to be stopped now.

Jerry Green published a feature article on Mark in *Sports Illustrated* and another in *Baseball Digest* soon after the big game. Jim Hawkins, who wrote the Tigers' weekly column for the *Sporting*

News, began regularly pumping Bird stuff to the national audience. Everything anyone wrote added to the frenzy.

People magazine sent a photographer and reporter to Mark's apartment, and they informed the world that he indeed lived simply in an apartment with a mattress on the floor for a bed, sheets over the windows instead of curtains, no television, and no phone. Mark told a reporter that he was generally neat, but sometimes did let his dishes stack up. "But they don't stack up too high," he added. "I only have four."

The tales of Mark's fun-loving antics were eagerly gobbled up by the press and the public. They loved it when Mark told reporters why he always threw the ball back to the umpire to exchange for a new one after a base hit. "That ball has a hit in it," he explained. "I want that ball to get back in the ball bag and goof around with the other balls. I want him to talk to the other balls. I want the other balls to beat him up. Maybe that'll smarten him up so when he comes out the next time, he'll pop up."

Mark, realizing he was on to something, began having fun with the reporters. "If I don't talk to the ball," he asked, "who will?" He told them, "If I want it to, I'll say, 'Ball, you curve.' If it doesn't curve right, I say nasty things to the ball when the catcher throws it back to me."

When asked the inevitable question of "Does the ball ever talk back?" Mark answered, "The only time that happens is when it's going over the fence, it yells back to me that I shouldn't have thrown that pitch."

Dave Anderson wrote an article in the *New York Times* entitled, "Detroit's 'Bird' Capturing Hearts." He reported that Mark was driving a compact Dodge Colt—and sweating out the payments. His mother told Anderson, "He had a '69 Chevy, a yellow two-door, but he didn't think it would get him to Florida for spring training so he bought the new car." His mother also volunteered that Mark enjoyed tinkering with cars and "when something isn't working, he talks to the car just like he talks to the baseball." She added that Mark had always loved baseball: "When he was small, he used to go to bed with his baseball hat on and with his glove under the mattress." Virginia concluded by telling Anderson, "I just hope Marky doesn't change. He sent me a dozen roses for my birthday two weeks ago. I put one of the roses in the Bible he gave me for Christmas, and when he phoned, I told him, 'Marky, please don't change.' He told me he wouldn't."

Marky? Perfect.

Through it all, Mark Fidrych was open and available with everyone—always trying to please. If he made one joking statement and it got a laugh, he repeated it for the next bunch of interviewers—and there was always a next bunch waiting. Mark's apparent innocence and his obvious joy on the field—having fun playing baseball—struck a nerve. His lack of pretense was appealing compared to the serious athletes who appeared to view the game only as a business. When he told reporters he was happy with what he was making, he was sincere and the public ate it up. Imagine, while everyone else in baseball was only concerned with how much money they could get, here was a guy who was happy with what he had. He was exactly what the public wanted, at the exact right time. His own father had told everyone what was plain to see: he loved the game so much he would play it for free.

Why do we want our baseball players to play for free? We don't ask that of athletes in other sports. We don't expect a pro wrestler to say, "I love pile-driving people's heads into the ground so much I would do it for nothing." Hockey players and football players deserve to get paid for playing their violent games. But we want our baseball players to play for free—to love it so much that they would do it for nothing. Because we certainly would. We all did, back when we were kids. We played for nothing then and we certainly would do it now. But in 1976, baseball players were not only playing for outlandish sums of money, they wanted more and were willing to jump teams to get it. All except The Bird. He alone loved baseball so much that he didn't care about the money.

Late in the week, a wire service article announced shocking but heartwarming news to the country with the headline, "Detroit Hero Fidrych Does it All for $16,500 a Year." It explained that although Mark was happy with his salary and did not want a raise, he did express concern over how he was going to answer all his fan mail on his limited budget. "Ten letters a day times thirteen cents is a lot of money," he said. It was also reported that he had turned down five offers from would-be agents in the days after the Yankee game. "Only I know my real value and can negotiate it," he told reporters, who gleefully relayed the information to their readers. If only all players felt that way—we could keep those suit-wearing, briefcase-carrying snakes away from the game.

Joe Falls finally weighed in and gave tacit approval of The Bird. Then, he devoted his next three columns to the subject and even allowed, "Forgotten in the fuss over his strange antics on the field is the fact he looks like a pretty good pitcher." As the week progressed and the unprecedented fury continued, Falls admitted that "no player, on any team, anywhere, has had quite this impact on the game as The Bird has in these last few days" and, "Mark Fidrych has taken a hold on this town as no athlete has done in years." But, refusing to bow like all the rest, he cautioned, "Let's hope he is a true character and none of this is a put-on," and also wondered, "How long can he keep his act going?"

Houk mentioned to reporters, "I have to say I'm concerned about what's been happening to him. So far, all the publicity hasn't seemed to bother him. But ever since that TV game, there's been a deluge. He's been taking it all pretty good, but I'm still a little worried about how he might react. I've never seen anything like it in all my years in baseball."

And all of this was in the three days after The Game.

Mark's next start was scheduled in Baltimore on Friday night. Advance ticket sales skyrocketed for the game. A rainout the day before, however, caused Houk to shift his rotation, and Mark's slot was delayed—to the dismay of Baltimore fans and officials—until the next night in Detroit. A Detroit television station had rearranged its prime-time schedule in order to broadcast the Friday game back to Michigan, but after the rotation was changed, they scrapped the TV plans. "He's (Mark) the only reason we added this game to the schedule—absolutely," said Frank Sisson, baseball coordinator for WWJ-TV.

In anticipation of Mark pitching his next game in Detroit, Joe Falls, now seemingly accepting The Bird, wrote, "Saturday night will be the greatest happening around here since last Monday night." Could he do it again? Could he possibly top Monday night's performance?

Before the season, with bleak prospects for attendance, the July 3 game had been designated as Windsor Night in hopes of attracting fans from across the Detroit River. It soon became apparent that much more than just Canadians were showing up, however. Fans lined up along Kaline Drive several hours before game time, hoping to be lucky enough to land one of the 10,000 bleacher seats for a buck fifty, which were all that were left. The Tigers opened three additional ticket windows and added five men to the ticket staff for the game. Again, thousands were turned away without a ticket, many of whom simply remained in the parking lot, listened to the game on the radio with other stranded fans, and had a great time. Others wandered down the street to the Lindell AC, which was overflowing. In all, 51,023 fans packed inside Tiger Stadium for the game. Writers quizzed fans to find a reason for the frenzy. "I really haven't been able to see much of The Bird on TV," said Lyann Fardell, who drove from Ypsilanti with four friends to see their first game. "I just heard about him on the radio, and I'm really impressed with his age. He's the same age as me and he's way up there. If he's that great, I have to see him."

Pat Seollin, a Providence Hospital secretary, said, "Everybody in the park gets excited. He gets into what he's doing. It's contagious." Seventeen-year-old Chuck Reardon added eloquently, "The Bird just freaks me out."

Oriole players were eager to get a look at Mark. They watched him warm up and watched the fans' reaction to him. Coach Jim Frey later said, "That's all we were talking about." During the game, Oriole first baseman Lee May looked over at Tiger first base coach Dick Tracewski and said, "This kid really enjoys the game, doesn't he? It's a lot of fun to him."

The Orioles got base runners on in the top of the first inning, but Mark worked out of the jam. Rusty Staub gave the Tigers an early lead with a three-run homer. A Jason Thompson home run made it 4–0. In the fourth inning, a walk, a single, and a fielder's choice loaded the bases for the Orioles with no outs. Mark then struck out the next two batters and got the third on a ground-out. As he bounded off the mound the crowd was sent into another stratosphere. The rest of the game was a repeat of Monday night. Taking only one hour and fifty-four minutes, Mark threw a shut-out, and the Tigers won 4–0. The fans were even louder the whole game than they had been during the Yankee game. The annual fireworks on the nearby Detroit River were going on late in the game, but in Tiger Stadium, The Bird provided all the pyrotechnics the fans needed. After the game, the Baltimore players stayed in their dugout to see how the crowd would react to The Bird and what he would do about it. Again the fans refused to leave until he returned for a curtain call.

Nine-year-old Greg Scupholm was a budding baseball fan who was watching the game from the left-field bleachers with his parents. "In the ninth inning, the crowd rocked with 'Go, Bird, Go!' over and over," he says. It was so loud, "you couldn't hear the fireworks not too far away. When he got the last out, judging by the fan reaction, you would've thought he pitched a perfect game. He didn't, but Mark was perfect in the minds of Tiger fans every-where: he was ours, we literally loved him, and weren't about to let go." As the crowd called for Mark to come out of the clubhouse, chanting, "We want The Bird," Greg could not help but notice that The Bird's appeal transcended generations and levels of baseball knowledge. "Even my mother, who had been coaxed to maybe five Tiger games her whole life and who had no idea how many balls it took to walk someone, joined the masses with a gleam in her eye and shout in her throat . . . my mom wanted Mark Fidrych to do a curtain call, and that was pretty darn amazing in my eyes." Mothers, grandmothers, old men, little kids—everyone loved The Bird. He had done it again.

In the warm glow of the aftermath of the evening, Lew Matlin of the Tigers' promotion office reflected on the gate, the game, and the incredible outcome and voiced the thought that everyone else was surely thinking: "We had our greatest Windsor Night ever."

Two games—100,000 fans. It was obvious that something was happening here. "Mickey Mantle used to draw crowds," said Houk, "but I've never seen a rookie do anything like this. I don't think I've ever enjoyed anything like this in my life."

"I saw Sandy Koufax pitch," said Dick Tracewski. "And he never got the reception this kid gets."

Reggie Jackson, the Oriole rent-a-slugger for the 1976 season, commented to reporters, "He was sincere in what he was doing out there. I never got the feeling he was ridiculing us. He's got great concentration for being so young. He knows what's going on. He's no kid on the mound. He's smart. . . . His game is to get you out on his pitch. You've got to respect him and admire him."

Earl Weaver was equally impressed. "I don't think he talks to the ball as much as he's talking to himself. . . . He's years ahead of his age. He's got some things that are just born into him—you can't acquire what he's got. He can change speeds and do it so natural that you just can't teach it."

Oriole pitcher Mike Cuellar added, "I talk to the baseball, too. But I speak Spanish and the ball is American."

Mark told reporters, "I'll never get used to all this. What I'm going through right now is really a trip. It's something that I'll always remember. Right now I'm a happy person and I plan to stay that way." He reminded the press that the fans weren't just coming to see him. "These people don't just come out to see me. They come out to see the Detroit Tigers. I'm only a third of the game. What about the hitting and defense? When people come out to the park they don't just see me. They see those great plays behind me that the guys have been making all year." Mark was named American League Player of the Month for June on the strength of a 6–0 record. His ERA of 2.18 was leading the league now.

The salary issue began to gain momentum. Larry Paladino of the Associated Press wrote an article on July 6 entitled, "Fidrych Is the Only One Not Worried About a Raise." He quoted Mark as saying he did not want a raise. "This is the most I've ever made in my life. What happens if he (Campbell) did give me a raise? It might go to my head and I'd start losing. I'm satisfied with what I'm getting. I don't need an agent." When questioned about the subject, Jim Campbell noted that the team was not in the practice of giving midseason raises. "So why start now?" But Campbell did indicate that the Tigers might reward him after the season.

"If it wasn't for baseball," Mark told reporters, "I'd probably be working in a gas station in my hometown. I'm not even working forty hours a week now."

"I couldn't ask for anything better than being in the big leagues," he happily added.

Mark's next start came on July 9 against Kansas City. The crowd of 51,041 in Tiger Stadium included Mark's family, who drove from Massachusetts. The total made 150,000 fans over the past three starts. And for the third straight start, Mark pitched brilliantly. The Royals starter, Dennis Leonard, a twenty-game winner, was just as brilliant on this night. It turned out to be a matchup of two pitchers in top form; seemingly every single pitch was perfect—not one pitch was above the knees for nine innings. Mark gave up one run, a fourth-inning score courtesy of two singles and an infield hit. Three times in the first four innings Mark erased base runners by getting ground-ball double plays. The Tigers could not muster a single run off Leonard, however, and lost the game 1–0. Then a strange thing occurred. Even though the Tigers had lost, the fans refused to go home, chanting, "We want The Bird, We want The Bird." A curtain call after a loss? Unheard of. Absurd. Mark was in the clubhouse, already out of his uniform when a stadium security guard found him. Speaking to other security men over his walkie-talkie, the frazzled guard told Mark, "You've gotta go out there so we can get these people out of here." Mark put on a pair of pants and his Tiger jacket and went back out—sixteen minutes after the game had ended. The fans erupted when he stuck his head back out of the dugout. Even in defeat, the lovefest continued.

Afterward, reporters delighted in writing that after conducting interviews, Mark suddenly thought of something. He rummaged around in the bottom of his messy locker and produced a box someone had sent him. Opening it up, he asked all the gathered reporters, "Anybody want a cookie?"

The next day, the *Detroit Free Press* ran a picture of Paul, Virginia, Carol, and Lorie Fidrych in the stands at the game—Detroit's new first family—on the front page (top half) of the paper. "There has never been a love affair in our city to match what's happened around here in the past month," Joe Falls wrote in his column, and no one could disagree. Think of it—when is the last time you saw a picture of a baseball player's family in the paper? On the front page?

And life just kept getting better. Mark found out that he would get a little help to provide for stamps to answer his mail—a $7,500 bonus that had previously been written into his first contract. The clause had provided for a bonus of $1,000 if he spent ninety days on a Class AA roster, another $1,500 for spending ninety days on a Class AAA roster, and $5,000 for ninety days on the major league roster. He had shot up through the minors so fast the previous year that he had never spent ninety days anywhere, so all the money came due upon his ninetieth day in the majors.

The Detroit area Ford dealers showed their appreciation of The Bird by presenting him with a new $10,000 Ford Thunderbird to use for the rest of the season. The whole Fidrych clan went down to the showroom. Paul Fidrych was soon on a first-name basis with all the executives, photos were taken, hands were shaken, and Mark happily roared off in the new car, still somewhat amazed at the bounty being bestowed upon him for merely doing what he enjoyed. Is this a great country or what?

Joe Falls—remember, if he writes a good column about you, watch out—quickly cast a pall over the gift. The fact that Mark accepted the offer of the car apparently offended Falls' sense of innocence—he had liked the carefree Bird driving a subcompact car, acting like he didn't want money or material wealth. "The Bird made a tactical error Friday," Falls wrote with great indignation.

"And the charm wore off—almost immediately. . . . Now he is like all the rest."

Mark told other reporters he was upset when Falls wrote the story about the car. "I'm only using it during the season, and my car that I'm still making payments on I gave to my little sister to use. I don't think it was right for him to knock me, but I won't say nothing to him about it." Mark had indeed given Carol the car for the year, and she was the envy of all her friends as she proudly drove the Dodge Colt with a Bird bumper sticker on the rear to Algonquin Regional High School in the fall.

That Sunday, just after the game had started, the Tiger Stadium public address announcer informed fans that Red Sox manager Darrell Johnson had picked Mark Fidrych to be the starting pitcher for the American League in the All-Star Game. As the fans erupted, Mark popped out of the dugout to acknowledge their applause with a wide grin on his face. Tears welled in his eyes as he thought, "It's everybody's goal and I've made it." The game was halted—the opposing pitcher stopped for three or four minutes—while the crowd roared. Before the game, Mark had told reporters, "I just want to pitch one inning to say that I've played in an All-Star Game."

Mark was so elated that he forgot to tone down his language for the flock of reporters who gathered around him after the game. When asked if he was surprised to be selected as the starter for the All-Star Game, only the second rookie in history to have that honor, he replied, "Shit, yes." A radio man shoved a mike a little closer and asked if he could repeat his answer, giving him a chance to sanitize it. "Certainly," bubbled Mark. "Was I surprised? F———in' ay, I was surprised."

The 1976 All-Star Game was held in Philadelphia to coincide with the bicentennial celebration. The game's biggest stars, along with President Gerald Ford, were in attendance, but they were all merely side attractions. The only real star as far as everyone was concerned, was Mark "The Bird" Fidrych. Bob Smizik wrote in the *Pittsburgh Press*, "The 1976 All-Star Game has turned into a gathering of Bird watchers. The great birdman of Detroit is on the scene and no one else matters."

The fact that no one else mattered appeared to especially bother San Francisco pitcher John Montefusco, who thought of himself as an outspoken media star. Montefusco wore a tight curly perm that would have made Mike Brady proud. He regularly challenged opposing hitters from the mound and in the press. He had once memorably guaranteed striking out Johnny Bench four times (Bench responded with a 450-foot home run). He called himself "The Count." The Count of Montefusco.

Initially, Montefusco decided to have fun at Mark's expense. He switched identities with National League starter Randy Jones, who was five inches shorter but also wore a perm, when they introduced themselves to Mark. Later, in front of reporters when it was time to take the standard photo of the opposing starting pitchers, Mark went up to Montefusco and said, "Come on, Randy, they want us." Montefusco laughed. "You don't even know who you're pitching against, do you?"

Montefusco told reporters he did not expect to have any trouble with American League hitters. He openly baited the American Leaguers in the press and at the banquet. Later, Montefusco told Mark he should be popping off in the press like he was. It was to no avail, however, as the media continued to ignore everyone but Mark. Finally, Montefusco admitted defeat, saying, "I'm using my best stuff and I still can't get anywhere. Mark's stealing all the press." And the thing was, he was doing it all without trying. He was just being himself.

The media crush was intense. An estimated two hundred reporters were in Philadelphia for the game, and each one of them, it seemed, had been sent there with one order: get the story on The Bird. In addition to the reporters, there were the radio and television people, photographers and journalists from an endless array of magazines—all wanting a few more minutes of Mark's time; a few more questions, a few more pictures.

At the scheduled news conference at the Bellevue-Stratford Hotel, Mark sat at the head table along with several other stars and dignitaries. Mark was initially at a loss for words when the microphone appeared in front of his face before the large audience. Someone said, "Say something, Mark." And he told them, "It's the thrill of a lifetime to be here." Then he asked the writers, "How was that?" and they broke up with laughter like so many Ed McMahons at a bad Johnny Carson joke.

While everyone else had on suits, Mark had shown up for the news conference in a pair of blue jeans and a loud flower print shirt. "They didn't tell me I had to wear a leisure suit," he said. He told the reporters that the most exciting thing that ever happened to him before this day was "when I bought a minibike when I was fourteen." He told them if it wasn't for baseball, he'd be working in a garage in Northboro.

When asked if his friends considered him kooky, Mark answered, "No, they're like me, too." When asked why he wasn't demanding a raise, Mark told them, "I don't want a raise. Don't you see? What's happening to my life right now is my raise."

The National Leaguers set the bar high as far as arrogance and trash talk was concerned. They said it would be a better game to just pick two squads from the National League and play each other. "Why don't you guys just collect your meal money and go home?" they said to the American Leaguers. The National League had won eleven of the previous thirteen All-Star Games and expected to continue their dominance regardless of The Bird.

"We won't be standing in the batter's box laughing," Joe Morgan said.

Pete Rose, perhaps irritated at having the spotlight stolen, was angry at the way he perceived that Mark was trivializing the game. "Pete didn't like him talking to the baseball," Phillies shortstop Larry Bowa said. "He said, 'My first time up, I'm going to hit one right back at him.'" Rose, who had faced Mark in exhibitions, told his All-Star teammates to lay off the low pitches and wait for something up high.

Mark's catcher for the All-Star Game was none other than Thurman (Who's he?) Munson. By this time, Munson had learned from other players that Mark had not been intentionally trying to put him down with his comment to the press after the Monday night game. Munson and Fidrych met in the American League clubhouse and talked. "He came over to me and said, 'How you doing, Mark?'" Mark later recalled. "He was laughing and shaking his head. He said, 'That was a pretty good quote you had about me.' After that . . . we had kind of like this friendship." Mark got a baseball signed by Thurman, which was later proudly displayed in the Fidrych living room years after Munson's death in a plane crash.

Before the game, Mark was in the clubhouse getting ready when he heard someone coming up behind him. "The Bird, how are you?" the man said. Mark, finally getting irritated at all the intrusions while he was trying to prepare, testily said without looking, "I thought we had a game to play." As he turned around, he recognized the speaker from television—it was President Gerald Ford, accompanied by a gaggle of Secret Service guards.

Mark recovered from his shock and asked the president, "Did you send me a thing in Texas?" A few weeks earlier Mark had received a congratulatory telegram in the clubhouse in Texas signed by President Ford. Tiger teammate Ron LeFlore, sitting next to Mark, poked him and reminded him that it had been a gag from his teammates.

"I tried to call you," the leader of the free world replied.

Mark asked the president about his son, Jack. "Now don't talk to those young fellows, talk to the old man," replied Ford.

"I just was wondering how he was doing with those dates."

"Come to Washington and he'll fix you up." Ford then invited Mark to the White House to take a private tour. Ford joked to reporters about the presidential first pitch, saying, "I hope he throws better than I do."

"Oh, I'm sure I will," Mark replied. Mark talked with Jack Ford a few minutes, and then it was time to take the field.

While it was widely reported that Mark had asked the president and his son to fix him up with tennis star Chris Evert, who Jack had publicly dated earlier, Mark later said that he only asked Jack about the pressures of trying to date a celebrity with media constantly hounding you—pressures Mark was suddenly facing.

Philadelphia's Veterans Stadium was packed with 63,974 fans for the All-Star Game—the largest crowd in Philadelphia baseball history. The players in the starting lineup were serious and businesslike as they introduced themselves to the television audience; all of them except for the American League starting pitcher, who wore a huge smile as he said, "I'm Mark Fidrych. I'm from Northboro, Massachusetts. I'm a pitcher," pause, even bigger smile, "and I'm in the All-Star Game." He laughed as if he couldn't believe the words he had just said. Then he looked off camera and asked, "How was that?"

The visiting American Leaguers went out quickly in the top of the first, and then Mark took the mound. Before throwing the first pitch he looked around at the packed stadium, including the Secret Service men on the roof, drinking it all in, committing the scene to memory. He later liked to tell reporters that he paused and thought, "Seventy thousand people here, and if I don't throw the ball, they're still waiting."

Pete Rose was waiting for a pitch up in the zone, and he got it on Mark's second offering and stroked it up the middle for a single. Steve Garvey followed with a slicing drive to right field that narrowly eluded a lumbering Rusty Staub. As it bounced past, Staub slipped and fell. Garvey cruised into third with a triple and Rose scored. After Joe Morgan popped out to short right field, George Foster hit a ground-out that scored Garvey, and the National League had a quick two-run lead.

In the second inning, Mark gave up singles to Johnny Bench and Dave Concepcion. With two outs, Pete Rose came to the plate again. This time Mark got him out on a grounder to the first baseman, who threw to the pitcher covering first.

Mark was due to bat in the bottom of the second inning, however, manager Johnson informed him that he was being lifted for a pinch-hitter—his night was done. Mark asked Johnson if he could just go up to the plate and see one pitch. "No," Johnson replied, "because I know you'll swing at it."

"Could I get in the on-deck circle with a helmet on?" Mark asked. Hal McRae, the pinch-hitter, agreed to let Mark hold a bat and kneel in the on-deck circle until his time at the plate came. And that's how Mark Fidrych's All-Star Game ended. He went through the dugout shaking hands with all his fellow All-Stars, thanking them for making his All-Star debut memorable.

The National League won the game 7–1. John Montefusco finally got his time in the spotlight. He pitched two scoreless innings and after the game told reporters, "Fidrych told me if the National League won, he was going to blow up my car. I think he was only kidding."

Mark shared a cab back to the hotel with Red Sox pitcher Luis Tiant, who told him, "Don't worry about it, buddy, we'll get them next year."

After the All-Star Game, the media circus around The Bird showed no sign of slowing down. Each day, wire reports added to the growing legend. Reporters continued to poke around Northboro, interviewing friends, trying to dig up more funny stories.

Everyone loved The Bird. He was a rock star in a baseball uniform. Bruce Kimm recalled seeing him get in a car after a game in New York and being immediately engulfed by worshipping fans, making it look as if he were riding in a vehicle built entirely of human flesh.

"He gets more mail in three days than I got in my whole career," John Hiller said. The area around Mark's locker was constantly stacked with packages and all manner of stuffed bird creatures that fans had sent. There were also uncounted cakes and cookies that arrived at the clubhouse door earmarked for The Bird. Jim Hawkins reported in the *Sporting News* that in the span of one month, Mark received 960 letters and postcards compared with 613 for the rest of the team combined.

"Initially when Ralph Houk asked me to locker next to Mark, I didn't think anything about it," says Hiller. "But by midseason when he was doing so well I could hardly get to my locker because of all the media attention he was getting. There wasn't much space in the Tiger Stadium locker room anyway."

Paul Fidrych was in heaven. The Fidryches drove to as many games as possible; sometimes the whole family would go, sometimes just Paul and Carol. Paul had gone from the giddy feeling of his son making a major league roster to the indescribable recognition that his son was the most popular sports personality in the country over a span of three months. In his wildest dreams when he was teaching his young son to play in the backyard he could have never imagined this. If he had made a Faustian bargain with the Devil, he would not have asked for all this because it would have been too impossible to conceive. "He was so proud," says Carol. "He collected every single thing that had The Bird on it; T-shirts, buttons, bumper stickers, you name it." One game two sisters created a giant sign on a bed sheet that caught Paul's attention. "We drew a picture of Mark and wrote, 'Sit on it, Fonzie, The Bird is number one,'" says Laura Floetke, who, unknown to Paul, was actually a friend of Mark's, having met him earlier in the season. "It was so big that we could only bring it out and walk around with it between innings. Mr. Fidrych spotted it and came over and talked to us. He was really nice. He introduced himself and asked if he could have the sign, so after the game we folded it up and gave it to him." Paul Fidrych's son: more popular than Fonzie. In 1976, you couldn't get any bigger than that.

Mark soon discovered that there was a price to pay for all the fame. The intense crush began to intrude upon every facet of his life, leaving him no privacy. Tom Veryzer, who became Mark's roommate on the road after Coleman was traded in early June, told reporters that Mark received at least twenty phone calls a day, even though they began leaving their phone off the hook until noon in order to get some rest. People found out where Mark lived and often waited in his hallway at all hours. "I'd come home at two, three in the morning, and there'd be people, men and women, waiting outside my apartment," Mark told Patrick Zier. "People would wake me up anytime and ask if I wanted a beer or could they have an autograph." A horde of kids would gather outside his apartment each afternoon, waiting for a glimpse or maybe a handshake or an autograph. Mark worked out a signal for friends to climb in through the laundry room to avoid the mob.

Mark's teammates couldn't believe the crowds—and couldn't

believe he hadn't gone crazy from them yet. They told reporters they would be at his apartment and someone would knock on the door and ask, "Can The Bird come out?" When Evansville pitcher Ed Glynn was called up to the Tigers, initially he was going to stay with Mark for a short time. After a few hours of listening to the noise from the crowd in the hall, he couldn't take it any longer. "That's it," he said. "I was thinking about staying here . . . I'm getting myself a hotel room. I want some sleep." He asked Mark, "How could you hack this the whole year? I been here three hours and I can't hack it."

Seeing the multitude in front of Mark's apartment wanting his attention, Mickey Stanley told him, "You oughta make it a meat shop. Put numbers out there, it's so bad. How the heck do you live like this?"

"When we went to Detroit, it was totally chaos," says Lorie. "It was unbelievable, like he was a movie star. We would drive to the game and people would be banging on top of the car and screaming as we drove in."

"I would go shopping with Mark in Detroit and everyone in the store would want his autograph," recalls Carol. "When we would drive through the tunnel in his Thunderbird people would honk and jump on the car."

"Once Mark drove us home from Tiger Stadium in his new Thunderbird," says Paula. "We got in it in the underground garage. He had to bolt out of there because people would follow him out and try to follow him home. He gunned the engine and had to lose them. That ride was the scare of my life."

"Mark shared his apartment in Southgate with me when I got called up in June," says Frank MacCormack. "After a few weeks, there was just a constant crush of fans. After the game, when we would try to get out of the parking lot a plain-clothes cop would sit on the hood and push people away so we could get out without hurting anyone. After a few games, when we would pull onto the interstate, a line of cars would be waiting by the interstate and would follow us. We'd take fake exits and try to lose them. Sometimes, people would just come by his apartment. One night the doorbell wouldn't stop ringing, people kept coming—people we didn't even know. By the end of the night there were seventeen cases of beer in the apartment and we hadn't bought any—people would just drop by and bring him beer, wanting to party with The Bird. But he had the ability to remain upbeat, be amicable no matter what. Of course, he could have had a conversation with a fire hydrant; that was just his personality."

Ralph Houk later said the public clamor around Mark was more than Roger Maris had faced in 1961. But where Maris' hair famously fell out in chunks due to the stress, Mark's glorious curls seemed to only grow longer. Publicly and privately he actually seemed to enjoy it. Sure, he was irritated by the pushy people who showed up at odd hours, or women who would butt in at a bar, but, for the most part, he had fun with the people and rarely gave them any indication that they were annoying him.

Sherry Stover-Conley was part of the large group of kids who gathered outside Mark's apartment during the season. "I remember when one of the kids came to school and said, 'You know where Mark 'The Bird' Fidrych lives? He lives across the street,'" she says. "We were like, 'No way.' It spread like wildfire through the school." They went over to the apartment complex and waited for a tall curly headed man to unfold himself out of a Dodge Colt. "Sure enough, he showed up," she continues. "The first time I saw him I thought, 'He really does look like Big Bird.' I don't mean that in a negative way. Big Bird was someone you could just run up to and hug, and Mark had that kind of charisma about him. At first, he wasn't that famous, it was just cool to have a Tiger player in our neighborhood. But as the summer went on, he was all anyone could talk about. We knew which car was his, so we would wait in the parking lot by his car when we knew he would be coming out to go to a game. He was so nice to us. He would always stop and talk to us kids and joke around. He was just unbelievable—it was like he appreciated our attention. He never acted like we were bothering him. He radiated kindness."

Jane Syzdek lived with her family in the same apartment complex as Mark and remembers his special appeal and thoughtfulness around kids. "They (Mark and the other players) used to hang at the apartment pool with us in the summer," she says. "I remember especially that Mark used to give my younger sister (age seven) dolphin rides in the pool. He was such a normal kind of guy making friends with the neighborhood kids." Once when some of the kids showed up at his door selling candy bars, he bought five from them, then gave the kids extra money to eat one for themselves.

Jane's sister, Vivian, remembers his kindness: "I was this skinny little Chinese girl with some teeth missing and my hair usually in ponytails, all of fifty pounds. Mark was very popular with all the kids in the neighborhood. I didn't appreciate who he was at the time, but got that he was someone special. I just wasn't all the way sure why. Maybe that's why I got special attention from him, at least that's how he made me feel at the time. He made me feel like I was one of his favorites among the kids, even though he was usually really open and interactive with all of the kids."

Vivian's favorite memory is "that Mark 'The Bird' Fidrych taught me to swim—how to hold my breath and stay under the water and swim. I think that I was probably just trying to impress him, but he got me to do what no one else had been able to get me to do, and something that I'd been afraid to do before then.

"One afternoon when the kids were swarming all around Mark, and I felt bad that they wouldn't leave him alone, he made up some excuse, like he had to move his laundry or something, always such a nice guy, and then he did this cool run and side hurdle over the fence and dashed off to his place. I was smitten, his biggest fan." And that, in a nutshell, was the secret to Mark Fidrych's extraordinary ability to handle the crush from the media and from fans—he appeared approachable, gave them his time, made each one feel special, and then, when he finally needed space, he made an excuse, did a cool run, and hurdled a fence—leaving them all smitten.

As his popularity skyrocketed, it became obvious that a potential source of trouble was the fact that Mark was now being bombarded, seemingly on a daily basis, by offers from agents, kooks, and hucksters—all with grand money-making schemes they couldn't wait to pitch. In order to keep some sanity amid all this, Mark signed with the New York–based William Morris Agency in July to handle his nonbaseball affairs. The Tigers had helped bring Mark together with them, wanting to prevent him from being swindled by the many people suddenly begging for his attention. The William Morris Agency was a nationally known, respected firm that included Olympians Mark Spitz and Bruce Jenner, as well as Bob Gibson, Hank Aaron, and Secretariat among its clients. Mark told everyone that he would continue to handle his baseball contracts, however.

Mark's first start after the All-Star Game was against the Oakland A's in front of 45,905 Friday night fans in Detroit. Knowing he was a fast worker, the A's batters decided to try to disrupt The Bird's timing and concentration by stepping out of the box and stalling. It did not work. Mark faced the minimum number of batters through the first six innings as the A's only had two base runners—one single and one walk—and, courtesy of a double play and a failed steal attempt, both were erased.

Claudell Washington of the A's, who normally took a lot of time between pitches anyway, was especially slow and intentionally stalling. When he led off the sixth inning for the A's he seemed intent on staging a one-man rain delay. After he finally got in the batter's box and took a first-pitch strike, he stepped out again, adjusted this, scratched that, then leisurely strolled about the park. Mark responded by squatting down on the mound to make Washington wait when he eventually got back up to the plate. Then Mark pointed with the ball. Washington stepped out again. Mark yelled to get back in the box and Washington yelled something back. The next pitch was a fastball inside—well inside—aimed at the knees, brushing the batter back. Washington yelled out to Mark and started toward the mound carrying his bat. Claudell Washington was a young outfielder with powerful, cordlike muscles that draped from his wide shoulders as if they were hung from a coat hanger. Detroit fans gasped as he started toward The Bird with menacing intensions. He was immediately intercepted from behind by Kimm as players from both benches streamed onto the field. When order was restored, Washington grounded out.

Only four years earlier, Detroit pitcher Lerrin LaGrow had narrowly averted injury when Oakland shortstop Bert Campaneris had thrown his bat at him in the playoffs. Perhaps with this on their mind, Detroit fans were ready to protect The Bird. "It's a good thing Washington stopped," says Frank MacCormack. "I could see fans putting their legs over the rail, getting ready to go out there to rescue The Bird. They were ready to run out there. They were not going to let The Bird get hurt. It would have gotten ugly if Washington had gotten any closer. But that's how the Detroit fans felt about him."

The game continued with Tiger hitters having their own problems as the zeroes mounted for both teams. The A's were eventually able to get seven hits and four walks, but each time runners got on, Mark worked out of trouble. After nine innings, there was still no score. Mark Fidrych refused to be the first to blink. With one out in the top of the eleventh, the A's got a runner to third base on a single, a stolen base, and a throwing error. Mark then struck out Don Baylor and got Joe Rudi on a fly-out to end the threat. The Tigers finally scored in the bottom of the eleventh on a Willie Horton single. Mark had pitched his third eleven-inning complete game victory in a span of six weeks. The crowd once again refused to leave until he came out to acknowledge them.

The rest of the summer was a love affair between a city and a player. Detroit had possessed plenty of sports heroes in the past, but none had seemed to touch the core of the hearts of citizens like Mark Fidrych did. While the rest of the country enjoyed hearing about The Bird and looked forward to his visit to their city, residents of Detroit knew they owned him. Area kids tried to impersonate him in Little League games and while playing wiffle ball. At least four bird songs were recorded and played over Detroit radio stations, including "Chirp Me Out to the Ball Game," by a group called the Fowls and the popular, "The Bird Is the Word." The Detroit newspapers had cutout iron-on transfers of The Bird. Helicopters bearing greetings to The Bird circled the stadium. Vendors sold Bird T-shirts, buttons, bumper stickers and, in the perfect confluence of seventies pop culture, there were even Bird mood rings.

Fans counted the days until his next start—making sure to at least listen on the radio or watch it on local television. The area outside Tiger Stadium resembled a carnival on days The Bird pitched; the stadium rocked. Fans stomped their feet so hard the whole place seemed to shake. Games were genuine happenings. The stadium felt different, sounded different, when Mark was on the mound. Part of it was the sheer number of fans, but also there was a different buzz, an electricity, a palpable static that ran through the crowd well before the game even started. There was an anticipation from the fans for what they were about to experience. They knew that Mark always came through—in fact, it was September 3 before Mark did not finish a game in Tiger Stadium—after four months and fourteen straight complete games at home.

"Me, Tom Veryzer, Mark, and Ben Oglivie used to drive to the games together," says Frank MacCormack. "Normally we'd get there at 4:30 for pitchers' batting practice—we'd play home run derby and the stands would be empty. Then the team would take infield, and the starting pitcher would go down to the bullpen at 7:10 to start warming up, usually in front of about 15,000 fans. On nights Mark pitched, coming up the interstate before the game there would already be lines, and when we took our BP, 25,000 people would be in the stadium. The place would be filled by the time he went down to the bullpen. The energy was shocking; it was tremendous."

And, of course, when the game was over the fun did not stop. After every game, fans called him back out and he happily obliged. "We would stomp and yell like crazy," says Laura Floetke, who attended every game. "Everybody would get into it. Even if you weren't a baseball fan, you got swept up in the emotion. Sometimes, he would stay in the dugout a few more minutes, to tease us. Then when he came out everyone would yell even louder."

There apparently were no limits to the things people would do to show their love for The Bird in 1976. Michigan state representative Dan Angel, R-Battle Creek, authored a resolution in the state legislature recommending that the Tigers raise Mark's salary (unfortunately, it was tabled while the legislators debated other less important issues such as jobs and taxes). A model, Peggy Bogart, showed off what she termed her Fidrych Frizzies—in which she had her hair curled Bird style. Her picture was carried all over the country on the wire services. In Warren, Michigan, a baby born to Mr. Donald Shoemaker was proudly named Mark Fidrych Shoemaker. When Mark got his first haircut after the All-Star break, the valuable locks were placed in several autographed boxes and auctioned off for charity by the Tiger Wives Club. A photo of the trimming was carried to interested readers in the nations' newspapers. According to Jim Hawkins, when discussing trimming his power-giving hair, Mark said, "It was like Samson and Goliath."

A campaign was organized by fans called Bucks for the Bird in which they sent checks to the team to pay their favorite pitcher. One town, Hell, Michigan, sent $103, all in one- and two-dollar checks. Alas, all the money was returned (although it was never documented whether or not it went in a handbasket). Ten-year-old Tim Kattreh had a school assignment to make a picture of three birds native to Michigan. He drew a cardinal, a robin, and Mark Fidrych. (He would find the picture almost thirty years later and send it to Fidrych, who signed and returned it.) A large number of family parakeets throughout the Midwest were renamed Mark Fidrych that summer.

Through it all, Mark tried to stay the same—concerned with winning games, and maybe having a little fun. The hype came so fast, it was hard to really make sense of it all; hard to appreciate the enormity of it. "The first time we came to Detroit this year, nobody even knew Fidrych was on the team," said Brooks Robinson in July. "We come back a second time, and they're set to name him mayor."

Mark interacted with fans as few players ever had before. "That year was unbelievable," says Fred Gladding. "Everyone would be screaming and hollering for him when he would just walk down to the bullpen to warm up. And he loved it. He would go over by the stands and high-five and shake hands all the way down to the bullpen, a huge smile on his face. Once he got to the bullpen, he flipped a switch and he was all business.

"I can remember him walking through airports," Gladding continues. "Crowds would come up to him. He would smile, lay his stuff down, and talk to them and sign autographs for as long as they wanted."

He routinely walked along the rails talking to fans before and after games in which he didn't pitch. He might spot someone in the stands with a Bird T-shirt and strike up a conversation. Often he would call other players over to sign autographs for kids.

Did he understand how much it meant to fans? Did he appreciate what a memorable experience he was creating for them? Or was he just enjoying himself, doing what came natural? Whatever the reason, there is no doubt to the lasting impact that he had on those members of the crowd he came in contact with. One such fan was six-year-old Rod Wharram, who was sitting with his dad near the rail for the Tigers–White Sox game in August. "As the game was ending a security guard nearby mentioned to stick around after the game as Mark was in the habit of coming over to the first-base side of the field to sign autographs," says Wharram. "We stayed nearby, and it wasn't too long that Mark came over, signed a few autographs, and talked to everyone. It didn't matter whether you were a fan of the opposition, a security guard, or a six-year-old kid. I was one of the last to go up to him, and his words were simple, 'Are you gonna play baseball one day?' I nodded my head yes, and with that he leaned over the fence and picked me up into his arms. Standing on the field at Tiger Stadium with Mark Fidrych was amazing! After a moment, he passed me back over to my dad and patted my head with the biggest hands I had ever seen. He had a baseball that was nearby and he signed the ball and gave it to me. I remember years later, my mom telling the story where I did not go to sleep that night." Wharram, who grew up to pitch in college, never forgot that meeting and still has the ball safely stored in the jar his mother put it in that night. It was a simple act—a smile and a few casual words—but a colossal event in the eyes of a young kid. And this was hardly a unique story—Mark did this over and over on a nightly basis.

On July 20, the Tigers played the Twins in Minnesota in a game in which the Twins, like every team, had heavily advertised the appearance of The Bird. Minnesota had been averaging barely 10,000 fans per game—only 5,005 showed up for a "beer night" promotion to watch the same two teams a night earlier—but 30,000 showed up for the Tuesday night game to watch The Bird. The traffic from the unusual crowd prevented so many fans from getting in on time that officials delayed the start of the game to allow fans to get to their seats. Players joked that a fat lady was stuck in the turnstile.

Someone in the Twins management had dreamed up some stunts for The Bird. As Mark finished his warm-ups and prepared to start the game, thirteen pigeons were released from just behind the mound, and the public address announcer spoke directly to him, saying, "Mark, I hope this doesn't scare you: thirteen birds on your thirteenth start." Mark, unaware of the stunt beforehand, was initially perturbed. "It was weird," he later said. "Here's this guy I didn't even see talking to me like the voice of God, and I'm saying to myself, 'I thought we were here to play ball.'" He remained focused enough to shut down the Twins as the Tigers won 8–3. In the seventh inning, the electric scoreboard, Twins-O-Gram, announced, "THANKS A LOT, BIRD! For filling the nest tonight."

Tony Oliva of the Twins had been one of the top hitters in baseball over the previous decade. He had become the first player to lead the league in hitting as a rookie in 1963 and had repeated the next year. By 1976, bad knees had ravaged what would have otherwise been a Hall of Fame career. Against Mark on July 20, playing designated hitter, Oliva went four for four. After the fourth hit, a single, Mark got a new ball from the umpire, then walked over toward first and tipped his hat toward the Minnesota slugger. Later, a reporter asked him why he tipped his cap to Oliva. "Who's Oliva?" Mark asked. After the reporter explained, Mark said, "Oh, that guy. I don't know his name, but he is a really good hitter. I just wanted him to know that."

After the game, Twins manager Gene Mauch told reporters, "That kid might be the best thing that's happened to this game in a long time."

But not every game was great. July 24, at Cleveland in a Saturday nationally televised game, Mark had one of his worst outings, giving up four runs on nine hits and leaving in the fifth inning. Before the game, when Mark picked up the ball on the mound, he found an unprintable message written on the ball by Indians players—a special note for The Bird.

After the game, a television interviewer told Mark it looked like he was going to cry during the game when he was being roughed up. Mark, taken aback by what he felt was a cheap shot by the interviewer, responded that he wasn't going to cry but that he was upset by his pitching performance. "I was just bullshit," he said. He quickly added, "Excuse me."

In the clubhouse after the interview, the Tiger players acted stunned that Mark had said a dirty word on the air and told him, "Hey, you can't do that. Bowie Kuhn is gonna fine you for that." Mark went home concerned. The next day, the clubhouse man brought Mark an official telegram signed by Baseball Commissioner Bowie Kuhn saying he had been fined the total of two hundred and fifty dollars for using an obscenity on television. Upon reading the telegram, Mark dropped the food he was eating and turned to John Hiller at the next locker and asked, "John, can he do this?" Hiller studied the telegram, noted that it looked official, and pronounced somberly, "Yeah, he can, we told you that yesterday." Mark responded, "He can't fine me like this. I can't afford two hundred and fifty dollars. He can't get me for a mental mistake."

Desperately, he ran into Ralph Houk's office. Houk apologized that his hands were tied and reluctantly told him, "Hey, I can't say anything. If he fined you, that's one of the things you have to find out. You just found out the hard way."

"Pull some strings," Mark begged him. "I can't afford this."

"I can't pull any strings," was the reply. "You did say *bullshit* on TV, didn't you? He's the commissioner; he can do what he wants. Bowie Kuhn overrules me."

Mark ran around the clubhouse seeking relief, but there was none to be found. "I'd like to help you," his teammates told him one after another, "but, after all, you did say *bullshit* on TV."

After half an hour, Mark's teammates could no longer pull it off and finally let him in on the joke. They had typed up the official-looking false telegram and had given it to the clubhouse man to deliver to Mark. The education of the rookie continued.

And the Bird media band played on. In early August, Mark was on the cover of the *Sporting News*. The cover story, written by Jim Hawkins, was a compilation of some of his best Bird tales from the preceding three months. By this time, most of these stories had been repeated numerous times across the country; however, they seemed in no danger of growing stale. There apparently was no sign of too much of a good thing as far as The Bird was concerned. He was good copy. Hawkins told readers, "He is fresh. He is funny. He is fantastic. . . . Everywhere you go, all anyone wants to talk about is The Bird. . . . Call it color. Call it charisma. Call it leadership. Call it inspiration. Call it magic. Call it what you will. . . . He's almost too good to be true. . . . Although he naturally prefers to think of himself as normal, Fidrych is a full-fledged flake."

Writers reported to fans of Mark dodging in and out of lockers having paper wad fights with his teammates in the clubhouse, of taking off his uniform piece by piece and firing jump shots over their heads into a laundry bin as he gave a postgame interview, and of playfully jumping Thurman Munson from behind and wrestling him to the ground when Munson came to the Tiger side of the field before a Yankee Stadium game to talk to his former manager Ralph Houk.

Meanwhile, Mark was enjoying the privileges his newfound celebrity allowed. He met and exchanged small talk with Elton John backstage before a concert in Detroit. "I was like shocked," said Mark. "He knew me, man! He goes, 'Oh, Mark Fidrych, how are you? How's Thurman Munson?'" He hung out with the Beach Boys before their concert, posing with them for photos for *Creem* magazine, receiving advice from Dennis Wilson and Mike Love to drink more carrot juice and try Transcendental Meditation, and politely turned down their offer to have him introduce them to the Detroit crowd before the concert—opting instead to watch the concert with a roadie sitting up in the lights. He clowned around with the real Big Bird in a photo session set up at Yankee Stadium. "I liked it!" Mark explained later. "I had a good time doin' it. You know why? . . . I met the guy inside the suit. My little sister, Lorie, she used to love it. Y'know? And I used to sit there and watch it, once in a while. And now here I am seeing that actual Big Bird and messin' with him. Just because back in '74 this guy called me Bird."

And, lest anyone forget, there was still some baseball to be played. On August 11, 36,523 fans watched Mark pitch against the Rangers in Tiger Stadium. Willie Horton later said that he spent the game in the trainer's room being treated for an injury. "Mark would come in after every inning to check on me. He'd ask, 'How's it going, Willie?' He'd say, 'Get ready, Willie, because we're going to need you tonight.'" The Tigers had a 3–2 lead before the Rangers tied it with a run in the top of the seventh. Mark retired the side in the eighth and ninth innings. Horton had put on his uniform and made his way to the bench in the late innings, and he was sent up to pinch hit in the bottom of the ninth and hit a limp-off home run for the win. Mark gave him a huge bear hug when he crossed home plate. "When he hit that I felt so happy for him," Mark told reporters after the game. "He needed that. He hadn't hit a home run in a long time." Mark brought Horton out with him for a bow after the game. Detroit fans were ecstatic in spite of the fact that the team was currently 54–58 and in fourth place.

Mark celebrated his twenty-second birthday on August 14. Birthday cakes poured in from all over. Mark happily told reporters he was going to eat them all—with a little help from his friends. Mark was sitting on the bench in the dugout, when the scoreboard asked, "What baseball player's birthday is today?" Then it answered, "Mark Fidrych." The crowd roared. The only thing unusual about that was that it occurred on the road in Kansas City.

August 17, a crowd of 51,822 showed up to watch Mark square

off with Frank Tanana of the Angels. It was the largest Detroit crowd since 53,863 had been on hand for Denny McLain's 1970 return from a suspension. Mark's battery mate Bruce Kimm was the hero this time, hitting his first major league home run in the eighth inning to break a 2–2 tie. It would turn out to be the only home run of Kimm's major league career. The fact that it came late in a game to help The Bird win was only appropriate.

August 25, after Mark beat the White Sox 3–1 for his fifteenth win, reporters gathered and wanted to know if it was true that the Detroit University coach (thirty-seven-year-old Dick Vitale) had offered him a basketball scholarship as rumored. "Naw, he hasn't contacted me," Mark answered. "It's probably just for publicity." Then he added, "I was pretty good in basketball in high school. I might take it if they have a good auto mechanics course." Dick Vitale doing something just for publicity? Mark may have been more perceptive than the writers believed.

In the other clubhouse, Paul Richards, manager of the White Sox, reflected on the phenomena of The Bird and said, "Babe Ruth didn't cause that much excitement in his brightest day." Richards, the oldest manager in the majors at the time and a man whose career began in 1932, was one of the few active men in baseball in a position to make the comparison.

Attendance in Tiger Stadium was 39,884 for the White Sox game—Mark had not pitched in front of fewer than 30,000 since mid-June. "Nobody ever pulled them in the way he does—nobody," said George Kell. "Everywhere we go, they ask only one thing: is the Bird going to pitch?" Other general managers, realizing what a box office bonanza Mark provided, badgered Houk to juggle his pitching rotation so The Bird could make an appearance in their parks. Jim Hawkins reported in the *Sporting News*, "The first thing the press and opposing players want to know whenever they en-counter the Tigers these days is 'When is that funny guy who talks to the ball going to pitch?'" Late in the year, Yankees general man-ager Gabe Paul wanted Houk to rearrange his rotation for the Yan-kees so that Mark wouldn't pitch on Jacket Day, which was already sold out. Having him pitch one of the other games of the series would assure the Yankees of two sellouts in the same series, but Houk refused. "Times have changed," Paul indignantly complained to reporters. "The Tigers don't care about money anymore."

On a late August western road trip, it was determined that Mark was scheduled to pitch in Oakland and would miss Anaheim. Dismayed over not getting to have The Bird perform at their park, Angels' officials arranged for Mark to appear and sign autographs before each of the three games of the series. "He heard the kids were disappointed he wasn't going to pitch and asked us to allow him to conduct an autograph session. Naturally we set it up," was the official announcement by an Angel spokesman. That, in and of itself, was unique—an autograph session for a visiting player; something that announcer Ernie Harwell later said that he only saw once in all his years in baseball.

Mark gave a slightly different account than that of the Angel spokesman of the reasons for the autograph session that winter while dictating his autobiography, *No Big Deal*: "The guy (from the Angels) comes up, he goes, 'We're trying to make a million people. . . . You're a good drawing card. Would you please come up and sign autographs before the game? He went through Ralph. And Ralph said, 'I know the guy. If you want to do it, do it.' . . . And I did it for him." The other Tiger players were concerned that Angel officials were overstepping the line of exploitation (especially after reporters wrote that Mark was placed in a "bird cage" for the autograph session after a temporary chain-link fence was erected to protect Mark and the line of fans) and cautioned him. "They asked me, 'What are you getting out of this?' They said, 'Hey you better not be doing that for nothing. . . . You don't have to do that. Because you're taking your time.' . . . They said, 'Don't let them take advantage of you . . . there's a point to draw the line.' And I said, 'Don't worry, I ain't doing it for nothing. I got my little TV (he was given a television by the Angels) out of the deal. . . . It was nice. It didn't bother me . . . I just was happy doing it.'"

Ken White, a friend from Northboro, was in California, and Mark got him tickets for one of the games. As he came into the stadium, he saw the huge crowd around Mark. "He was signing autographs, posing for pictures with fans, hugging some pretty girls and laughing," recalls White. "He was having a blast with everyone. A camera crew was there trying to get shots of him. He spotted me in the crowd and yelled, 'Hey, there's my buddy Whitey from my hometown. Get a shot of him.' So the camera crew focused on me and took some shots. That night on the L.A. news the whole sequence was televised. Some people I know saw me, which was neat."

When viewed according to all accounts, this episode provides some insight into the attitude and outlook of the twenty-two-year-old Mark Fidrych: eager to please everyone, perhaps reluctant to say no. And where older teammates worried about exploitation and the need to get something out of it, he professed to be relatively unconcerned, and, once in the presence of the crowd, he thoroughly enjoyed himself.

In September, *Detroit Free Press* writers Jim Hawkins and Jim Benagh released *Go, Bird, Go*, an unauthorized biography. Reportedly produced over a two-week period, the book was largely a retelling of material previously published in the *Detroit Free Press*. The prologue stated, "It's a bird. It's a plane. It's Superm—! No, it's a bird after all. The Bird, to be exact. The one and only. Even Superman would have a difficult time following Mark (The Bird) Fidrych's act. The Bird swooped down out of nowhere in 1976, stole the game of baseball away from the mercenaries, who considered it merely a business, and gave it back to the fans. Thousands of men have played major league baseball in the past century. Hundreds of them have been heralded as heroes. But no one has ever turned the fans on like this twenty-one-year-old Detroit Tiger rookie. It's his ball, his game, his fans. 'If somebody told you to write a script about a young ballplayer,' said Tiger general manager Jim Campbell, 'and you wrote what has happened to Mark Fidrych, nobody would believe it. They'd lock you up.'" One could accuse the writers of hyperbole, however, viewing the sentiment at the time, perhaps they were actually guilty of understatement.

The *Worcester Telegram* reported that *Go, Bird, Go* was "selling like hotcakes" in the Northboro area. "We've sold 180 in a week and a half," local pharmacy manager Bernie Tourigney said. "I have my fifth order coming in tomorrow. He's the local boy who made good and people are happy about it." Some residents were upset, however, that Mark wasn't getting anything from the book sales.

Lawyers from the William Morris Company sent Benagh a letter demanding he stop publishing the book on the grounds that it "may cause irreparable harm or injury." Also, they charged that it invaded Mark's "personal right as well as his property rights." Nothing came of the protests, and the book reportedly sold over 75,000 copies in less than a month. Mark later mentioned that he did feel taken advantage of because he didn't receive anything from the book. Also, there were some mistakes regarding his background. "If they had asked me I would have told them everything," he said.

Everyone wanted a piece of The Bird now. Mark made numerous promotional appearances around Detroit at malls, grocery stores, and fast-food joints. He made a series of autograph-signing appearances at Detroit area Little Caesar's Pizza places—an upstart company owned by a forty-seven-year-old ex-Tiger minor leaguer named Mike Iltch. Late in the season, Mark signed to do a series of thirty-second commercials for the Highland Appliance Company on "What the Bird is really saying to the ball." In one commercial, he told the ball to meet him at Highland Appliance. He threw the ball, which was then hit out of the park and landed at Highland Avenue. He also found time to make goodwill visits to hospitals and schools.

In August, while the Tigers were in California, Mark was invited to appear on Bill Cosby's TV show, *Cos*. "They gave me some lines to read, but I couldn't read them," Mark later told reporters. "So they said, 'Go ahead, do it your way.'" *Sports Illustrated* reported that the director screamed at Mark when he had trouble reading the cue cards. "Hey, man," Mark screamed back, "this isn't my field. I'm a baseball pitcher."

The media offers continued to pour in, but Mark couldn't do everything—he had to play a little baseball from time to time. He turned down invitations to appear with Johnny Carson, Mary Tyler Moore, Dinah Shore, and on *Good Morning America*. Newspapers reported that promoter Allan Carr, who was planning a movie version of the play *Grease*, wanted Mark in a supporting role. "If he can fill stadiums, he can fill theaters," Carr said. Everybody wanted a piece of The Bird.

Late in the year, the constant demands seemed to be taking a toll. Team physician Dr. Livingood (who Mark laughingly referred to as Livingbad) advised him to settle down and not to think that he had to be nice and talk to everyone. Mark later admitted, "There were times I thought I'd crack." But where other athletes had been ruined by so much attention, Mark seemed to remain unchanged as far as his outlook and approach to people and life. While he assured Dr. Livingood he would settle down, once people approached him, it was against his nature to turn them down. As Patrick Zier noted in the *Lakeland Ledger*, "He is still outgoing and uninhibited, still determined to live his life and have fun."

On the field, Mark's pitching success slowed down a bit late in the season as he had a 4–6 stretch, but one of the losses was 1–0 and another was 2–1 in twelve innings. He rebounded to finish strong, winning four of his last five games. On October 2, in his last start of the season, Mark threw a five-hitter for his nineteenth win, beating Milwaukee 4–1. Reporters noted that on two straight plays when Bruce Kimm chased after foul pop-ups, Mark rushed to the catcher's box to retrieve his cap and mask so Kimm wouldn't have to bend down to get them, a habit he had performed throughout the season.

Mark concluded the 1976 season with a record of 19–9 for the fifth-place Tigers, who had an overall record of 74–88. His ERA was 2.34 in 250 innings. He threw twenty-four complete games and four shutouts. The ERA and complete games led the American League. Four of the complete games were extra-innings jobs; three of eleven and one of twelve innings. Only once in twenty-nine starts did he fail to get a decision. Amazingly, with all the tight late-inning situations, he only gave up one run in the twenty-three ninth innings that he pitched.

"I think Mark Fidrych was the best pitcher in baseball that year," says Kimm. "He was great when he got close to the end of the game. It was like he could go into another gear to close the game. And his stuff would be just as good at the end. One thing that helped him get so many complete games is that he didn't try to strike a lot of guys out and he didn't waste any pitches. I remember one game where he had a complete game on 81 pitches."

"He loved to win," adds Houk. "The team played good behind him because he worked fast. And when he had a lead in the eighth or ninth inning, I knew the game was over—he really bore down. I never needed to worry about the bullpen; he just got stronger and stronger at the end of a game."

Suddenly, it was time to talk about a new contract for the next year. The day of reckoning had arrived for the Tigers to pay for all those large numbers The Bird had been writing in his locker after each game. The Tigers were silently hoping that Mark would not hold them up with an outrageous demand. Several recent rookie stars, such as Vida Blue and Fred Lynn, had held out with very contentious salary demands and ruined their second seasons. Mark Fidrych certainly was in position to ask for anything he wanted. What could the Tigers do—turn him down and risk public relations disaster? The Tigers were anxious to conclude things as quickly as possible. Agents had been telling Mark they could get him $1 million for four or five years, but, true to his previous assertions, he did not enlist the help of an agent for the negotiations. When Jim Campbell asked Mark, "Who's going to help you?" he told him his dad would.

Campbell paid to fly Paul Fidrych in for the contract talks. School was back in session, so he flew in on Saturday and left Sunday. Mark and his father went into Jim Campbell's office to discuss the contract and soon shook hands and walked out. The negotiations were taken care of quickly and painlessly for the Tigers, who reported that the talks actually took less than half an hour. Mark later said, "I looked at my dad and he gave me a signal that said it was okay, and that was it." He said he was happy with the way the Tigers and the city of Detroit had treated him and was satisfied that Campbell had offered him exactly what he wanted.

October 1, the Tigers announced that Mark had been given a bonus for 1976 and had signed a three-year contract that would take him through the 1979 season. He was only the second Tiger ever (after Staub) to receive a three-year contract. His 1976 salary of $16,500 had been increased to $19,000 (the new league minimum) under the contract with the Baseball Players Association that went into effect during the season. Mark was given a bonus estimated at $34,500 as a reward for his 1976 performance. At the press conference, Mark was asked if he got a hundred grand for next year. "Naw," he answered, "I took a cut in pay." Everyone laughed, but when viewed in detail, Mark actually did take a cut in pay: his salary of $19,000 for 1976 was bolstered by the $7,500 contractual bonus for staying in the majors ninety days and the $34,500 end-of-year bonus—making a total of $61,000. The new three-year contract called for a salary of $55,000 for 1977. "An agent probably could have gotten me more money," Mark said. "But then maybe I wouldn't have been happy. . . . I could have signed a one-year contract for a lot of money, but what if I died out next year? This should make it easier for me. Now I know I'll be able to pitch next year and the next year and the next year without anybody asking me all the time if I'm going to get an agent. . . . I can take my mind off my contract and concentrate on playing baseball." The Bird die out next year? Impossible. Inconceivable.

Overall it was a great bargain for the Tigers. During the 1976 season, Mark drew 901,239 fans in his twenty-nine starts. The Tigers averaged 33,649 fans at Tiger Stadium when he pitched—605,677 in nineteen home starts. For the rest of their games, the Tigers averaged 13,893. At an average ticket price of $3 per ticket, Mark was responsible for an extra $60,000 a game, or over one million dollars for the season in ticket sales alone. When the attendance figures are compared to the rest of the league, an even more startling fact is revealed: the Twins and A's each drew less than 800,000 for the entire season, and the White Sox and Indians drew a little more than 900,000—Mark Fidrych almost single-handedly outdrew four teams.

"The whole season was like one giant trip," Mark told reporters soon after the season ended. "I can't explain it any other way. It's all been unbelievable." He admitted that he was exhausted from all the attention and would like to "hibernate" a while, but was looking forward to next season. "I get excited when I think about my future." The Tigers were also excited when thinking about the future. Things could only get better.

The awards and accolades flooded in. Mark was named Tiger of the Year by the Detroit chapter of the Baseball Writers Association of America. He was later named the top Michigan sports story of 1976 by sportswriters and broadcasters. He received a watch as the *Sporting News* American League Rookie Pitcher of the Year. He received a trophy for selection to the Topps Rookie All-Star team. In October, the Michigan Senate voted to set aside November 23 as "Bird Day" to honor "the migration to Michigan of a particularly unique species, the Mark Fidrych."

Not to be outdone, back in Massachussetts, Mark Fidrych was declared "State Bird of the Day" on October 15 in a ceremony conducted by Governor Michael Dukakis. Mark tossed a dozen pitches to the governor on the statehouse lawn. Legend has it that Mark called the governor "chicken" when Dukakis asked him not to throw hard. Wearing jeans and a dungaree jacket for the ceremony, Mark was asked by reporters if he was a Democrat. He replied, "I don't vote. Some people are happy voting. I'm happy playing baseball."

Dukakis' proclamation read: "Whereas Mark Fidrych has awakened the boy lying dormant in every man's breast, Whereas he has reminded us all that, in an age of free agents and no-cut contracts, baseball is still a game, he has proven baseballs, like people, respond best to kind words and constructive criticism and not to saliva and Vaseline, he made Big Bird as popular with fifty-year-olds as with the playpen set . . ."

Jim Palmer, who went 22–13 with a 2.51 ERA for the Orioles, won the Cy Young Award, with Mark finishing a not-too-distant second in the voting. Although no rookie in either league had ever won a Cy Young Award, there were many who felt The Bird deserved it. A strong case can be made for Mark in view of his nineteen wins for the fifth-place Tigers, his league-leading ERA of 2.34, and the fact that he accomplished all this after May 15. Unlike today, however, in the seventies the Cy Young Award usually went to the pitcher with the most wins, regardless of the other factors.

In December, it was announced that Mark had been selected Rookie of the Year for the American League. The voting was not close. Mark received twenty-two of twenty-four votes, with Twin catcher Butch Wynegar getting the other two.

Mark told reporters he planned on spending the winter in Northboro, "hanging around with my buddies." In reality, it would be a very busy winter for Mark as the William Morris Agency had lined up a number of speaking engagements and promotional appearances to go with his award banquets. There was also a commercial for Aqua Velva aftershave to be shot in December. Mark later joked, "They know I'm no good, and I know I'm no good," about the commercial, which took three or four hours to shoot for the thirty-second spot. "They had to do it for the lotion, not the shaving cream, because I don't shave yet."

Back home in Northboro for the off-season, Mark Fidrych was eager to relax and become Fid again. Friends and townspeople welcomed him back, but it was different now. "You never felt that he was totally comfortable with all the attention," says Paul Beals. "He was like, 'It's just me guys.' He never lost sight of who he was or where he came from. Even after everything else later." Although he had been the toast of the national media, had rubbed elbows with Elton John, the Beach Boys, and President Ford, he was still the same guy who had left the small town two years earlier. The big difference now, though, was the reaction of other people. The Bird had been too big, too hyped, too much fun for Mark Fidrych to ever be viewed as just Fid again. There was no going back.

"The hype was sort of overwhelming," says longtime friend Wayne Hey. "It came so sudden, no one expected it. Everyone was just along for the ride."

Those close to him were concerned that the fame and constant attention would have an affect on Mark. Friends resented the journalists who played up the flaky stories and made fun of his New England accent. "When I come home now, my friends say to me, 'Hey, man, what're they doing to you?'" Mark told a reporter that winter.

"I worry about Fid," said Dave Pierce, the thirty-one-year-old owner of Pierce Oil and Gas, Mark's old boss. "But I think he's all right. . . . He's just not used to being in public. . . . What were you like when you were twenty-one, twenty-two years old?"

"I don't like this Bird thing at all," Virginia Fidrych told a reporter. "Marky's not a bird. He's a human being. He's my only son. And I don't know what this flake business means." She had earlier been reported to be upset when he was called flaky, thinking that flaky was a slang term having something to do with drugs. "To me, my son is not flaky. He's just got a lot of nervous energy."

One friend told a reporter, "I slipped up one day and asked another guy if he was going to the big party for The Bird. 'Bird,' he says, shocked. 'For Chrissake, he's Fid. The name's Fid. Don't give me any of this Bird stuff.'"

The "big party for The Bird" was Northboro's celebration of the hometown hero's success. As the 1976 season neared a conclusion, a meeting was held in the town hall auditorium to discuss the best way to show the town's appreciation of Mark. "We want to make it a day for all of us in Northboro who consider ourselves as (Mark's) friends and neighbors," said selectman Robert Gabriel. "His is a Cinderella story in baseball, which will probably never be paralleled again." Since Mark had previously said that he wouldn't feel comfortable with a parade, they decided to hold a "Roast the Bird" banquet, with the proceeds going to charity.

The more than 500 tickets to the banquet sold out within hours. It was held at the White Pines. Located on the east edge of Northboro, the majestic White Pines had originally been the summer mansion of Daniel Wesson (the gunmaker of Smith and Wesson fame) in the 1860s. After a few ownership changes through the years, it had been converted into its present use—the place in town where all big events were held. The audience stood cheering when Mark walked into the room wearing a plaid shirt, corduroy jeans, and a huge grin. Mark and the Fidryches sat at the head table along with Bruce Kimm, who was flown in by the organizers, and Mark's former coaches Jack Wallace, Tom Blackburn, and Ted Rolfe. Although he didn't appear nervous to the audience, Mark was worried about being in such a spotlight in front of his friends and neighbors. The twenty-two-year-old baseball player was especially worried about having to give a speech. "Mark initially didn't want to do it," says Paula. "He was kind of embarrassed by all the attention. But he made sure that all the proceeds from the night went for lights on the Little League field." Whether he wanted the attention or not, Mark was definitely getting it, even in his hometown. But everyone at the White Pines was happy to see that he was still Fid—he had not let the celebrity go to his head. Mark gladly signed scores of autographs, endured bad jokes from the speakers, and cheerfully answered the same questions over and over. He wandered from table to table talking to the guests while they were eating. One woman was quoted in the paper the next day as saying, "Now I know why everyone likes him so much. He's really being nice to everyone."

The whirlwind off-season continued. In December, after a deer hunting trip in northern Michigan with Bill Freehan and Mickey Stanley, Mark flew to Los Angeles to accept the Man of the Year Award at the Major League Baseball winter meeting. It was obvious as soon as one entered the main lobby of the L.A. Hilton and was greeted by a large portrait of Mark Fidrych that baseball was holding him up as its number one selling point for the future. One writer attending the event noted that when first meeting Mark at the All-Star Game, he had been skeptical of Mark's sincerity. "He seemed just a little too pat, a little too perfect. . . . But now, six months later, my skepticism has vanished. He is still wide-eyed, innocent, and refreshing. Nobody could maintain a naiveté act that long without going bonkers. He has to be genuine."

During the banquet, in front of over 1,000 baseball and showbiz celebrities, Mark was worked over by the comedians. One said, "Fidrych has been talking to my steak for the last twenty minutes." Don Rickles added, "Fidrych, you look like Harpo Marx's brother;

you belong in a home. They oughta throw him in some home and throw away the key. But then you'd see the owners of Detroit going, 'Please let him out.' "

When it was time for the award, Vin Scully introduced Mark: "Because he was individually responsible for putting more people in ballparks than anyone since Sandy Koufax, the National Professional Baseball Association names Mark Fidrych its Man of the Year."

Thrust in front of the microphone, Mark told the audience, "I didn't really know what was going on a couple of years ago, when the Tigers signed me right out of the gas station and the R & T Furniture Store, and I don't know what's going on now. I'm not really intelligent enough to speak any funny lines. But I do know that I'm up here, and all these coaches and managers are down there in the audience, so I guess I'm doing something right."

After dinner, a reporter, noting Mark's late-season bonus and raise, asked him, "Has the money changed your life?"

"Well, I can just about buy anything I want now."

"What have you bought?"

"Nothing yet."

"What are you going to do with your money?"

"I'm just saving it."

Mark wandered through the banquet hall mixing with Hollywood celebrities. "I'll clue ya, these actors, man, they were neat," he said. "My mother woulda went nuts to meet Cary Grant. And Frank Sinatra! She'd have been goin' nuts! . . . Monty Hall (of the game show *Let's Make a Deal*) was probably more of a highlight to *me* because I've *watched* Monty Hall." Mark had his picture taken with a tuxedoed Frank Sinatra. He was introduced to Walter Matthau. "Do you know me?" the actor asked Mark.

"I've seen you around," Mark replied. "You look familiar."

"Did you see *The Bad News Bears*?"

"No."

Matthau explained that he had been in a few movies, including the popular one about the ragtag youth baseball team, and Mark then moved on—continuing his happy, occasionally oblivious existence—galaxies removed from the little gas station on Route 20 in Northboro.

As 1976 came to a close, it was hard to fully appreciate all that had happened—difficult to see the entire picture while immersed in it. Mark had lived through a year unlike that experienced by any individual baseball player in the history of the game. Why was Mark Fidrych so popular? Why did he affect people of all ages so much? Other pitchers have had better years, but no one has ever had a year in which he affected the fans and the game like Mark Fidrych did in 1976.

Writers strained to put into words an explanation for Mark's unimaginable popularity. Joe Falls seemed particularly perplexed—and also disturbed—by the whole phenomenon. "No player in our time—not any of the greats, not Ted Williams, Mickey Mantle, Hank Aaron, Willie Mays, Sandy Koufax—none of them, ever pulled people out to the ball park the way this 22-year-old phenom has done this summer," he wrote in the *Sporting News*. "The whole thing is a little frightening. At least to me it is. They cheer him every minute he's on the mound and then when it's over, they won't leave until he comes back and waves to the fans. When, if ever, has a ballplayer ever been asked to take a curtain call every time? They never even asked that of Babe Ruth.

"What scares me is that I feel a tremendous overreaction taking place," Falls continued, "and I asked myself what causes it. . . . I don't think it is Mark Fidrych the fans are cheering for so much. I get the overpowering feeling the fans are really cheering for themselves. They see in this young man something that is good and exciting and alive and this is what we all want out of life. . . . These people are crying out for a better life and at the moment they are getting it, vicariously, through the exploits of one young ballplayer."

Not happy with his own explanation, Falls sought professional help. He wrote an article that was carried by the wire services in which he consulted two Detroit-area psychologists regarding the phenomenon of The Bird. "What we've got is a nobody becoming a somebody—a 'Joe Doakes' reaching for a million dollars," said Dr.

William Lucken. "We all dream about getting lucky in our lives, even once—and here is a young man who made it. We need someone like Mark Fidrych every once in a while to let us know that our dreams can come true. He's given us a thrill—he's given us a big ride—and that's beautiful."

"The principle of contagion is at work," added Dr. Ed Staniec. "What we've really got is gross over reaction in a deprived situation. We haven't had very much in Detroit in recent years, not even in the way of sports. Our teams never seem to win anything. We've needed something to give us a lift—to give us hope—and we've found it in a person. He is humble and he is from humble beginnings and he fulfills our Great American Dream. I don't think it's his antics per se that turn everybody on—it's just an excuse for us to relate to him. We are living in a violent, materialistic society and along comes this kid. He tells us he'd like to drive a truck for a living. Who wouldn't be turned on by something like that?"

A *Newsweek* profile stated the appeal more simply: "In an era of self-important, pampered athletes, Fidrych is a throwback who communicates with the fans and gives all he has on a minimum salary of $16,500."

In the *Christian Science Monitor*, it was written: "Sports fans have become fed up with all the legal hassles intruding upon their games—the talk of money by players and owners, and all the emphasis on contracts, agents and courtrooms. Suddenly, here was a refreshing new star who obviously loves to play ball, who responds enthusiastically to success, who is a bit of a character, and who has focused the attention of the public back where it belongs—on the field."

The Lindell AC's owner, Jimmy Butsicaris, weighed in and explained why there were so many little old ladies among Mark's devoted fans, when a few years earlier Mark would have been the kind of kid adults didn't like—different with long hair: "He's everybody's son. People are used to that kind of kid now."

It is impossible to overstate what Mark Fidrych meant to the city of Detroit during the 1976 season. Detroit was no longer just a punch line for late-night comedians. It was not a crime-ridden city to be feared—it was the place to be. He gave the citizens of this downtrodden, tough, blue-collar city something to be proud of; a reason to venture back into the city. And he made about the same amount of money as the workers did—they could relate to him.

But it was not only in Detroit that he had an impact. He did something for all of baseball. People remember becoming baseball fans in 1976 solely because of Mark Fidrych. People who weren't Tiger fans became Mark Fidrych fans. Whole families would gather around the television to watch him pitch—at least one thing to bring parents and kids together at a time in which they desperately needed something to bring them together.

Mark's teammates certainly enjoyed the excitement of the year. Late in the 1976 season, Kimm told reporters, "This is the greatest thing that has happened to the game in a long time. . . . And when I get old, I'll be able to say I played with him—I caught him."

"He electrifies the fans and the players like nobody else I've ever seen," said Rusty Staub. "Everybody can see the enthusiasm in Mark. He brings out the exuberance and inner youth in everybody."

"When he pitched, we felt like we were playing in the World Series," said Aurelio Rodriguez in 1977.

Later, with the perspective of time and age, teammates still tried to explain his appeal. "He just caught the imagination of the youth of America," said Staub in 2002. "Because he was real. It was not contrived. To be that unique and have those little idiosyncrasies on the mound and to be able to perform as he did was an incredible combination and it was fun."

"He was so popular, I think, because when he went out on the field there was no doubt that here was a guy who loved to play the game," says Kimm. "He was just playing the game like we all used to play as kids. I think that transcended to the fans." And true to his statement of 1976, Kimm adds, "I'm proud of the fact that I got to catch all his starts in 1976. I got to be part of the most exciting thing in baseball that year."

"All the stuff with Mark kind of saved our year," says Hiller.

Mark (second from the right) on the bench during a basketball game at Algonquin Regional High School, circa 1972. Immediately to the left is Mark's friend, Brad Ostiguy.

(Courtesy of Brad Ostiguy)

Playing for the Northboro American Legion team, Summer 1973.

(Courtesy of Carol Fidrych-Duda)

The Bird. Spring 1976.

(Courtesy of the National Baseball Hall of Fame Library, Cooperstown, NY)

Grooming the mound. "You've got to make your own hole."

(Courtesy of the National Baseball Hall of Fame Library, Cooperstown, NY)

Mark prepares to pitch during his rookie season. "Gotta flow, let it flow."

(Courtesy of the National Baseball Hall of Fame Library, Cooperstown, NY)

Signing for fans at Tiger Stadium, June 30, 1976. Note the excellent examples of mid-seventies hairstyles.

(AP Images)

The Roast the Bird banquet in Northboro, Massachusetts, November 1976. From left to right: Paul Fidrych; Tom Blackburn, coach at Worcester Academy; Mark Fidrych; Bruce Kimm; Jack Wallace, coach at Algonquin Regional High School; and Ted Rolfe, Northboro American Legion coach.   (Courtesy of Jack Wallace)

Mark with Massachusetts governor Michael Dukakis on the statehouse lawn, October 18, 1976. Legend has it that Mark called the governor "chicken" when he asked him not to throw hard for their photo-op game of catch.

(AP Images)

Mark waves his hat to the crowd at Tiger Stadium on August 13, 1980, in response to a tremendous ovation as he walked from the dugout to warm up before his first appearance in Detroit following his recall from Evansville.

(AP Images)

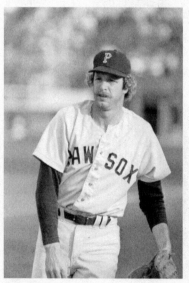

With Pawtucket, June 14, 1982. "You lose your pride, but it's still baseball."

(Courtesy of the Walter P. Reuther Library, Wayne State University)

Mark demonstrates his famous dancing moves at sister Carol's wedding, 1985.

(Courtesy of Carol Fidrych-Duda)

Mark and brother-in-law Rick Duda (far left) with a happy camper at a Red Sox fantasy camp in Winter Haven, Florida, circa 1990.

(Courtesy of Carol Fidrych-Duda)

Mark making a speech on behalf of the Wertz Warriors for
the Michigan Special Olympics
Winter Games, 2009.

(Courtesy of Wertz Warriors)

Signing autographs and talking to fans for the Wertz Warriors.
"It's a chance to give back where you can."

(Courtesy of Wertz Warriors)

Mark gathers family in the living room of his house. Wife Ann, with dark hair, is in front of Mark, flanked by his sisters Paula and Lorie. Mark's other sister, Carol, is in the back row. (Courtesy of Lorie Karolowicz)

Mark shows an old friend around the farm.

(Courtesy Joe McNally Photography)

"We didn't have a very good ball team, but that took away a little bit of the pressure of winning and losing. The team drew well. When he pitched, the atmosphere in Tiger Stadium was like a playoff game."

"I never had so much fun in my life as I did watching him and playing that year," says catcher John Wockenfuss. "I was glad to have been able to be a part of it and participate in that."

"I don't know of one person on the team who was jealous, who didn't enjoy it," says MacCormack. Teammates also appreciated the fact that the crowds The Bird brought in helped make them money when contract time came around.

Far from feeling upstaged or angry, the majority of opposing players enjoyed the atmosphere The Bird provided also. "I remember one time Ralph Garr (the White Sox .300 hitter) told me, 'Make sure you tell The Bird that he can really pitch,' " says Kimm. Some opponents even joined in the fun, such as the Yankees' Graig Nettles who stepped out of the box, held up his bat, and told it not to listen to anything that Fidrych said—and later complained to reporters after a hitless game, "The damn bat was made in Japan."

Earl Weaver later said, "The strange thing about it was the ballplayers didn't get mad. When you're winning and he keeps getting you out, a guy like Frank Robinson is going to say something nasty. The guy talks to the ball and does the dirt and then gets Frank out. Frank woulda went nuts, I think. But he (Fidrych) just entertained everybody."

But perhaps it was the fans' reaction to Mark and his to them that made the season so special. His appeal extended from the youngest to the oldest of fans. Young children liked him because he was called The Bird, and they were told he looked like Big Bird, someone they could identify with. Kids taken to the ballpark by their parents were captivated by his boyish charm. They enjoyed watching his unusual behavior on the field, wondering, "What's he going to do next?" Teenagers liked him because here was a guy with long hair who listened to loud rock music, wore jeans and T-shirts, and still was able to play Major League Baseball. Older fans loved him because of the old-school way he pitched, completing every game, going right at hitters. Everybody loved him because he won. Everyone loved him because he had been the underdog, the unknown rookie, the embodiment of every kid's dream.

Whatever the reasons, 1976 was a baseball season unlike any other. Mark Fidrych had won the Rookie of the Year Award, replaced state birds in two states, drawn almost a million fans to his games, remained engaging and friendly—and survived—while being pummeled by an ever-demanding press, and had given dolphin rides and swimming lessons to little kids. What could he possibly do for an encore in 1977?

6

"Slow Down"

Mark Fidrych began 1977 just as he had finished 1976, on top of the world, living large. He could do no wrong. He was the center of attention everywhere he went. There seemed to be no end in sight to the love from fans and the frenzy from the media.

More than 5,000 people lined up to get his autograph at the Worcester Center Galleria early in the year. The fans didn't seem to mind waiting up to four hours to see him, and, of course, he obliged them all. Then it was off to New York where, unusually dressed in a tuxedo, he attended the New York Baseball Writers Association of America Banquet to accept their Player of the Year Award. He sat on the dais with new Hall of Famer Ernie Banks, plus Johnny Bench, Joe Morgan, and Sparky Anderson, for the black-tie gathering of 1,400. He admitted to reporters that the event made him so tight that he couldn't give his prepared speech, but he managed to charm the audience nonetheless. With all the practice, he was becoming more comfortable and more accomplished at public speaking. The attendees laughed when he told them, "I don't ever have to worry about going back to the gas station. I own the station now." Afterward, Dave Anderson joked in the *New York Times* that Mark "smoothed out the tablecloth and talked to his fork" during the evening and remarked that his speech was given without notes. "He exists extemporaneously. Saying and doing what comes naturally is what makes Fidrych different from hermetically sealed ballplayers."

There were other banquets and ceremonies, almost every week. He was honored by the Detroit chapter of the March of Dimes for being selected Sportsman of the Year by Detroit's United Foundation. A few weeks later he was the guest of honor at the annual Detroit Sportswriters Dinner for being selected the 1976 Tiger of the Year. In between, he was the star attraction at a Detroit auto show.

Mark took time off from the banquet and appearance circuit to join other Tiger players and officials on a press tour of Michigan in late January. Along with Ron LeFlore, Dave Roberts, Ben Oglivie, and Jason Thompson, as well as Houk and Campbell, he visited St. Clair, Flint, Saginaw, Lansing, Grand Rapids, Kalamazoo, Jackson, and Toledo—spreading Tiger goodwill, signing autographs, and encouraging people to buy tickets. Wire services ran a picture of him trying his pitching grip on a snowball during the trip. Jim Hawkins wrote about the tour and told readers of the *Sporting News* that "The Bird is flaky as ever." Hawkins wrote that Mark wore his customary dungarees full of holes, ate a sauerkraut sandwich for breakfast, tortured tour members on the bus with his attempts at playing the harmonica, and only brought one pair of red socks on the trip, which he wore every day. "When asked, he also offered such enlightening information as, 'Rome wasn't built in a day.'" When Roberts and Oglivie teased him about the remark on the bus later, he responded, "Hey, I took history in high school, you know!" (even though the statement was taken from his college-level Grodzicki 101 course). He also advised young ballplayers throughout the state to "get your rest and don't be fooling around with the ladies all night."

Hawkins noted that, "If The Bird is at all aware of the incredible pressure that is going to be heaped on him this season . . . he sure doesn't show it. . . . After last year, it will no longer be sufficient for Fidrych simply to be good. Anything less than sensational, or at least 19–9, will be judged unsatisfactory."

While Mark enjoyed interacting with people on the tours and at the banquets, it made for an extremely busy winter, and the constant attention and repeatedly answering the same questions began to take its toll. He longed for some personal time to just relax and goof around. He memorably told *Sports Illustrated*'s Ron Fimrite, "It got so I felt like saying, 'Hey, it's my vacation, let me vacate.'"

When the weather warmed up, it was time to put on the cleats and get out the glove again. If there was any question that The Bird would be a one-year phenomenon and that something else might replace him in the baseball public's fancy, it was quickly extinguished. Hordes of reporters eagerly waited to expound on Mark's every action. He participated in a slow-pitch Major League All-Star softball charity game in Tarpon Springs, Florida, in mid-February to benefit the Sickle Cell Disease Foundation. A pro-am golf tournament was also part of the festivities. Mark was noted to thoroughly enjoy himself on the links. Wearing a tan shirt and lime green slacks, he howled with laughter as his tee shots ricocheted through the woods. Major league stars such as Robin Yount, Johnny Bench, Tom Seaver, and George Brett were all secondary to Mark with the gallery and autograph seekers. The players hammed it up during the softball game, which was televised by CBS. Bench talked to his bat before stepping in against Mark, then pounded a pitch over the left-field fence. The next time Bench came up, Mark looked awed and fell to his knees bowing. Mark legged out a triple later in the game, and Phyllis George, a former Miss America and NFL commentator, could be heard squealing with laughter from her third-base coaching box as he joked with her while standing on third.

Writers reported that Mark had moved over the winter to a new apartment, one with a security guard that could keep people away from his door. The new apartment cost $305 a month and came with a washer and dryer and a view of a lake. "It's even got curtains," he bragged. "People say, 'Hey, why don't you get a more expensive place, you can afford it.' They don't know, man, I gotta be careful. I really got hit hard with taxes this year. I can't write anything off. I gotta save. . . . I don't blow my money on dumb things. . . . I'm saving so I can buy me a garage someday." Mark had also been nailed with a $2,000 tax bill for the Thunderbird. While being careful with his money, he did admit to spending some of it to send his parents to Fort Lauderdale in February to see his uncle Arthur for his mother's Christmas present.

Mark was constantly questioned about the sophomore jinx. "What's the sophomore jinx?" he responded. "I made it through my sophomore year in high school, didn't I? Your hardest year is your first year if you play in the big leagues. I've got nothing to worry about. Whatever happens, happens. I can't change it, right?"

When asked to compare his salary to that of the Indians' Wayne Garland who had won twenty games for the Orioles in 1976, went the free-agent route, and signed for $2 million, Mark gave his own unique view of personal economics: "It's enough to live on for a job, right? I go home and my friends don't make a third of what I make. If they can live on what they're making, why can't I?"

The Tigers arrived in Lakeland for spring training with high hopes. "You never saw such optimism as there is here in the Detroit Tigers' camp," wrote Milton Richman of UPI, discussing Ralph Houk. "It's not a man or some superman he's carrying on about, it's a bird."

Mark's spring pitching debut was scheduled against the Red Sox in Winter Haven. Cars started lining up two hours before the game. The Red Sox's ballpark was jammed to capacity with many fans standing in the aisles. Thunderous applause broke out as Mark took the mound. He immediately dropped to his knees and spread the mound dirt with his hands, then proceeded to throw three shutout innings. "I've never seen anything like it," said Hal Middlesworth afterward. "This kid is the greatest draw in baseball."

Mark blanked the Cardinals over four innings in his second start; however, on March 20 he was shelled by the White Sox in a twelve-run second inning in which he blew up, screamed at the umpire after several questionable calls, and threw his glove. He immediately felt bad about his on-field tantrum and apologized to reporters after the game. The next morning, Houk called Mark into his office for a fatherly lecture on the danger of losing one's temper on the field. At the conclusion of the talk, Mark stuck his hand in his pocket, produced the skipper's watch, and handed it to him. It seems that during the same argument the day before, Houk had waved his arms so wildly while yelling at the umpire that his watch had flown off and disappeared into the plush Florida infield grass. Unable to find it, he had given it up as lost. Mark had found it lying in the grass and picked it up.

The White Sox game notwithstanding, life was grand. Mark was pitching great. The fans loved him. At twenty-two years old, he had a new contract and his future was limitless. And then, suddenly, it wasn't. How long does it take for everything in a life to change? How long does it take for it all to be turned upside down and lost? Sometimes, it only takes a second.

March 21, 1977, was a beautiful Florida day, like any other in spring training. Mark was in the outfield talking to Rusty Staub and Bob Sykes, shagging flies for batting practice before an exhibition game with the Reds. Normally, shagging flies is a low-key, relaxing activity. But Mark never did anything normally or low-key or relaxing.

"I can remember it like it was yesterday," says Sykes. "Tony Perez had come out of the visiting clubhouse down the right-field line and was walking toward the infield. Bird knew him from the All-Star Game and other places; everybody in baseball knew Tony Perez. Bird was yelling at him, badgering him, having fun." Mark was zipping around the field, laughing, enjoying life.

Staub said, "OK, we got two weeks left of spring training. You've had a great spring—slow down."

"Rusty, it's baseball," Mark answered. "I'm having a good time."

A few minutes later a fly ball was hit near them. "You want this one?" Mark asked. "No, you take it," Staub replied.

"Mark took off after it," says Sykes. "As he got close, instead of just catching it, he gave a goofy bird call and lunged, kind of dove for it." Mark left the ground as the reining Rookie of the Year, the most popular player in the game. He had no way of knowing that when he came down, things would never be the same again.

"He came down kind of straight-legged," continues Sykes. "It was kind of an awkward landing. You could tell he hurt it. He immediately started limping."

"I don't know which hurt worse, my knee or my head after Rusty whacked me with his glove and said, 'What did I just tell you?'" Mark later said.

Mark knew right away that something was wrong with his left knee. He tried to work it out and later did his scheduled running, but when he came in he told trainer Bill Behm the knee felt funny. That night it stiffened up on him. He called his father crying, "I had everything and now I've lost it." By the next morning the knee was swollen and painful to walk on. It was x-rayed and examined by doctors at Lakeland's Watson Clinic. Ralph Houk, hoping for the best, told reporters, "They said it was a strained knee and that he should rest it for three or four days and then come back again." Houk tried to sound relaxed, but it was certain that a deathly chill was being felt throughout the entire Detroit Tiger organization.

Dr. Glen Barden of the Watson Clinic told reporters, "It does not appear there is a more serious underlying injury than the sprain." Reporters noted that Mark limped noticeably when he walked at the game that night but didn't seem overly concerned.

But he was soon very concerned, along with everyone else. After starting to feel better with a short rest, the knee popped again during a light workout. It was reexamined by Dr. Barden on March 28, and this time the results were not good. Suspecting torn cartilage, plans were made to fly Mark back to Detroit for a more thorough examination at Henry Ford Hospital.

Dressed in his usual outfit of blue jeans and a plaid shirt, Mark was met at Detroit's Metro Airport by Lew Matlin and whisked away from the gauntlet of photographers and reporters and into a chauffeur-driven limousine. Upon arriving at Henry Ford Hospital, he walked into the lobby carrying a knapsack and his omnipresent tape player. "How do I get to the sixteenth floor?" he asked the lobby receptionist, as patients and visitors turned to watch the lanky, curly headed patient check in, whispering, "There he is. That's him, that's The Bird."

At Henry Ford, Mark was examined by Dr. David Mitchell and Dr. Edwin Guise. He had an arthrogram, a technique used at the time in which dye was injected into the knee and the knee was then x-rayed—this was before MRIs and CT scans. The severity of the injury was confirmed—there was cartilage damage that would need surgical repair. Surgery was scheduled for March 31, the next day. The Tigers said they expected him to be hospitalized for a week and hoped that he would be on crutches not more than three weeks.

Everyone scrambled to understand the implications of the injury. Mark Fidrych expected to miss thirteen starts if he was out the eight weeks team physician Dr. Livingood predicted. Ralph Houk told reporters, "They told me the worst it would be is he'd be out until June 1 and then he'd be 100 percent." It was reported that the Tigers figured to lose 130,000 to 200,000 extra fans the first two months of the season while The Bird healed. It was easy to calculate the impact in dollars. Everyone marked their calendars. Eight weeks. June 1. Then the real season could begin. And things would be just like last year. One hundred percent.

The one-hour operation to remove damaged cartilage from the most important knee in Detroit was declared a success by doctors. "There was a large tear in the medial left cartilage but no additional damage," said Dr. Mitchell after the operation. "The entire cartilage was removed and a large compression dressing was used but no cast."

Meanwhile, anxious fans made life miserable for switchboard operators at Henry Ford Hospital. "There were hundreds of calls," said a hospital official. "Most of them wanted to know his room number so they could send flowers or notes. But we're getting some real funny ones. We had people call and say, 'Put me through to Mark Fidrych,' just like that. Like we'd just ring his room for them."

In order to give the special patient any peace, room 608 at Henry Ford Hospital became the most heavily fortified room in the city. It was made off-limits to almost everyone other than doctors, teammates, and personal friends. Guards blocked access to the floor. A hospital security man, Mike LaBrecque, was placed in an ante-room outside Mark's private quarters, where potential visitors were stopped and all calls were screened. LaBrecque told *Sport* magazine that he prevented numerous people from sneaking in. One man came to the door wearing a white doctor's gown and told him he was there to examine the patient. LaBrecque, who knew all the doctors in the hospital, didn't buy it, and upon intense question-ing, the man cracked and ran off. "Oh yeah, it's crazy," LaBrecque said. "This chick calls and says she's the secretary of Jim Camp-bell . . . and wants to talk to Mark. I ask her what her name is and she gives me a name and I know she's lying. I know Campbell's secretary and her name ain't that. Guy calls up and says he's Camp-bell himself. Had a lot of them. Houk, some guy said he was Ralph Houk. Mark's father, his mother, his brother—hell, he hasn't got a brother. People shove notes under the door. Nurses keep trying to get in."

A worker for Michigan Bell showed up in Mark's room. "Switchboard's going crazy," he said. "I don't know if we can han-dle all the calls for him." The worker claimed that he saw Mark that morning hanging out of his window yelling, "Help me! Help me! Get me outta here! Save me! Save me! I'm going crazy in here, somebody get me outta here!"

As if there wasn't enough to worry about, Joe Falls, who ear-lier in the year had publicly ripped Mark about his choice of clothes at the United Foundation banquet, created extra controversy. Ever the curmudgeon, Falls had mentioned concern in a column in early March over such a valuable team property as Mark running around the field with reckless exuberance. "If he doesn't calm down, he's going to hurt himself," Falls wrote. He later wrote in a book, "The moment he showed up on the field in Lakeland (in 1977) he was leaping over fences, jumping up and down, and racing around like a young colt. It was almost as if he were saying, 'I'm still the same guy, world. Do you still love me?'"

After the injury, Falls suggested in his column that the injury was a "blessing in disguise" because it would temper the expectations and give Mark an excuse if he got off to a bad start when he returned.

Later, Falls seemed to delight in telling the story (which he did in at least two books and several interviews) of the press conference at the hospital. With the room packed with doctors, nurses, writers, and broadcasters, Falls said, "When Fidrych saw me, he pointed at me and started crying. He said, 'There's the man who wanted me to get hurt. That's him over by the wall.'"

Among the writers who followed the Tigers, Falls seemed to have had the hardest time understanding Mark Fidrych. This could be due to the fact that, since he admittedly never socialized with the players he wrote about, Falls never got to know the real Mark Fidrych. He may have felt, like others who didn't know him personally, that Mark was putting on an act—how could anyone possibly be that way naturally? Several times in his columns Falls lamented the fact that Mark acted immature—rather than acting like a thirty-five-year-old veteran. The point Falls seemed to have missed was that the enthusiasm and effort were the things that had made Mark Fidrych. Falls hadn't seen Mark in spring training in 1976 because he wasn't looking for the unknown rookie then, but by all accounts Mark was not acting any differently in the spring of 1977 than he had his whole life on the baseball field. You could not ask Mark Fidrych to curb his enthusiasm any more than you could ask Nolan Ryan to throw the ball slower, or Pete Rose to relax his ego and take it easy, or Gale Sayers to just run straight up the field—to do so would have been to rob him of the very thing that distinguished him from other players of similar talent.

Ralph Houk, who managed many very good players over the years and knew a thing or two about talent and performance, understood. "In 1977, when he hurt his knee, it was just because of the way he played," says Houk. "I'm surprised he didn't get hurt earlier because he played so hard."

Mark quickly learned just how fleeting glory could be. *Sports*

Illustrated pulled him off the cover of its Opening Day issue soon after the injury. "So I got hurt. I ain't dead, right?" he complained to a reporter. He had spent four hours for the photo shoot that coupled him with Big Bird.

Mark talked about the injury from his hospital room a few days after the operation (the day before Opening Day) for a *Sport* cover story. "When this happened, I couldn't believe it, man. I kept asking, 'Why me, God? Why me? What did I do to deserve this?' I still keep asking that. I'm religious, you know. I don't go to church much, but I don't have to; I can talk to God right here in this room. I think this is His way of showing me that, hey, I'm human, I'm just like anybody else, and don't start acting like some kind of a big shot."

The 1977 season did not start with Mark Fidrych on the mound in front of a crazy, sellout Tiger stadium crowd as planned. It began with Mark Fidrych lying in bed in the hospital listening to the game on the radio with Dave Roberts pitching for the Tigers. Mark spent a fretful April resting the knee. Aside from daily visits to the hospital, he could do nothing but sit around his apartment the first two weeks. Sitting still and keeping quiet had never been his strong points. The inactivity was difficult.

"It was hard on him, but he kept his spirits up," says Bob Sykes. "My wife and I went by his apartment after his surgery. He was upbeat. He figured it would work out. But that was Mark—I never saw him worry one minute of his life. Nothing bothered him. He always figured that things would work out."

After an eternity (a few weeks) it was time to get rid of the crutches and begin slowly working back into shape. The knee felt good. He couldn't wait to get out on the field and start throwing. He started jogging in mid-April and was throwing lightly the first of May. He was soon running a mile a day. It was announced that he would be placed on a modified spring training routine to get his arm into shape. He began throwing batting practice before games and pitching on the side. It was tough watching and listening to the Tigers struggle. Mark began pushing for an earlier start, but Houk refused, telling reporters later, "He's so young and eager, but we wanted to bring him back slowly, so that the first time he started, he'd be ready to go nine."

The inactivity was driving Mark, and everyone else, crazy. He almost gave Houk a heart attack during a trip to Texas by trying to lift a car that had gotten its bumper locked with the Tigers' bus. Soon after, he took batting practice using a bat that was fifty inches long and weighed sixty ounces. "I asked the Louisville Slugger people for the biggest bat they make," he told reporters. "Why not?"

Mark's autobiography was due to be released soon. "I haven't read it yet," he said. "My agent went through it. The agent said there were too many swear words, but other than that it's a good book. I'm dying to see it." He had earlier joked in *Sports Illustrated*, "I'm supposed to be writing a book and I can hardly read."

The book, titled *No Big Deal*, was like its subject—different. Mark's coauthor Tom Clark, a prolific writer of poetry and prose, had once hitchhiked across England with poet Allen Ginsberg. Clark extensively chronicled the beatnik and countercultural genera- tion of San Francisco and Berkeley and was the distinguished edi- tor of the *Paris Poetry Review*—not your basic sportswriter. But Clark was also a huge baseball fan and had previously written two baseball books and several baseball-themed poems. He met with Mark and interviewed him for five days while Mark was in Los Angeles to accept the baseball executive award in December of 1976.

Clark explained in the introduction that "interviewing Mark is like being thrown into the water at an early age. You learn how to float in time, then you take a few strokes, then you're in the swim of it. . . . His thoughts and responses moved in large wave- like periods (he called them trains of thought), and as interviewer it was the best I could do to hang on." Mark had originally wanted to name the book *How They Made Me*, as an acknowledgment of everyone who helped make him a success. Clark had chosen *No Big Deal* as a title because it was one of Mark's most frequent expres- sions and it seemed to be appropriate for how he viewed himself and his accomplishments.

The book was written in an interview style—Clark's questions and Mark's answers, mostly unedited. This makes it somewhat difficult to follow as it sometimes strays from subject to subject, but it captures the rapid-sequence thought patterns and language of the twenty-two-year-old Fidrych, leading to paragraphs such as this when Mark talks about his first car: "I got a—I bought it off my schoolteacher, man. It was a '65 Chevy Bel Air Standard. Y'know? And the schoolteacher was funny, man. This is a joke. Like we're goin' home, man—this is funny, though. We're comin' home, and like I'm bringin' the teacher home with the car, y'know? He's gonna show my parents. And me and my buddy are in the back, Jerry Milano, right? And Mr. Eaton, one of the teachers. And he's drivin' down there, he's showin' me—he goes, Yeah! 'Cause he's really enthused, he's glad I'm buyin' it. 'Cause all it needed was one little part in it, y'know? I think a little solenoid, it needed. Because sometimes it just wouldn't turn over. And so he goes, Y'see, the radio works good! He goes, The heater works good! The fan! The windows roll up and down! He's showin' me everything—the blinkers both ways work! The lights work! And he goes, pushes in the cigarette—Even the cigarette lighter works for your roaches! I just went voom—I just cracked up laughin'. I go, C'mon, Mr. Eaton! I said, I don't do that, y'know? We're just laughin' our heads off! But I got that car for a hundred bucks, right? I had it a week. And it ran great, man! Ohh, I loved it, man! That car was good. And I had it a week. I sold it for a hundred dollars."

Carefully reading Mark's comments, one can find examples of his attitude and mind-set at the time, particularly his inability to find anything wrong in his fellow man (or woman). When he talks about the people who broke into the trailers in Bristol, he says, "You know what they were? They were hippies. Druggies." Still, Mark refused to be mad at them or think they were bad guys. "I *knew* the people. 'Cause I met 'em different than the other guys did . . .'cause I walked and thumbed a lot of places with a lot of 'em. They picked me up, 'cause I had to thumb."

Also, Mark mentions that singer Joni Mitchell took him out

to dinner. She gave him some store-bought tapes of herself and told him that she had dyed her hair dark so no one would recognize her. Clark, who knew the real Joni Mitchell, saw a picture and informed Mark that the girl was definitely not Joni Mitchell the singer. Maybe she disguised herself? Not a chance, this was an imposter. Mark thought a moment, then didn't seem too upset and mentioned that he had fun anyway. "I think it was a good joke, now. But it might not be, people change."

The book was panned by serious critics. "It's even shocking to realize that an author of poetry and an editor of the *Paris Review* [Clark] should be content to allow an almost nonverbal young baseball player to butcher the English language page after page," wrote one reviewer in the *Sporting News*. "Clark, who seems overflowing with hero worship when it comes to baseball players, has not even written a book in the accurate sense of the word." Others were kinder, however. Jonathan Yardley wrote in *Sports Illustrated*, "[Fidrych] is a very, very funny talker and he loves to tell stories . . . it may well prove to be the funniest sports book of the year. Voom!"

The press was everywhere during Mark's time off. Every day when he showed up at the stadium, a crowd was waiting. One more interview, one more question—it never ended. The media seemed to be ignoring the rest of the team. They only wanted to know about Mark. The toll of the inactivity, the Tigers' struggles, and the constant badgering by the press began showing in late May. "I don't want to hear any more questions about my knee," Mark snapped at reporters after throwing seven strong innings against Cincinnati in the exhibition game on May 26.

"I've got to be different this year," Mark said. "I can't go on the way I did last year, letting anyone take advantage of me. I'm going to charge $100 for interviews, with the money going to cerebral palsy, the March of Dimes, or some kids who need it. I hope it keeps people from interviewing me, because I can't come to the park without being interviewed. I can't be like anyone else. And the things people write. My mother's always calling me." Mark—and his mother—was particularly upset by the *Rolling Stone* article that needlessly contained a crude description of Mark's postgame activities.

The *Rolling Stone* issue of May 5, 1977, was historic in that it had an athlete on its cover for the first time. *Rolling Stone* magazine was founded in San Francisco in 1967 as the voice of the new countercultural generation. The name was taken from the Muddy Waters song of the same name and not the British rock group. Sports had historically been viewed to be dominated by conservative squares—even, gasp, Republicans—just the type of people the magazine was against. Mark Fidrych seemed to be the perfect athlete to break the cover barrier—young, unconventional, famously casual in his attire, hair style, and language, and with a reputation as a fun-loving party dude. He regularly blasted Lynyrd Skynyrd, Marshall Tucker, The Who, and The Grateful Dead from his tape player. And The Bird was already a pop cultural icon. The cover shot, taken by famed photographer Annie Leibovitz, was a classic. With his hat turned sideways, blond curls falling from under it, Mark was holding a baseball to his face with a perfect, teeth-exposing smile. His eyes seemed to ask, "What do we do for fun next?"

In the article, Mark offered his view of his sudden stardom: "I've done the best I could possibly do, not winning games, but in popularity," he told associate editor Dave Marsh, who noted that Mark seemed a little hurt by assertions that he wasn't aware of this. "I could win twenty games, but it won't be the same this year, the enthusiasm, the way it exploded. People are gonna come to the ballpark and all that, but it isn't gonna be like a madhouse anymore. People don't think I know—I know that. . . . People don't think I know what's going on. I . . . know what's going on. If I didn't, I wouldn't be here. Right?"

Finally, the wait was over. Mark took the mound in Tiger Stadium on May 27 for his first game of the 1977 season. The fans were ready. "Two things keep this city alive," Nancy Szczukowski, a Detroit secretary, told *Sports Illustrated*'s Peter Gammons, "the automobile industry and The Bird."

Mark anxiously arrived almost four hours before the game—an hour earlier than normal. Appearing relaxed, he talked and joked with everyone. He walked up to groundskeeper Frank Feneck. "Don't you ever change your shirt?" he asked, jabbing Feneck in the chest with his finger. When the groundskeeper looked down, Mark flicked his finger up to tweak his chin and walked into the clubhouse howling with laughter.

Vendors were ready with Bird buttons, posters, and records. Two fans were dressed in Big Bird costumes. Bird T-shirts and posters filled the stands. Mark received a standing ovation when he walked down the left-field line to warm up. After warming up, he threw a ball to a kid in the stands as was his custom. He had trouble standing still during the national anthem, shifting his weight from foot to foot and hopping up and down. He received another standing ovation when he took the field. The game was superfluous. Mark pitched a complete game, but the Tigers, who got only three hits, lost to Seattle 2–1. The two Mariners runs were the result of a dropped fly ball, a bloop double, and an error. It was noted that Mark didn't talk to the ball or landscape the area on the mound quite as much as usual, and Jim Hawkins reported that, even though the crowd of 44,200 went through the expected motions, it was relatively reserved compared to those of the previous year. "The special magic was undeniably missing." Was it due to the delayed gratification of the late start? The fear of wondering how he would hold up? Or was it just impossible to match the feeling of the previous year?

To everyone's relief, Mark's arm and knee felt fine. The score was not a cause for concern. The main thing was this: The Bird was back. "I feel like I let the people down by losing," he said afterward. "But, boy, I'm happy to be back. It felt so fine. When I started warming up and heard all those cheers, I felt tingly and got half tears in my eyes. Lemme tell you, I felt good."

Tiger management also felt tingly and good—especially where it counted: on their ledger. Because six of Mark's ten missed starts would have been at home, it was estimated that the Tigers lost nearly $500,000 in gate receipts due to Mark's knee. They hoped to soon start recovering the lost money. *Sports Illustrated* dusted off the photo shoot with Big Bird and ran it on the cover that week, making The Bird's reappearance official.

Mark lost to the Indians 6–4 in his next start, going only six innings. Thereafter, he was on a roll: a shutout over the Angels, a five-hit win over the A's, and a 4–1 victory over Toronto in which he threw just 81 pitches in a complete game.

On June 20, Mark faced the Yankees in Detroit before the largest home crowd of the season. He won 2–1, limiting the Yankees to a measly three singles. Mark had given up just three runs in his last four games. He was selected American League Player of the Week for his efforts. And the Detroit crowd was demanding curtain calls after every game once again.

Baseball talk at the end of June 1977 was dominated by two subjects: Rod Carew's pursuit of .400, which was currently at .411, and the reemergence of The Bird. On June 29, Mark won his sixth straight game 7–2 over the Red Sox. He gave up a home run to Butch Hobson, the first in sixty-seven innings on the season. After the home run, Houk walked to the mound. The crowd of 51,745 booed Houk's appearance, not wanting The Bird to be removed. Houk only wanted to talk, however, and the crowd cheered when he left the mound with Mark still holding the ball.

Writers once again took pleasure in reporting on the zany antics of The Bird. In early July, Dave Anderson ran a syndicated article entitled, "Out in left field with The Bird." He reported on various adventures, including a recent incident in which Sy Berger of the Topps Company handed Mark two photos that he said couldn't be used for baseball cards: Mark had posed as a left-handed pitcher. "You didn't get away with it. We spotted it," said Berger. "Lew Burdette tried that twenty years ago."

"You mean I wasn't the first to do that?" Mark replied. "I was just having fun."

Ralph Houk noted that at this point a lot of The Bird stories were being exaggerated or invented. "I think some people are making up stories about him now. Like they did with Yogi Berra."

Mark remained as popular or even more popular than the

year before. According to Hal Middlesworth, Detroit director of publicity, between 3,000 and 4,000 picture postcards of Mark had been mailed to fans who had sent requests by mid-June. No player in Tiger history had ever received as much mail.

The Red Sox game lowered Mark's ERA to 1.83 and improved his record to 6–2. He was dominating hitters even more than in 1976. Despite the late start, he was named to the All-Star squad for the second consecutive year. Life was grand. Full-house stadiums were cheering madly for him. He was pitching great. It was just like last year, or even better. Then, suddenly, it wasn't.

Mark took the mound against the Orioles on July 4. A crowd of 45,339 showed up to watch his first career appearance in Baltimore. The Tigers took an early 2–0 lead, and Mark didn't allow a base runner to get as far as second base until the fourth inning. The Orioles still had not scored when Mark warmed up before the sixth inning as Fleetwood Mac's "Dreams" played on the public address system. Mark did not know it, but his baseball dream was about to turn into a nightmare.

After two quick ground ball outs, Ken Singleton fought off a 2–2 pitch and fisted it into left for a single. Rookie Eddie Murray homered on the next pitch. Lee May then doubled to the left-field fence. After an intentional walk, Rick Dempsey lined a single to the outfield. Mark Belanger blooped a double just fair down the right-field line. Al Bumbry grounded a single up the middle for the sixth straight hit (not counting the walk), and Mark was finally relieved. He got a standing ovation as he walked off the mound and tipped his cap to the fans; however, nearing the dugout, frustration took over and he fired his glove into the dugout, which turned some of the cheers to boos.

"I was watching him pitch that game against the Orioles," says Dave Rozema. "Mark threw a pitch, and I thought, 'That really looked weird.' His motion was different. And the velocity of the pitch was way off. I said, 'Wow, something happened.' I saw it happen. The next pitches were all hit hard. I don't think it had anything to do with his knee. I think his knee was okay."

"All of a sudden, he couldn't get anybody out," says Kimm.

When Houk came out to the mound to relieve him, Mark said, "I feel fine, but the ball went dead." Ralph answered, "Yeah, it seems like you're throwing change-ups."

In his next start, July 8, Mark lost to the White Sox 10–7, giving up six runs in less than six innings. Kimm noted that Mark was a much different pitcher. "That was the first game his stuff just didn't look very good," he says. "He really didn't have anything on the ball. I could tell something was wrong. In the clubhouse after the game, he said, 'Bruce, my arm is killing me.' And I told him he should say something. He was just the kind of guy who didn't want to complain and was trying to work through it."

Four days later, Mark started and pitched to four batters against Toronto in Detroit, then signaled that he was having arm trouble. Houk immediately pulled him out. Houk said after the game that there was "a slight muscle pull on the side of the right shoulder in a place not usually too dangerous."

"I threw three or four pitches that hurt," Mark told reporters. "They were all fastballs. I didn't throw any sliders." He noted that he had been throwing well in warm-ups. He added, "I'm not worried like with the knee injury." Newsmen on the team's charter plane reported that he did not seem to be "as exuberant as usual" but didn't appear downhearted either. It was announced that he would not be available for the All-Star Game now. He would need to rest the arm over the All-Star break so he could come back strong for the second half of the season.

Mark rested, but it didn't get any better. A week later, he was examined at Henry Ford Hospital and diagnosed with tendonitis in the shoulder. A little bit more rest and it should be fine he was told.

But it wasn't fine after a little bit more rest. July 24 he was placed on the twenty-one-day disabled list. Mark had tried lobbing a half-dozen balls to test his arm, but it still hurt. "The hurt is still there, what more can I say?" he told reporters. "Same pain, same location, same everything. It hurt every time I threw, and I was just tossing the ball soft." It was noted that he would be eligible to pitch again August 10. The season was slipping away.

So began a long odyssey.

The cause of Mark's arm injury has been debated over the years. Was it due to the excessive load he pitched as a rookie in 1976? Did he try to come back too soon from his knee surgery before his arm had time to get in shape? Was there really a cause, or did it just happen? It's all conjecture. "I thought his mechanics were different after he came back in 1977," says Bob Sykes, who had watched him pitch since rookie ball in 1974. "It wasn't his normal pattern. I'm not saying he came back too soon, but it just changed his mechanics and that led to the injury."

"I think he tried to come back too soon from the injury (to his leg)," says John Hiller. "He didn't have time to get his arm in shape after the knee surgery."

"One thing you have to remember," says Frank MacCormack, "is that he had grown up playing ball in Massachusetts, where the seasons are very short. And then he threw in relief a lot his first two years in the minors. So he had never pitched a whole lot of innings before his rookie year. I think that played a role."

"I think pitching in front of all those crowds was part of it," says Dave Rozema. "Think about it. When a full stadium is on its feet cheering like crazy for you, yelling your name, you're going to get an adrenaline surge and throw harder. Mark did that almost every inning, every single game he pitched. That had to affect it."

In March of 1978, Patrick Zier ran a series of articles in the *Lakeland Ledger* questioning why so many of the Tigers' young pitchers had developed arm trouble. In addition to Mark, Vern Ruhle, Dave Rozema, and Jack Morris had also experienced similar problems in the past two years. Ralph Houk denied that they were being used too much. "They pitched every fifth day. I didn't pitch any of them with three days' rest," he told Zier. "There's no way they pitched too much. I don't know what happened to Mark. Maybe people wanted him to get well too soon. Maybe he went out there and just overthrew. He's so competitive; he might have got behind somebody and just cut loose. Anything could have happened. Even if they pitched every fourth day, it shouldn't have hurt their arms."

Jim Campbell also denied that the young pitchers had been

misused. "I don't buy that at all," he said. "I think Ralph handled them exactly right. He pitches them with four days' rest. Every arm is different . . . last year was the first time we ran into that (arm problems). But it wasn't because anybody was misused. I really don't know what did it." He denied the suggestion that Mark came back too soon. "After Mark had the operation, whether he subconsciously changed his motion when he came back, I don't know."

Mark Fidrych agreed with his bosses. "Naw, I don't think they pitched me too much," he said. "I don't worry about it. I just work here. I pitch when they tell me to. That's not my decision to make." Mark also denied that he tried to come back too soon, although he said that John Hiller told him not to try it, that the long layoff enforced by the knee surgery would put him behind and increase the chance of injury. "I used to work more in high school. I'd pitch and then go play the outfield. . . . If I thought they were working me too much, I'd say so. But I don't think they are."

When questioned over thirty years later, Ralph Houk is still adamant. "There's no way he came back too soon," he says, a slight edge creeping into his ninety-one-year-old voice. "And I don't think he was overworked. I think his arm just went out because he threw with such effort on every pitch. I think it was inevitable that it would just go out."

While many observers have blamed him for overusing Mark Fidrych in his rookie season, in all fairness to Houk, it's hard to hold someone to 2012 standards for conduct in 1976. In that era, starting pitchers expected to finish games. Workloads routinely reached levels that would make a modern-day pitching coach scream in terror. In 1971, the Tigers' Mickey Lolich threw the astounding total of 376 innings. He came back the next year to throw 327 and win twenty-two games. Mark's total of 250 innings as a twenty-one-year-old in 1976 looks pedestrian compared to some other numbers that were logged by young pitchers of that era. Bert Blyleven threw 278 innings in 1971 as a twenty-year-old. He followed that with 287 in 1972 and 325 in 1973. It hurt his arm so much that he was only able to pitch for twenty-two years in the majors and win 287 games. Vida Blue threw 312 innings in

1971 as a twenty-two-year-old. A holdout for more money cost him the next year, but he was still able to win 209 games over seventeen seasons. Frank Tanana threw 268 innings in 1974 as a twenty-one-year-old. He followed that with 257 and 288 the next two seasons. He eventually developed arm trouble, but not enough to keep him from winning 240 games over a twenty-one-year career.

Whatever the cause of Mark's injury, one thing is certain: he wanted to get back to the mound as soon as possible. "He later told me that his arm hurt earlier, but he wouldn't tell anybody," says Patrick Zier. "He wanted so badly to continue with baseball. He just didn't want anyone to think that he wasn't trying hard."

"He had a blue-collar work ethic," says Bruce Kimm. "He would have worked all the time without complaining. He should have told them earlier that his arm was sore, but that just wasn't in his makeup. He wasn't a complainer."

To add insult to injury, urban legends grew and circulated on how and why he injured his arm: some said he really hurt it in a bar fight, some said he didn't take good enough care of himself, that as a fun-loving party guy he didn't work hard enough and that led to the injury. Another myth had him hurting his shoulder while trying to hop a wall to make curfew one night. All of this was hogwash. Game accounts leave little doubt that the injury occurred in the sixth inning of the Baltimore game—he pitched great before that inning, and never really pitched well after it.

When August 10 arrived—the day Mark was supposed to come off the disabled list—the arm had not improved. He remained inactive. Mark went to the bullpen and played catch for a few minutes before a game a week later, but the pain was still there. Finally, the Tigers announced on August 27 that Mark had been sent home for the remainder of the season and would rest his arm for the next two months. They hoped he would be able to join the Florida Instructional League team in late October.

A few weeks later, Mark tried his hand at a second career. ABC hired him to do expert analysis on a regional Monday night televised game between Texas and Minnesota; however, he did not draw raves from the critics. He was teamed with play-by-play man Al Michaels, who introduced Mark as "a refugee from Disneyland." Mark played it straight early in the game, seeming determined to prove how serious he could be. He pulled it off for three innings, then 205-pound ex-teammate Willie Horton tried to steal second, and Mark thought it was hilarious. "That's weird . . . seeing Willie run with his body," he remarked.

When Dave May came to bat, Michaels asked Mark if he knew him. "No, I never met him," he replied.

"Well, he's the guy Atlanta got when they traded Hank Aaron," Michaels pointed out. "Don't forget that now."

"Ask me again in about four innings and I probably won't remember," Mark confessed.

Later, Michaels mentioned the Phillies' Richie Hebner. "Who's Richie Hebner?" Mark asked.

Incredulously, Michaels responded, "You really don't know who Hebner is?" He recovered and said, "He's the Phillies' first baseman. Do you just follow the American League?"

"I don't follow no league."

Between innings, Michaels plugged the *ABC Evening News* with the popular team of Harry Reasoner and Barbara Walters. "Do you watch Harry and Barbara?" he asked.

"Harry and Barbara who?" was the reply.

Midway through the game, the camera in the booth went on and Michaels found himself alone. A moment later, Mark reappeared. "Where'd you go?" Michaels asked.

Mark hesitated a moment, then replied, "I hadda go to the commode."

"From what we saw and heard," wrote John Valerino in the *Lakeland Ledger* afterward, "The Bird better stick to changing tires during the off-season."

In 1990, Michaels was still talking about sharing the booth with The Bird. "It was unbelievable," he said in an article in the *New York Times*. "The ultimate example of someone having no clue what television is about and not caring. When I asked him to talk about a particular pitcher who'd come into the game, his response was, 'Who's he?'"

Mark seemed to enjoy himself, however, oblivious to Michaels' disdain. When asked about the TV gig later by a sportswriter, he said, "That was neat, even though I don't know anything about baseball, at least not what those guys know, ya know stats and back in the past, ya know, people that I guess were good in the game, things like that. I don't know anything like that, so I was weak in that area."

In Mark's defense, he was not prepared for the job. Network executives felt his magic could just come through the microphone. His old nemesis, reading, came back to haunt him again. Also, the network could not have picked a worse partner for him. Michaels was not a former player; his job was announcing and he took it very seriously, worked at it hard, and was a professional. Three years later at the 1980 Winter Olympics he would yell the immortal call, "Do you believe in miracles? Yes!" as the U.S. hockey team defeated the Russians. Michaels became renowned for being difficult to work with in the booth, however, as he often had chilly relations with his coannouncers. He did not suffer amateurs well. The network might as well have paired Mark with Joe Falls to cowrite an article for the *Sporting News*. It was doomed from the start.

The Tigers finished the 1977 season in fourth place with a record of 74–88, the same record as in 1976. In September, team officials still talked, perhaps wishfully, as if Mark's arm problem was not serious and rest would cure it. "I don't think any of us think of it as a critical thing," said Dr. Livingood. "We don't look on this as ominous to his career."

"With any young pitcher, without a prior problem, the chances are better than not that he will come back," added Dr. Mitchell of the Henry Ford Hospital. "You can't rule out that he'll never come back, but its highly unlikely."

Mark had also been examined by Dr. Harvey O'Phelan of Minneaspolis and Dr. Frank Jobe of Los Angeles. They had agreed there was no reason not to expect a complete recovery.

By mid-October, Mark was throwing regularly without pain

in Florida, and it looked like his troubles were behind him. Jim Campbell skipped a World Series trip to New York to detour south to Florida to monitor Mark's progress. In early November, he was throwing close to full speed and felt strong enough to throw in a game. He was able to pitch in several Instructional League games under careful restrictions and did well.

He was noted by reporters to be somewhat more reserved—not exactly acting like The Bird. His answers to questions were polite but dull. He was not running around with his normal energy. He was concerned, and rightly so. "I never really had an arm problem like that before," he explained. "I was just wondering if I could ever throw again. But I said, 'Aw, don't worry. Your arm'll come back.'" He told reporters he planned to remain with the team in St. Petersburg until the Instructional League ended on November 13 and then planned to hunt deer and attend a teammate's wedding in Mexico.

The teammate getting married was fellow pitcher and good friend Fernando Arroyo, a native of Mexico. Mark and Dave Rozema went to Mexico for the wedding, staying two weeks. Rozema was surprised to find that The Bird's popularity did not end at the border. "It was just a little town with gravel roads and donkeys running around," says Rozema. "But everybody knew about The Bird. They worshipped him. We went over to another town to see Aurelio Rodriguez's team play and Mark was just mobbed."

Mark spent most of the winter living in Detroit—a drastic change from his commercial-shooting, banquet-attending, promotional whirlwind of the previous winter. He worked out regularly at the University of Michigan with fellow pitchers Rozema, Wilcox, Sykes, and Ruhle under the guidance of a physical therapist in an effort to work the sore wing back into shape. Mark ended 1977 full of hope for the future. His arm was feeling good. He was ready to put 1977 behind him. It was just one year. He was still only twenty-three years old. He had his whole career in front of him. Next year things would be back to normal.

Later that winter, at a banquet, Bowie Kuhn announced that baseball was still the favorite pastime due to what he called, "The

Fidrych Syndrome." Kuhn stated, "Baseball is attracting more young people than any other major sport. More and more, these fans relate to the game's personalities. Mark Fidrych is a manifestation of it—a unique individual that has brought new stimulation to the sport." Mark Fidrych, the Tigers, and baseball in general were all eagerly awaiting the healthy return of The Bird for 1978.

7

The Long Road Back

The Detroit Tigers gathered in Lakeland in the spring of 1978 as a team on the way up. They were loaded with young talent that was expected to produce a pennant in the not-too-distant future. Jim Campbell's plan of building through the farm system and not with high-priced free agents seemed to be working perfectly. However, the hopes of the team still rested with their best and most popular pitcher, Mark Fidrych. Everyone nervously watched to see how his arm would hold up in the spring.

On February 24, Detroit newspapers breathlessly reported that The Bird threw from the mound for eight minutes and his arm felt fine; no pain. A ten-minute session from the mound three days later produced more optimistic results. Hopefully, the problems of 1977 were in the past.

Mark pitched very well in the spring of 1978, winning his first four decisions with a 0.60 ERA. Jim Hawkins reported good news to fans in the *Sporting News* under the headline "Tigers Give Fidrych 100 Percent Mark." He noted that those around the Tigers "couldn't help but notice how much more mature the 23-year-old Tiger pitcher seemed this spring." He also reported that "Fidrych still goes out of his way to cooperate with the press. And he didn't even complain when a little old lady woke him up at 8 o'clock in the morning on the day of his first spring start, just so she could get his autograph." The Tigers ended spring training with more wins than any team in baseball and had high hopes for both the season and Mark Fidrych.

Mark was on the mound for Opening Day in Detroit. He was in control of the Blue Jays most of the game, cruising to a five–hit, 6–2 win. There were a few tight spots, but he managed to bear down and get out of them. With two outs in the ninth, Mark paused to pick up some trash that had blown across the infield, chasing one piece of paper all the way to first base as the fans cheered his efforts. He then returned to the mound and got the batter to ground back to him for the final out. Mark jumped into the air, shaking his fist. He shook everyone's hand and headed to the dugout, only to reemerge for the curtain call. He was back!

Mark won his next start, another complete game, against the Rangers, 3–2. The whole team looked good. Veteran Jack Billingham, obtained from the Reds, added leadership to the young pitching staff. Blossoming catcher Lance Parrish, along with the keystone combination of Lou Whitaker and Alan Trammell, appeared to provide the Tigers with strength up the middle for years to come.

Mark talked to reporters in April about his comeback. "I was a different person (last year)," he said. "I had the bad leg and the bad arm and I was trying to get my head together. Everything I count on, my bread and butter, was missing, and it got me down. The doctors told me to relax, and some of the older players told me how they had come back from injuries, but I didn't really know about myself until I went down to the Instructional League in October. Then I knew for sure. I said, 'Oh wow! I can throw.'"

The Bird was back, the Tigers were playing great, and rival teams were once again calling Jim Campbell and Ralph Houk, inquiring when The Bird was scheduled to pitch, trying to arrange an appearance in their park. Mark appeared on the cover of *Sports Illustrated* on April 24. By the time it hit the shelf, however, the situation had changed drastically.

On April 17 against the White Sox, Mark threw 40 pitches and gave up two runs through four innings. He told Ralph Houk his shoulder was stiff and painful after the fourth inning, and Houk immediately removed him. The following Saturday, Mark couldn't get his arm loose in the bullpen before his scheduled start and had to be scratched minutes before the game. The disappointed fans booed the replacement pitcher, twenty-three-year-old Jack Morris, when he took the mound instead of The Bird.

Mark rested his arm a few days, but it didn't get better. "I expect him to get back," said Dr. Mitchell after examining him at Henry Ford Hospital. "I don't think it is terribly serious." Doctors tried a cortisone injection in the shoulder in hopes of relieving the pain and inflammation. Mark attempted to throw in a pregame test in Seattle a week later but gave up in disgust after less than five minutes because of stiffness and pain. Houk told reporters, "I'm going to take it slow and easy with him. I'm not going to set him up to pitch again until I'm satisfied that he's throwing 100 percent." The Tigers soon put Mark on the twenty-one-day disabled list. Jim Hawkins summed up the feeling of the press with the title of an article in the *Sporting News*: "Tigers Sing Sad Bye-Bye to Bird, So What's New?" Mark was sent to Los Angeles to be examined by Dr. Frank Jobe, the man who invented Tommy John surgery. Jobe gave him a second cortisone injection and advised that he do nothing with a baseball for a week, then start throwing gradually. Jobe told reporters he was confident Mark would be able to pitch again in 1978.

After a week of rest, Mark tried to throw, but the pain was as bad as ever. Both Mark and the Tigers were frustrated by the lack of progress, and there didn't seem to be any plan for making it better. Opinions and offers of help flooded in from all over. A dentist said it had to do with his bite, causing the muscles to stiffen. Some people said it was nutritional and recommended all kinds of hokey diets, including one in which he was supposed to eat nothing but chicken. People told the Tigers to use horse liniment on him. Some said to use snake oil. A farmer wrote and said to rub cow udder ointment on it. A man said the Tigers should have Mark wear three heavy sweatshirts twenty-four hours a day. At least fifty chiropractors offered their services for free. One fan wrote to ask Mark why he didn't just learn to pitch left-handed. It was all great advice, to be sure, and it was actually about as helpful as what he was hearing from the experts he was seeing, but none of it seemed to help.

The Tigers sent Mark to Lakeland by himself in late May. Not on any special program, he was on his own to run and throw a little. Hopefully, the sunshine and rest could do something the Detroit doctors could not. The plan was to reevaluate him at the end of two weeks. "I'd like to contribute, I'd like to be out there," Mark told Patrick Zier when he arrived in Lakeland. "After two weeks, I'm gonna go back up there and they're gonna decide something. I guess I'm gonna find out whether I have to get another job." Both the Tigers and Mark were beginning to realize that things were getting serious—Mark's career might be in jeopardy.

Another reason for sending Mark to Lakeland had been to get him out of the national limelight. All anyone had wanted to talk to him about for a year was his arm. "How would you like all these guys coming up to you every day and asking the same thing, 'How's the arm today?'" Mark later said. "Guys you probably never saw before who just come to get a story. It's like a broken record." Mark stayed at the home of Lakeland Tigers president Frank Decker. Mark spent his mornings in Decker's backyard pool, his evenings playing pinball at Zimmerman's bar, and worked out at the Tigers' field in the afternoons. He also signed autographs for elementary school kids and made an appearance at a local high school sports banquet in which he told the players they ought to go on to school or learn a trade so they have something to fall back on if sports don't work out. "Look at me," he told them, "I had one good year and haven't done nothing since. Who knows? I might have to go back to pumpin' gas."

In Lakeland, Mark renewed his friendship with Jim Leyland, the Lakeland Tigers' manager. Leyland was a former catcher in the Tigers' minor league system who was working his way up the managerial ladder. He had coached Mark in the Florida Instructional

League back before The Bird became famous. In Lakeland, Leyland caught Mark in the bullpen before the other players arrived each day, offering encouragement, trying to help keep his spirits up. Jack Homel, former trainer for the Tigers and Dodgers, had been hired by the Tigers in the spring exclusively to work with Fidrych. He continued to work with him in Lakeland. He told reporters the problem was a "muscle spasm in the deltoid muscle, not tendonitis," and predicted that Mark would pitch again in the 1978 season.

Mark failed to make any progress at all in Lakeland, however. Instead of the originally planned two weeks, the stay ended up being almost a month. Still, Mark was unable to throw full speed without pain. He was sent to New York to be treated by Dr. Maurice Cowen, the Yankees' team physician. Tiger officials had seen the success of Cowen's treatment of a similar ailment in Don Gullett earlier in the season and hoped he could perform magic on Mark as well. "I agree with previous diagnoses of tendonitis in Mark's shoulder," Cowen told reporters. "I found that repeated episodes of inflammation resulted in tightening of the right shoulder, limiting complete movement of the arm." He went on to explain his treatment, which had never been used on baseball players before the current season: "Under a general anesthesia, I manipulated the shoulder, stretching the scarred tendons, muscles, and ligaments so he could get his arm into a cocking position, which he had not been able to do before." He told reporters that, in addition to Don Gullett, he had done the same thing with the Yankees' Catfish Hunter.

"I don't know if it's going to work on me, but at least it worked on two other people," Mark optimistically told reporters after the procedure. "That's what makes me happy. I want to start pitching as soon as I can. Maybe I can be a reliever or a mop-up guy for a while. Anything to get some innings in." They did not know it at the time, but this was possibly the worst thing that could have been done for Mark's shoulder. It should be noted that Gullett and Hunter, two of the best pitchers in the game at the time, were not cured as originally believed. Gullett did not pitch after 1978, retiring at the age of twenty-seven, and Hunter pitched only nineteen more games, retiring at thirty-three.

For Mark, once again, medical science had failed him. His arm still hurt every time he tried to throw. He later admitted that he was very depressed at this time, struggling with the unknown, unable to pitch, wondering if his career was over. He credited his teammates with helping keep his spirits up. "But the older guys really helped me there," he said. "Guys like Mickey Stanley, Rusty Staub, Jack Billingham. They kept telling me I was too young for my career to be finished—that I'd be okay. Billingham really talked to me, and I didn't even know Jack that well. . . . It was almost like a father-and-son relationship. He'd say, 'Look Mark, I've seen this before. You'll be back. You're too young not to be back.' And I was able to react to it a little better."

"Mark was just such a nice kid," says Billingham. "He was trying hard to make a comeback. I felt if anything he might have gone about it too hard. Nobody worked harder than he did— running, throwing, arm exercises, weight program—he just did it and did it. The only time I ever saw him down was on the days he didn't pitch very well. But the next day, you would see Mark Fidrych the way Mark Fidrych always was: smiling, excited, bouncing around full of energy, joking. It was another day and he would work hard to try to improve. Everybody gets down, but when he was down, he bounced back quicker.

"When he came to the ballpark, he just brought a spirit every day that you wish everybody could have—you wished you could have," continues Billingham. "Even when he was on the disabled list, he brought something to the clubhouse. You knew he was there trying to rehab, but he brought positive feelings to the clubhouse. He wouldn't come in hanging his head, feeling sorry for himself. He came in with a great attitude, like, 'Come on guys, let's go get them.' He was always backing the team, always patting you on the shoulder, 'Great game, Jack,' and 'Nice play, Tramm, Whitaker.' He was always pulling for the other guys to do well."

"When he was on the disabled list in 1978, he was still around the park a lot," adds Bob Sykes. "And he was as optimistic as ever.

He kept thinking he would be back. He was realistic. He knew baseball wouldn't last forever. He always talked about going back home after baseball and owning trucks. He planned for life after baseball. But that year he was still optimistic that he would get better."

Unfortunately, Mark did not get better. The Tigers finally decided not to keep Mark around the team taking up a roster spot. He was optioned to Lakeland—officially sent back to the minors. Houk and Campbell both told reporters they talked to Mark, who agreed to the move. The plan was to build up his arm gradually by pitching short stints against minor league batters. It was announced that he would receive no special treatment with the minor league team other than a private room on the road, which he volunteered to pay for. "It's not so bad. I don't mind the bus rides," Mark told reporters, trying to sound optimistic even if it was killing him inside.

Mark gradually worked his arm back into shape and was eventually able to pitch with reasonable effectiveness and without too much pain at Lakeland. Although the old zip was still not there, in early August, the Tigers announced that Mark would rejoin them in a week. An elated Mark told reporters, "This time I'm not going to hold anything back." Detroit fans ecstatically looked forward to his return.

But it was not to be. Three days later it was announced that Mark Fidrych would be sidelined for the rest of the season. On August 5, at Lakeland in his last appearance before heading to Detroit, he had to be removed from the game after complaining of stiffness in his shoulder after only eight pitches. The Bird was done for the year. Once more, reporters flocked to him for quotes. "Sure I've worried about my arm and wondered if my career will end as suddenly as it started," Mark told one. "Who wouldn't worry? All my hopes center around baseball. Without it, I'm nobody." He would not play winter ball this year. He would not touch a baseball until next spring.

Days later, Mark turned twenty-four years old. In the midst of despair over his career, he found time to reach out to make someone else feel good. The Associated Press reported that Mark had called the Cleveland hospital room of Sue Sechen on her fifteenth birthday. Sue was recovering from a bone marrow transplant—an experimental procedure at the time—for aplastic anemia, a potentially fatal condition in which the bone marrow shuts down its production of blood cells, and had been hospitalized in a sterile room for over a month. According to her family, Mark Fidrych called when he learned that Sue, a huge Bird fan, shared his birthday. The young girl was ecstatic to hear from her hero; it was the highlight of an otherwise drab hospital stay.

In December, Jim Campbell arranged for Mark to attend a seminar in Orlando conducted by the Association of Professional Baseball Physicians. Mark was examined, and his case was reviewed by the top doctors in the country. Afterward, the chairman of the group told reporters that Mark Fidrych would be unable to pitch for at least another year due to atrophy in the shoulder muscles and scar tissue in the shoulder. The statement made headlines across the country. Both Mark and Campbell were upset with the public announcement. "It was supposed to be behind closed doors," Mark said later, "but when I got back to Detroit, my employer called me up and said, 'Hey, you see this in the papers where you're not going to pitch again until 1981?'"

"Hey, who's he to say?" Mark asked reporters. "I can't wait till spring training starts." He maintained to reporters that he was not worried. "There are too many problems in life to worry about. I've been in worse. Like living. Getting through school. . . . In ten more years, I'm going to retire and go live on a farm."

Jim Campbell arranged for Mark to remain in Detroit for the winter, undergoing special therapy treatment three days a week. Campbell told reporters that while he was optimistic about Mark's chances, "Right now he's on the back burner. We're not counting on him."

Mark Fidrych was slowing sinking in quicksand. The more he thrashed, the harder he tried, the farther his career slipped away. And no one knew why. He had been to the best doctors in the country. Medical science did not have a way to even diagnose his problem in 1978. And that was the worst part for Mark—no one knew what was wrong with him.

It was a different Detroit Tiger team that awaited Mark Fidrych in the spring of 1979. Ralph Houk had resigned as manager of the Tigers after the 1978 season and was replaced by Mark's old manager from Montgomery, Les Moss. All the veterans who had been so helpful to Mark were gone now. Mark Fidrych was entering his fourth major league season. He was the veteran now. Mark talked optimistically to the press. "I'll be in the rotation come April," he vowed. "If I wasn't planning on pitching this year, I wouldn't be here. Why come down here and waste the time?" He was anxious to earn his $125,000 salary. "I won't hang around anymore, I'll tell you that. Either I pitch this year or I'm gone. You just can't hang around a club. You've got to contribute." Entering the final season of his three-year contract, it was suggested by the press that this was his make-or-break year.

Mark was spotted with a picture of St. Jude, the patron saint of lost causes, posted on his locker early in the spring. "Thank God my arm feels better," he said a few days after hanging the picture when he threw without pain for the first time in ages. "I've prayed a lot. I've become more religious. But that doesn't mean I've stopped cussing or anything like that." Jim Hawkins later reported that Mark was reading the Bible daily in the clubhouse and packed the Bible with him on trips. "I ain't no religious freak," Mark told him. "I'm not going around saying 'This is the right way.' I just do things my way. I do what I think is best for me. And every day I pick up this book, it helps. I'm not much of a reader. I can't start from the beginning and just read. But every day I read one little passage. This way, there's something different every day. It seems like every time I read it, I find a problem I've already had. It explains it. It helps me out. Right now, I'm searching for something. So why not try Him again? I used to try Him when I was a kid, why not now?"

The thing Mark was searching for most was his old fastball. The agonizing process of one step forward and two steps back continued. After initially throwing well, back spasms caused Mark to sit out. The arm continued to progress slowly, and Mark was on the twenty-one-day disabled list as the team prepared to head north for the season. The plan was to allow him to throw on the sidelines until he was ready.

Mark made his return to active status amid tepid expectations. He pitched four shaky innings against the Twins, then was hit hard by the Brewers. He lost to the Yankees on May 16, giving ups six runs in three innings. He was at a loss to explain the result when he talked to reporters after the game. "I feel fine," he said. "I threw with no pain." Then he added, "At least I can pick up a ball. I'd rather be pitching than sitting on the bench. Do you know what it's like to have to open the door with your left hand all the time? At least I can open the door with my right hand now."

Although not painful, the arm was just not the same. John Grodzicki, now the Tigers' pitching coach, noted that Mark was not able to throw hard: "He's throwing about 60 percent of velocity." The old location at the knees and corners, where he had lived in 1976, was much harder to hit now. Too many sliders were hanging.

Mark was put back on the disabled list on May 23. Dr. Edwin Guise announced that the shoulder was fine, but there was weakness in the triceps because of the long period of inactivity. "He will go through a program of exercises with weights and resistance devices to restore his strength," he said.

Mark had pitched in four games in 1979 and had an 0–3 record and a 10.43 ERA in fourteen and two-thirds innings. He tried to put on an optimistic face for reporters. "My confidence will hold up," he told them.

The Tigers wanted to send Mark to Evansville to work things out, but an American League team, later identified as the White Sox, claimed him—not allowing him to clear waivers. The Tigers were mad at the team's lack of regard for his rehab but were forced to choose between keeping Mark on the major league roster or lose him to the White Sox. They withdrew the waiver request. The 1979 season was over for Mark Fidrych.

In late July, Mark was sent to San Diego to undergo treatment by Dr. Paul Bauer, a leading Pacific coast orthopedic specialist and team physician of the Padres. He had examined Mark over the All-Star break and agreed with the previous diagnoses. But he offered nothing new in the way of treatment. Or hope.

The once-fawning, ubiquitous press that had fed The Bird Media Circus now turned against him—disappointed that he could no longer make easy copy for them with his antics and victories. One writer remarked, "It is sure to help the Detroit players' morale not to have The Bird constantly around and still getting attention from media persons." Writers made backhanded comments about how much money he was making to sit on the disabled list.

Even worse than the press turning on him was the fact that the Tigers seemed to be giving up hope. Jim Campbell said, "Essentially you can forget Fidrych, something nobody wants to do but which people are going to have to accept." Mark stayed alone in San Diego for a month to receive treatment and therapy. On August 14, he turned twenty-five years old. There were no scoreboard messages, no stuffed birds this time; no multitude of cakes sent by adoring fans. He no longer needed the William Morris Agency to sort through offers and keep people away from him. Mark Fidrych was a forgotten man.

With his three-year contract expired, Mark hired an agent to negotiate a new contract for 1980. This caused some snide comments by the press as might be expected, but the business of baseball had changed enormously in the past four years—almost every player had an agent now. Even though he had yet to sign, Mark showed up in Lakeland two weeks early and, along with John Hiller, got an early start getting in shape for the season. Jim Campbell soon arrived in Lakeland and, two days later, had Mark's name on a new contract. Terms were not announced, but it was later reported to be $133,000 for the 1980 season.

Mark appeared to be throwing well in February and was optimistic as usual even as the Tiger organization continued to change around him. Sparky Anderson had taken over as manager the previous June and was busy making the team his own. There were a lot of young pitchers in the system waiting for their chance. Anderson did not have time to wait for Mark Fidrych. He had never seen a healthy Mark Fidrych; never seen the reaction of a sold-out stadium to The Bird.

It had been three years since Mark had lit up stadiums, but fans, opposing players, and teammates still paused whenever he took the mound—anxious to see what he could do. Fans showed their encouragement and kept up a steady demand for Mark's attention and autographs in the spring. "It's like I haven't been gone at all," he remarked to reporters. "It surprises me. I haven't pitched in three years, but people still come up and say they're behind me, that they're pulling for me.

"Sure I was disillusioned at first," he said. "I wondered if the world was against me. Now I have rationalized. I have no bitterness at all. I'm happy to be playing baseball. If it's ordained that I don't make it, I can always become a carpenter or pump gas."

Although Mark told anyone who asked that his arm felt fine, he struggled once the exhibition games began. In his third start of the spring, he strained a triceps muscle and had to leave in the third inning. The arm pain didn't get any better with rest over the next week. The frustrating cycle was repeating itself once more. Detroit writer Tom Gage wrote, "The Fidrych comeback (has become) an annual hoax. He wasn't close to being his old self, despite his hope and optimism and pronouncements otherwise."

Mark was optioned to Evansville, and it was announced that he would be under the control of Jim Leyland, now the Triple-A club's manager. "When Jimmy says he's ready to pitch, he'll pitch," said Anderson. "We won't do anything with him until Jimmy says he's ready."

Mark's honesty and openness with the media soon caused him trouble. In his disappointment he made some comments that he thought were off the record, criticizing Anderson and the team for demoting him and then not showing up to watch him throw in a minor league intrasquad game. He was quoted as saying, "All this is doing is cutting into my pension time . . . this thing is nothing but business with them, and it's costing me money. I might be wrong, but I'm pretty sure I haven't lost any money for the Detroit Tigers."

When told of the comments, Anderson blew up. "I think all the crutches have got to be knocked out from under the arms," he told reporters. "It's got to be now: production. How many big crowds has he drawn in the last two and a half years? Have the Tigers paid him? Looking at all the things that they have done and all the doctors they have sent and all the things they have tried to do—and they have paid the salary—is there a balancing point?" Anderson said that he felt the Tigers, if anything, had been giving him too much attention, sometimes to the detriment of the rest of the team. "Mark Fidrych, at this time, is no different to me than Dan Petry, Bruce Robbins, Mike Chris, or any of the others. The day has come to an end . . . that Mark Fidrych is no more important . . . something has been wrong with us. Now it's over. . . . There is no more importance put on Mark Fidrych than on any other individual in this organization."

Fans reacted negatively also and piled on. "He's a spoiled kid, another self-centered, overpaid ballplayer," wrote one letter writer to the *Lakeland Ledger*. "He is definitely no longer an asset to the Tigers. I am surprised they keep him on," said another. There were others: "The Bird has finally shown his true colors. All he is worried about is money." And "He sure loses enough games."

Mark claimed he was misquoted. "Hey, it was a misunderstanding. I was a victim of circumstances. The guy who wrote that . . . he wasn't even a real reporter. He didn't have a notepad and pencil or nothing. I'm a Detroit man all the way. Me and Sparky get along fine. I have no desire to be traded or anything. They have sent me to the finest doctors and everything."

He later publicly accepted the demotion to Evansville and had no more negative comments for the press. "Going back will not be easy," he told reporters. "But I figure it's just another part of life. It isn't the crossroads of my career, just another side street."

Mark reported to the minors for the 1980 season, this time not as part of a rehab assignment, but as part of the team—trying to work his way to the majors the same as everyone else. The biggest step on the ladder of professional baseball is between Triple A and the majors, and it's much bigger stepping down than up. Nowhere was the difference more evident than in the clubhouse, especially the clubhouse at ancient Bosse Field in Evansville. Only eight to ten showers and not all of them working at the same time, lockers with chicken wire between them, rusty nails for the players to hang their stuff on, no air-conditioning, no free snacks or soft drinks, and paint peeling off the walls in flaky chunks—little things that weren't too noticeable on the way up—told Mark that he was a long way from Detroit.

A few weeks into the season, Mark spoke to a reporter about the adjustment. "I'm still the same person I was three years ago. I still like the same music: The Grateful Dead, The Allman Brothers. This (baseball) is where the life is . . . these are a bunch of level-headed guys on this team. They treat me equal."

He refused to believe he was washed up. "I don't know what I'll do if I don't make it this time. . . . I keep seeing improvement. That's what keeps me going."

Mark was desperate to try anything that might help. "He put horse liniment on his arm that gave him a horrible case of bad breath," catcher Steve Patchin later recalled. "It was worse than any garlic. Mark was also the hardest worker I've ever seen. He didn't get back to the big leagues for lack of trying."

"He was working very hard trying to get back," says Triplets general manager Chuck Murphy. "That horse liniment was awful stuff. It stunk up the place. But we were just trying anything."

Mark quickly became popular with his new teammates. "There wasn't a pitcher I ever played with that I loved to play for more than Mark Fidrych," says second baseman Dave Machemer. "He made you feel special when you did something good. I remember the first time I made a good play when he was on the mound—he ran over and jumped up and high-fived me. I thought, 'Wow, that was really neat.'

"He made you feel like we were all in it together," Machemer continues. "He was such a team player. We were all trying to get to the majors, but he made it feel like the most important thing was to win the game, not for him, but for the team. There was nothing fake about him, it was all genuine. It wasn't an act. You could tell it was coming from his heart, his soul."

Infielder Glenn Gulliver had been a student at Eastern Michigan University in 1976. He had watched The Bird perform at Tiger Stadium that year before being drafted by the Tigers himself. Now he was on the field with him. "It was awesome to get to play with him after seeing him that year in Detroit," he says. "You thought it was an act back then, but when I was on his team I realized that it wasn't an act, it was genuine. It was cool when he made a big deal after you made a good play. All the sudden, he's got you by the head and you're in the spotlight now. He had so much enthusiasm; he made it fun to play behind him."

Evansville had a loyal fan base, and the fans all remembered Mark from his stay there in 1975. He had won their hearts then, and they had followed his success in Detroit. They happily welcomed him back. Fans on the road were just as eager to get a glimpse of The Bird in action in their hometown parks. The Triplet players enjoyed playing in front of the big crowds The Bird brought. "Everywhere he pitched, he filled up the stadium," says Gulliver. "Back then, you weren't used to that, it was never like that. They just didn't draw those kinds of crowds in the minors back then. They started advertising ahead of time when he would be pitching and the fans came out to see him. They would really get behind him."

Even though he was struggling with his career, Mark's outward personality remained the same. "He was happy-go-lucky," said Larry "Bubbles" Pollock, manager of The Pub, a popular postgame hangout for players. "He never met anybody he didn't like. It wasn't a show. He just enjoyed life."

"Back then, we would all go out together after a game," says Gulliver. "Mark picked up a lot of checks. He was on a major league contract, and most of us had never been up yet. He was glad to help out."

Famously thrifty in his early years and once described as having "deep pockets and alligator arms," Mark was cognizant of the fact that he was by far the highest-paid player on the team and was generous with his money in Evansville. "Everywhere we went that year they wanted to have a press conference when Mark came to town—to promote the games," says Murphy. "In Denver, after the press conference, their GM gave Mark a hundred dollars for appearing. When we got back to Evansville, the next day was Father's Day, and we had a game. I was standing near the gate and Mark came through. He handed me the hundred dollars and said, 'Give that to some father tomorrow.' So we had a drawing at the game and gave away the money to a fan."

Dave Johnson of the *Evansville Courier & Press* remembered interviewing Mark in the dugout at Bosse Field and watching him sign autographs and talk to fans. "He was unbelievable. He was so exuberant."

Another reporter watched Mark in the bullpen in Evansville during this period and was struck by how gracious he was with fans, especially children. He stayed on the field after the game, signed their gloves, told them to work hard and be happy, and posed for pictures. The reporter asked Mark if it wasn't a comedown, after being in the major league spotlight, to be here in the minors. "Hey pal," Mark replied, "It was good enough for me on the way up, it's good enough for me on the way down."

Mark and Jim Leyland renewed their friendship in Evansville in 1980. The thirty-five-year-old Leyland, who had moved up from Lakeland in 1979, was the perfect manager to help Mark at this point. He brought a unique perspective to life and the game. He had signed with the Tigers as a catcher in 1964, but knew as soon as he showed up in Lakeland that he would never play in the major leagues. "I'd had hopes," he later said, "but once I saw those other players and how good they were, I knew I didn't have a chance." He toiled as a minor league catcher for six years, never rising above Double A, rarely hitting over .200, but doing anything the club needed—warming up pitchers, driving the bus, coaching base—and he impressed everyone with his attitude and aptitude for baseball. He learned something from each of his managers, filing away pearls for later use. In 1970, at the age of twenty-five, he was offered a job coaching at Montgomery. The next year he was managing Bristol. He became an organization man and worked his way up. Each winter he returned to live in his parents' house in Perrysburg, Ohio, usually working a winter job, and waited for his next assignment from the club.

Leyland was popular with his players. He had rules and expected maximum effort, but he was extremely supportive of his players and treated them as adults. Like Ralph Houk, he was a player's manager. He was honest, brutally so when necessary, but fair. "Leyland expected a lot out of his players," says Machemer. "The team wanted to play hard for him. You knew that if you didn't play hard, you would be on the bench. He was the first one to call you in to straighten you out, but he was also the first one to back you up anytime there was a problem. You knew he always had your back. I loved playing for Jim Leyland."

"Leyland had fun in the locker room; he joked around a lot back then," says Gulliver. "But then on the field, he was all business. If you messed up, he would be all over you, but the next day, it was forgotten and he was your best supporter again." His rough, gravelly smoker's voice surprised everyone with its ability to turn into a beautiful tenor while entertaining on bus rides or in the clubhouse and led to his nickname "Humpy," short for crooner Engelbert Humperdinck—although some thought the nickname referred to the Humpty Dumpty way he had hit as a player.

Mark Fidrych and Jim Leyland formed a special bond. Leyland was determined to help Mark get back to the major leagues and not to just use him as a gate attraction as some people suspected. At the beginning of the season, he told reporters, "I refuse to treat him as a gimmick. We won't pitch him until he's completely healthy." Leyland worked on both Mark's arm and his head. Mark later said, "He would sit down with me and say, 'Are you okay?' He would go over things about life. When I hurt my arm, I lost the big leagues, and here was a man who was never in the big leagues. He was a man you could talk to."

In Mark's first start in eleven months, he suffered from wildness, and Evansville lost 5–4 to the Iowa Oaks. Mark lasted just three and two-thirds innings, giving up five earned runs, four hits, and six walks. He struggled similarly in his next outings—the wins that he had earned almost every time out in 1976 now seemed impossible to come by.

"Mark was such a good guy, we all wanted him to do good," says Machemer. "One game I'll never forget, we had a chance to get a win for him. He hadn't had a win in something like two years. We had the bases loaded in the last inning, but I hit into a double play. I was so mad after the game that I threw a trash can in the clubhouse. I usually didn't do things like that, but I was just that mad because I wanted to get the win for Mark so badly. Well, the wall of the clubhouse at Bosse Field was so thin that the trash can made a big hole in the wall. I looked through it, and on the other side of the wall was the general manager, Chuck Murphy, looking back at me. Leyland made me pay to fix the wall—it cost $350. But that lets you know how badly we all wanted to win for Mark."

By mid-May, Mark was struggling terribly. His record was 0–2 with a 9.39 ERA. He was being battered by minor league hitters. There was nothing on the ball. It was openly speculated in the newspapers that the professional career of Mark Fidrych might be over. It was noted that he needed ten more days on the Tiger roster to qualify for his pension. Jim Campbell had promised Mark that he would get that no matter what (being on the disabled list of the major league team would qualify), and reporters questioned whether Campbell would stand by his promise now that a decision seemed imminent.

Mark had tried everything. He had even seen a motivational hypnotist. Lee Silen, who lived in Evansville and also worked with University of Evansville swimmers, was brought together with Mark by sportswriter Dave Johnson. "Jim Leyland and Mark came over," Silen explained. "We talked about what hypnosis was and what it wasn't. I told them, 'I'm not going to take over his mind.' We've worked on his fears and phobias. Without realizing it, Mark may have had a fear of failure in Detroit. . . . We've tried to remove that fear." Silen said that he had a mental block holding him back from throwing hard. "In his subconscious mind it was hard to stand up to the fantastic image he had. He not only had to be Mark, the person, but he had to be Mark, 'The Bird,' too." Unfortunately, unlocking the secrets of The Bird's subconscious mind and overcoming mental blocks did not help him throw a baseball any better. He continued to flounder.

Three and a half years. The magic of 1976 seemed so long ago. Different teammates, a different era, a different decade. Three and a half years of an endless cycle of pain, rest, rehab, optimism, then pain again. Mark had to wonder if it was ever going to end. Was it worth it?

Mark reached the bottom in Oklahoma City in early May. He started the game but couldn't get out of the first inning. After the first batter was out, hits started raining all over the park, and Leyland eventually had to rescue him. The shell-shocked pitcher trudged off the field, visibly shaken. "Mark was really down that night," says Machemer. "He felt like he had let the whole team down. He didn't know what to do. You never saw The Bird down, but he was down that night."

"That was probably the most frustrating period Mark's ever had," Leyland said later. "I sensed how he felt. So after the game I took him with me and we had a few drinks and talked about things. Mark was really confused. He wondered if things would ever work out for him. He said, 'Maybe this is it. Maybe I should be back working at the gas station. Maybe it's just not meant to be.'"

Leyland talked to Mark late into the night, encouraging him not to give up, reminding him of how much hard work they had invested the past few years, of how much Mark wanted to make it back. "Mark Fidrych wouldn't quit anything," said Leyland. "But that night he was really down, really frustrated. It was just a complete low for him. I'd never seen him so low. I told him to wait a couple of days and see how things worked out."

Jim Campbell flew to Evansville, presumably to tell Mark he was finished as a pitcher. With Campbell on the way, Mark, bolstered by Leyland's pep talk, begged for one more chance to pitch. Suddenly, The Bird was back—keeping the ball down, hitting the corners, getting batters out. The fans, recognizing the old talent, were soon swept up and grew louder with each pitch. The noise from the crowd brought back the animation and fun on the mound. Mark pitched three good innings, striking out five, not giving up any runs, and the stadium was rocking by the time he finished. "That was the first time he pitched with good velocity," said Leyland. "And the first time he was really into the game emotionally. That was the first time we saw his old antics, and the crowd really got into it. He turned that ballpark upside down." After witnessing another strong relief performance three days later, Campbell returned to Detroit cautiously optimistic.

Mark continued to pitch better and inched his ERA down. "He was throwing really well (by midseason)," says Gulliver. "I thought he was all the way back." Rumors began swirling around Detroit in late July that The Bird might be returning. Mark continued to pitch well, winning five out of six games, and in early August, the Tigers announced that they would be recalling him after his next start. In Mark's final appearance in Evansville, 5,781 fans showed up to offer thanks and wish him well.

"We filled the park for Mark's last game in 1980," recalls Murphy, who appreciated the crowds Mark brought that year. "It was a big deal; everybody was happy for him. And he was throwing pretty well—didn't have the same velocity, but we thought he was back. Well, it was time to start the game, but we looked and Mark wasn't on the mound. We looked around and he was in the outfield. He went around to each player on the field and shook each player's hand and thanked him for helping him get back to the majors. That's the kind of guy he was."

Mark then shut out Indianapolis over seven innings in the ninety-five-degree heat. He was given three standing ovations. The game improved his record to 6–7 and lowered his ERA to 3.92 in 117 innings at Evansville for the year. The next morning, Mark Fidrych was on his way back to Detroit. He had made it. That night, Jim Leyland found a baseball in his locker. "Hi Jim," it read. "OK City, Thanks, Mark Fidrych." The tough manager found tears building up in his eyes and a lump in his throat as he thought about the past few months and how hard his friend had worked.

On August 12, fifty thousand fans showed up in Detroit to watch the Tigers take on the Red Sox with The Bird on the mound. The stadium was full an hour before the game. Mark delighted the fans with most of his familiar antics in the early innings and looked good pitching. The Red Sox scored four early runs, but the Tigers rallied to tie the game. Jim Dwyer hit a home run in the eighth, and the Red Sox took a one-run lead that would hold up. Mark gave way to Aurelio Lopez in the ninth and tipped his cap to the cheering fans as he walked off. Afterward, Sparky Anderson seemed converted. "He's as good a competitor as I ever sat on the bench with. He has the courage. I see now why he throws off that electricity. He means it. He's no phony." Anderson was also impressed by the reaction of the fans and the atmosphere in Tiger Stadium. "I've never seen anything like this, I've got to admit," he said. "And I've been in four World Series."

Mark pitched inconsistently in his next three starts, and when he faced the White Sox on September 2 his record was 0–2. He responded to the near-sellout Tiger Stadium crowd by beating Chicago 11–2 with his first complete game of the season and first major league win since April 12, 1979. Late in the game, with a comfortable lead, Mark faced his former catcher, Bruce Kimm, who had been traded to the White Sox a year earlier. "When I came up, he tipped his cap to me," says Kimm. "Kind of like, 'Hey Bruce.' Then he laid one right in there for me—instead of trying to strike me out. He was trying to fight back to stay in the majors, but it was like he just gave me a good pitch for old-time's sake. Of course, I did what I usually did, I hit a weak pop-up."

In the ninth inning, going for the complete game, Mark was a bundle of nervous energy. It wasn't easy, but he was determined to finish it. As he prepared to pitch to Bob Molinaro with two outs and two men on base, he windmilled his arm, jumped up on his toes three or four times, and walked around the mound talking to himself. He then threw a slider that was popped up to right field for the final out. The fans, who had been chanting "Go, Bird, Go" in the last inning gave him a standing ovation when he left the field. They kept it up until he returned to doff his cap at the top of the dugout steps—just like old times.

Mark then went over to the box seats next to the Tigers' dugout and presented the game ball to James and Veronica Leyland of Perrysburg, Ohio—Jim Leyland's parents. "I wanted this game for them," he told reporters in the clubhouse. "I met them this winter. They're neat people." He added, "Sure that ball is important to me. But it will make them happy and that will make me happy. . . . I don't remember the last time, baseball-wise, I was this happy."

Jim Leyland told reporters, "I know it will go down as one of the biggest thrills of my parents' lives." He explained that Mark had accompanied him to his house while they were on their way to Florida the previous spring. Mrs. Leyland had been impressed with Mark's appetite at breakfast and worked her way into his heart by piling on the bacon and eggs.

Unfortunately, that was to be the high point of the comeback. Ten days later Mark was removed after throwing six pitches in Cleveland, complaining of stiffness and soreness in his shoulder. He rested and came back to face the Blue Jays in Detroit on September 24. He walked five of the first seven batters as the Tigers fell behind 6–0, and he was taken out after two-thirds of an inning. On October 1, Mark pitched five innings and picked up the win against the Blue Jays. His record was 2–3. He had struggled, it had been a battle, but he had managed to finish the season with the Tigers. It would be his last season in the majors.

It was obvious in Lakeland in 1981 that Mark's career was in jeopardy. He could not get his arm in shape. Mark was out of options, meaning that he had to stick with the Tigers. If they sent him to Evansville, another team could pick him up. Fans were still supportive, following Mark's every move, but he threw poorly in camp—no speed and no control. His ERA for the spring was 11.40.

After four agonizing years of comeback attempts, most people felt that The Bird was a thing of the past—a brief glorious chapter of baseball history, but a thing of the past. But Mark, alone, would not give up.

"I think I can do it," he told reporters. "I think I can pitch again like I did in 1976. If I'm healthy, I don't see any reason why not. Last year, I was inconsistent, but I still managed to get in over 150 innings. It's been a long time since I've thrown that much."

He added, "I just want to stay with the club. If shining shoes would help me make this staff, then I'd shine shoes." He noted that he had come to value life in the big leagues. "Last year when they sent me to Tiger Town (Detroit's minor league training complex) I just got over there and I broke my shoelace. So I went up to Brons (trainer John Bronson), and I said, 'Hey Brons, I broke my shoelace; you got another one?' He said, 'Yeah, you got fifty cents?'"

Joe Falls reported that Mark was the first one on the field every day and always led the pack in running. He was the only pitcher on the staff who attracted a crowd of fans just by throwing batting practice. His hair was shorter and he was not as animated on the field. "I'm calming down a little," Mark told him. "I'm taking things a little slower. I've got to get them out down here or I'm not worth anything to them. They're going to send my butt back to Evansville. I know that and that's the way it should be. They can't carry me at the expense of some young pitcher."

Unfortunately, Mark didn't get them out down there. The spirit was willing, but the arm was weak. The Tigers made the move on April 4—demoting him to Evansville. "Sending Mark down was the most unpleasant decision I've faced since I've worked in baseball," said Jim Campbell. "Right now, Mark just isn't one of the best twenty-five players on the club and I'm damn sorry."

Mark cleared waivers—no other team claimed him for the $20,000 waiver price. Nevertheless, he remained outwardly upbeat. "I consider myself lucky," he told reporters. "Because I know a lot of guys that have had arm problems and been released. . . . I'm surprised I didn't get picked up on waivers, but I'm glad I didn't."

"If he had been claimed by another club, we would have had to let him go," said Campbell. "All the other clubs have scouts down here, and they can see what's happening . . . he has not pitched well down here." Campbell then added, "I don't know of any kid I've ever pulled harder for to come back."

Mark vowed to return to the majors. "I'll be there again. You watch."

As Mark toiled as a twenty-six-year-old minor league long reliever and spot starter for Evansville he watched as Fernandomania dominated the national spotlight. Twenty-year-old Mexican rookie Fernando Valenzuela won his first eight decisions for the Dodgers and took Los Angeles and Major League Baseball by storm. The hoopla over Valenzuela made writers reminisce about The Bird's 1976 season. The average major league salary was now $185,000. Good pitchers were going for over $1 million. But Mark refused to publicly indulge in self-pity. "Feel sorry for me? Why?" he responded to a reporter's question. "I've got a lot of things other people don't have. I've got some land. I've got some cows and pigs. I've got a new car. . . . I succeeded in ball where other guys wanted to and didn't. The only thing I haven't gotten is to play in a World Series. . . . Ball has given me everything. Of course, it bothers me that I'm not in the major leagues. Sometimes, I say, 'Dang it, I wish I was still there.' But then I say, 'This is life, Mark. Be happy you were there.'

"People don't understand that I was never really into ball when I was a kid. . . . I repeated the first and second grades. It was hard for me to read, so I didn't read the *Sporting News*. . . . If I hadn't been drafted, I wouldn't have lost any sleep over it. I never was really excited (about pro baseball) until I signed. Then I said, 'Give it your best shot.' The man upstairs gave me the ball. He didn't give me a scientist's mind. He said, 'Here's the ball, see what you can do with it. . . . I'll keep trying until the Tigers don't want me anymore."

That time came soon. In mid-August, Campbell informed Mark that he would not be brought up to the Tigers in 1981. Mark finished the season at Evansville with a 6–3 record and 5.72 ERA. On October 5, the Tigers placed Mark on waivers for the purpose of giving him his unconditional release. Any team could have picked him up. None did. "The Tigers have done everything they possibly could do," Mark said in a prepared statement distributed by the club. "That's the one neat thing about it. I had a chance to do something very few people do, and a lot of people stuck with me."

Mark's mother, who in 1976 had told reporters she often cried worrying that Mark would hurt his arm, was more open and less diplomatic. She had a hard time controlling her anger to reporters when they called wanting a comment. "I told Campbell before and I'll tell him again, Mark was too young to be pitching that much. They shouldn't have kept pitching him. That was how he hurt his arm."

Mark considered his options in professional baseball. A few teams had showed mild interest, but there were no offers. Mark Fidrych went home to Northboro to await calls from other teams. No one called.

8

Pawtucket

"You see, you spend a good piece of your life gripping a
baseball and in the end it turns out that it was the other
way around all the time."

—Jim Bouton, *Ball Four*

Mark Fidrych refused to give up on his baseball career. He consulted the Red Sox's team doctor, Arthur Pappas, an orthopedic
specialist at the nearby University of Massachusetts in Worcester.
Pappas later stated that when he first examined Mark, the right
shoulder was wrapped tighter than a watch spring. The arm would
not stretch fully in any direction. The five years of overcompen-
sation, using muscles that weren't meant to be used, had taken its
toll. "It was excessive compensation," said Pappas. "And it was the
worst case I've ever seen. The first thing we had to do was teach
him to use his shoulder again. Not to pitch. Just to use his shoulder." Pappas gave him a regimen of stretching and other exercises
to do on a daily basis. By midwinter he was throwing without pain
again. Red Sox coach Walt Hriniak and catcher Rich Gedman,
who also lived in Worcester, caught Mark over the winter and

could see potential. Mark signed a minor league contract with Paw-tucket, the Red Sox Triple-A team, and reported to the Red Sox camp in Winter Haven.

It helped that the Red Sox manager by then was none other than Ralph Houk. "If he was going to come back, I would have hated to see him do it with someone else," Houk told reporters that spring. "Naturally, I'm a strong believer in Mark. I felt if anyone could do it, he's the type. I told him I didn't expect him to show me anything, to just come on down and continue the rehabili-tation. I think he felt I wouldn't exploit him." Houk later said that, if the experiment worked, in a few months general managers all over the league would be calling him to juggle his rotation so The Bird could pitch in their parks.

After arriving in Winter Haven, Mark showed that he could still draw crowds of fans and writers. He told reporters that he had bought thirty hogs and become a pig farmer after being cut by Detroit. When the Red Sox called with an offer to give it an-other try, "I fed the hogs and packed my bags." He told them he had been working on his old knuckleball, which might relieve some of the stress on his arm. He said he missed the excitement of base-ball. "Feed thirty hogs on a farm twice a day, 365 days a year, and you get a different perspective on the good life of a major leaguer."

Mark worked out in Winter Haven under the careful eye of Dr. Pappas, staying behind and continuing the rehab regimen af-ter the Red Sox headed north. He slowly gained strength, and his arm felt pretty good when he joined the Pawtucket team in mid-May. He was on a minor league contract, making minor league money—$18,000 a year—a far cry from the $133,000 he made his last year in Detroit. He joined the mix of young players on the way up, eagerly awaiting their chance at the majors, and a lesser num-ber of older players on their way down, holding on to the hope of one more shot. None of his teammates or opponents had reached the heights Mark Fidrych had. None of his teammates had a Rookie of the Year award at home. No one else in the league had ever ap-peared on the cover of *Rolling Stone*.

Despite being in the minor leagues, Pawtucket held some attraction for Mark. Since it was barely an hour's drive from Northboro, he was able to spend a lot of time at home, and family and friends were able to regularly attend his games. He often dropped in on his father's sixth-grade class to play with the kids and pass out PawSox tickets. His visits were always a hit with the kids, who would look out the class window, spy him coming up the walk, and shout, "Mark's here again."

Despite the years, Mark's name was still popular with fans and he remained a major drawing card. On May 23, nearly 9,000 fans came to Pawtucket's McCoy Stadium for his first start. It was the largest crowd in the forty-year history of the stadium. Mark pitched five and two-thirds innings of respectable ball and didn't seem to have any pain in his arm. Manager Joe Morgan lifted him with two outs in the sixth because he wanted to let the standing-room-only crowd mark the occasion with an ovation.

The next day, Mark showed up at the park at 7:30 AM before a Sunday afternoon game to work out. The owner of the PawSox, Ben Mondor, was stunned to see him there and opened the gate to let him in. Mark then ran, did his exercises, and lifted weights alone for several hours. Realizing this was his last chance, he was doing everything possible to make sure he was prepared. But the season became a struggle to find consistency.

No longer possessing lightning in his right arm, Mark was forced to rely on his brain to keep hitters off-balance, but it was not easy. Whatever it was that had robbed the arm of its ability to throw 90-mile-per-hour heat had also taken his two most valuable assets with it: the precision control and the movement on the ball. Paradoxically, he threw slower but had less control. Some nights there was very little left in the arm and he was hit hard by the minor leaguers. Other nights a combination of guile, wits, and will seemed to propel him to get just enough outs to escape. Whatever the result, he was still able to generate energy in the minor league parks with the fans, home or on the road.

"I can't think of anyone who affected the gate the way Mark Fidrych did," said Jim Weber, Toledo's longtime radio voice, in 2000.

"There's not anyone close—he is the hands-down winner. He pitched in Toledo twice when he was with Pawtucket. Those were two of the largest crowds in the history of the stadium, and there weren't any giveaways or freebies either. There wasn't an open seat anywhere. He never changed his ways—he still was jumping over the lines, talking to the ball, and patting the mound."

In mid-June 8,236 fans showed up in Toledo to watch Mark's scheduled start. It was sixty miles and six years away from his rookie season in Detroit, but the northwestern Ohio and southern Michigan fans had not forgotten. Mark took the field for warm-ups to a thunderous welcome. He pitched six innings to get the win, 6–2, his first victory with Pawtucket, and basked in a standing ovation en route to the clubhouse in the seventh inning. An hour after the game, a couple hundred fans still stood outside the clubhouse, chanting, "We want The Bird." Mark was informed that there was another door he could sneak out to avoid the crowd, but he said, "No, I owe a lot to these people. The fans have stuck with me. I appreciate that a lot." He walked out of the clubhouse and plunged into the crowd, signing autographs for forty-five minutes.

As always, Mark was popular with his teammates because of his attitude and personality. "His enthusiasm and fun made coming to the park something to look forward to every day," said one Pawtucket player. He was both an instigator and frequent target of clubhouse pranks. All of his teammates had heard of him and were not sure what to expect prior to the season. "He was a competitor on the mound," says pitcher Keith MacWhorter. "He was totally focused on throwing the ball. It didn't matter if there were two people in the stands or thousands, he was the same. I had thought it was an act when he was in the major leagues, but when I saw him from the bench in Pawtucket I realized that was just his personality. He was 100 percent pure and genuine. Also, he was the type of guy who was always there for you, always ready to do anything for you. If you needed a ride somewhere or something like that, Mark was always that guy. He was a good teammate. And he was a fun guy to be around.

"To be honest, by the time he got to Pawtucket, his arm was gone," continues MacWhorter. "I think the Red Sox knew he couldn't throw anymore, but he kept hoping he could make it back to the majors, that his arm would come back. Of course, it never did, but he was still a great guy to have around and the fans loved to watch him."

"If we had an All-Good Guy team, he (Mark Fidrych) would be on it," PawSox official Lou Schwechheimer later said. "He had a green Mercury Marquis when he was playing here. After a game, he'd sit on the hood of that car and sign autographs until the last fan left. I remember coming in early one Sunday morning, about 7:45. The Bird was sitting on the hood of his car—whistling. I asked him, 'What are you doing here at this hour?' He smiled and said, 'I'm just waiting for someone to open the ballpark.'"

There was just a little bit of magic left in that right arm; enough for one more unforgettable night. On July 1, Mark started against Dave Righetti in Pawtucket. Righetti had been the Rookie of the Year in the American League for the Yankees in 1981, but had struggled in 1982. The Yankees had sent him to their Triple-A Columbus team for a couple of starts to get straightened out. Mark Fidrych entered the game with a 2–3 record and had not pitched a complete-game victory in over a year. The matchup between the two pitchers was only announced a few days before the game, but the media quickly fanned the flames. Cars were packed around the stadium by six o'clock for the 7:30 game. A crowd of 9,389 squeezed into the 5,800-seat stadium. Included in the crowd were 124 media members, representing almost every paper from Boston to New York. Pictures of Mark shaking hands with Righetti had been quickly printed and were being gobbled up for two bucks each. Fans in the old stadium were normally close to the action and seemed to be on top of the players, but with this crowd the feeling was magnified. In anticipation of the sellout, temporary bleachers had been brought in. Fans crowded into a roped-off section outside the right-field foul line and stood two deep in the aisles. Mark warmed up within five feet of fans down the right-field foul line and chatted with them. "You gotta love it," he said to pitching coach Mike Roarke. "You have to get pumped up with something like this." The fans, media, and players, no matter how pumped up, could not have anticipated the spectacle they were about to see.

In front of the thunderous crowd, Righetti, anxious to return to New York, blew away the Pawtucket hitters to start the game, striking out the first five batters and six of the first seven. Righetti, who would pitch a no-hitter at Yankee Stadium soon after, threw smoke for six innings, striking out twelve. He left the game satisfied with a 5–3 lead. Mark Fidrych doggedly tried to stay to the end. Like an aging boxer, he survived on guts and know-how, by bobbing and weaving, feinting and jabbing. He grudgingly absorbed body blows but managed to avoid the knockout punch. A two-run homer in the sixth, followed by two run-scoring singles in the seventh, put him on the ropes, however. "About the seventh inning, he was in a jam," manager Joe Morgan later recalled. Morgan considered taking him out, but "I said to myself, 'We've got this crowd, this big mob here, and they came to see this duel.'" Morgan decided to give Mark just a few more batters. The next hitter stroked a base hit to the outfield, but the runner was thrown out at the plate, and another runner was gunned down trying to advance. The unlikely double play got Mark out of the inning and kept him in the game.

Pawtucket, seemingly inspired, clawed back with four runs in their next two at-bats, and Mark sprinted out of the dugout holding a 7–5 lead in the ninth inning. Visibly worked up, he fidgeted on the mound and pulled on the bill of his cap. His first warm-up pitch sailed to the backstop. The crowd, already packed on top of the field, seemed to surge closer and rose to their feat screaming. In the PawSox dugout, Joe Morgan, determined to win the game, had a reliever warming up and thought to himself, "One guy gets on base and he's gone."

The first Columbus batter of the ninth grounded out to second baseman Marty Barrett. Mark rushed across the infield and shook Barrett's hand. The fans, sensing something special, began chanting Mark's name. Suddenly, it was 1976 again. "Mark was actually timed at 90 miles per hour that last inning," says Mac-Whorter. "And he hadn't been able to reach 82 before." Mark struck out the next batter, then, with two outs, faced Butch Hobson. A dangerous hitter, Hobson had just been sent down by the Yankees. He had hit twenty-eight home runs for the Red Sox in 1979 and had touched Mark for a run-scoring hit earlier in the evening. Hobson took a huge swing at the first pitch and missed. The second pitch was low for a ball, followed by a slider for a swinging strike two. The crowd was delirious. Mark assumed his familiar stance on the mound, focusing on the plate. He reached back for one last pitch. As he released the ball, he threw with such effort that his foot slipped on the follow-through. He spun a three-quarters turn to the left and went to a knee, his hat falling off. The pitch was on the low edge of the strike zone. Hobson swung and missed, and the park exploded. Mark grabbed his hat, jumped with both hands straight up in the air, and then ran around the field shaking hands with every teammate, waiting behind the mound to catch the outfielders as they came in. Amid the increasing roar of the crowd, the Pawtucket players swarmed Mark just like, well, just like he was back in Detroit in that magical summer of long ago. As they headed for the clubhouse, the crowd stayed on its feet and got even louder. The other Pawtucket players looked with awe at the stands. They were unsure how to react—they had never seen a crowd like this, but Mark Fidrych had been here before; he knew what to do.

"When it was over, the fans wouldn't leave," said general manager Tamburro. "When he walked off the field, everybody was standing and applauding. Even after he went into the clubhouse, the crowd stayed on its feet, cheering. After a few minutes, he went back onto the field and tipped his cap. The place went nuts."

Mark bathed in the cheers of "Bird, Bird, Bird." When he faced the bleachers and raised his clenched fists like Rocky, the stands ignited like Dad's Fourth of July grill doused with lighter fluid. "The scene after the game was like out of a movie," said Tamburro.

"I get gooseflesh even now just thinking about that moment," says MacWhorter. "I've been to World Series games, but nothing in baseball affected me as much as being in that moment. I actually had tears in my eyes watching that last inning. We all knew he had worked so hard and this meant so much to him." In 1990, Keith MacWhorter was asked to write about his most memorable moment in professional baseball for the *Providence Journal*. He picked that moment. He wrote that "the baseball gods made their presence felt." Mark Fidrych threw in that last inning "as if he were being rewarded with one final moment of glory after six years of unsuccessful comeback attempts." It would be the last time Mark Fidrych would ever hear the rapturous cheers of fans at the end of a baseball game.

Mark finished the season with Pawtucket, compiling a 6–8 record with an ERA of 4.98 in twenty games. He had some good games and some bad games, but he never again came close to the heights that he reached with the Righetti duel. He filled McCoy Stadium with every appearance—over 8,000 each time—not 50,000 as in Detroit, but a packed stadium nevertheless. Pawtucket general manager Mike Tamburro later reflected on Mark's ability to fill stadiums: "When he got to us in late June, every place he pitched in the league was a sellout. Six years after his great year he was still selling out minor league parks."

During the winter, Mark continued to work with Dr. Pappas five days a week. The work wasn't all physical. "He was tremendously depressed," Pappas said later. "Obviously, you can't go through that range of high to low without that. I saw Mark five or six times a week, just spending time, trying to discuss his arm."

Mark arrived early to Winter Haven in February of 1983, determined to make the major league club. But it was soon obvious that his arm had other ideas. Finally seeming to accept that his arm would never allow a return to his status of 1976, Mark talked of just being able to find a role—any role—to help the team.

Players still talked of the old Bird to reporters in camp, as if discussing a dead relative. "Forget all that bull, all that stuff he did on the hill," Carl Yastrzemski told them. "He just came at you, and at you, and at you. If he wasn't overpowering, he was damned close to it. He had this zone between the shins and the lower thighs, and he never missed it." Unspoken was the unfortunate reality that the old Bird was a thing of the past, never to be seen again.

Mark talked reflectively to a reporter that spring. "He (God) gave it to me. He took it away. Now He's given it back. He said to me, 'Hey, you're goin' too fast, buddy. You've got to slow down . . . just slow down and look at what you have in life.' . . . Someone sent me something that really hit me a few years ago. It was a story about how you're walkin' along and there's four footsteps, yours and His, then there's suddenly only two, and you say to God, 'Where'd You go?' But it turns out the two footsteps are His. He's carrying you. See? I relate to that."

Players and coaches were cautiously optimistic. "The thing about Mark is that if he makes it, it wouldn't be good only for the Red Sox, but it'd be good for all of baseball," said Red Sox pitching coach Lee Stange. "Everybody is pulling for the guy; everybody loves him."

But as the spring progressed it became painfully clear to everyone that he would not make it back. In his third outing, against the Mets, Mark was hit hard, giving up five runs in two innings. After the game, Rusty Staub, who had a run-scoring hit for the Mets in the first inning, told reporters, "I didn't even want to get my bleeping hit off him. That's the way I feel about Mark. I had a real love for the kid. There was something special about him from the start. I'd been in the fishbowl, too, so I knew what he was going through. It was such a shame. You'd ask him if his knee hurt, and of course a kid is going to say no. So he just kept going out there, and eventually I guess everything went akilter."

Other major leaguers seemed to be rooting for Mark. Tom Seaver and Jim Kaat spent time going over mechanics with him and offered tips. But it was a struggle. Mark's fastball was timed at just 73 miles per hour.

After the Mets game, Mark was returned to the Pawtucket

club. He voiced optimism to reporters: "I have no doubts whatsoever that I will be back."

"He just wasn't the same pitcher in 1982 and 1983," says Ralph Houk with a touch of sadness. "The arm just wasn't close to what it had been. The life wasn't there anymore. I loved that kid. I would have done anything for him. It really was hard to let him go."

Back at Pawtucket for the 1983 season, Mark was slated for middle relief. "I'm just glad to get this chance," he told a television interviewer after his first game, in which he gave up three runs in three innings. "It's like Gates Brown told me—I've known the top and I've known the bottom, and how many guys ever get to say that? I figure it's made a better person of me."

While he may have been a better person, he was a much worse pitcher. He had a hard time in 1983, becoming the eleventh man on an eleven-man minor league staff. "His control just wasn't consistent," pitching coach Roarke later said. "But he never blamed anybody except himself. If somebody told him that a guy walked because an umpire missed a pitch, he'd say, 'I shouldn't have been in that situation.' Or if somebody made an error behind him when he had a one-run lead, he'd say, 'I had a one-run lead. I should've kept that one-run lead.' And he didn't dwell on the past. I never heard him feel sorry for himself that his arm went bad."

Mark was just hanging on. He was beginning to realize that, despite all the effort and optimism, his arm was not going to come around. Gone forever were the carefree days of setting the league on fire, of goofing off in the back of the Tiger bus with friends, of dominating opposing hitters. "It's still baseball," he told a television reporter. "It's still played the same way. You lose your pride, but at least you're still playing baseball."

"You could see the disappointment in Mark," his sister Carol said. "He felt like he was letting his fans down."

"It was frustrating because you were going into battle without all your weapons," Mark later said of trying to win at Pawtucket with a bad arm.

"Everybody in the organization wanted him to come back,"

says Roger Weaver, a teammate at both Evansville and Pawtucket. "But it was painfully obvious he didn't have it anymore. He was very candid with teammates about it. No one worked harder than Mark; he trained more intensely and worked on his pitching more than anyone in the organization."

"He was one of the hardest-working and most team-oriented players in the organization," 1983 manager Tony Torchia said.

Mark Fidrych knew the end was coming. "When I left the Tigers," he later said, "one thing Mr. Campbell told me was 'Mark, I know you're probably gonna try and play somewhere else, but don't end up being a Triple-A player. Don't end up bumming around the minors for five years." Mark loved baseball. He wanted to continue pitching forever. He later said, "My father always said that if you can find a job that you like to do, consider yourself lucky." Mark had always considered himself lucky to be in professional baseball. He kept hoping his arm would get better; kept hanging on to a small thread of hope that somehow it would bounce back. One night, talking over a beer with teammate Keith MacWhorter, who was also nearing the end, Mark asked, "How do you know when you're all done?" MacWhorter answered, "The hitters will tell you when you're done." With a 2–5 record and an ERA of 9.68 in twelve games, Mark was getting a not-so-subtle message from the hitters. On June 28, he was called into manager Tony Torchia's office for the conversation every professional player knows is coming but still dreads. The club needed space on the roster to make room for pitcher Brian Denman, who was coming off the disabled list. Mark was the obvious choice to go. He voluntarily retired on June 29, 1983, rather than face the indignity of being cut. It was finally over.

After the game, he remarked to reporters, "I told someone that I probably would go over to the mall and get a lunch pail." Then, it was time to break the news to his family.

"Mark called and told me to go over to see Dad," says Paula. "I went over there, then Mark called my dad, and Dad was saying, 'Okay Mark, if that's what you want to do.' Mark was telling him he was going to retire. Mark was crying, Dad was crying, and I was crying. Mark said he was tired, there was something wrong with his arm. The team needed someone on the roster who could do the job."

"I've had enough," Mark said. "I don't have it anymore. But didn't we have a great ride, Dad?"

"Yes, son," Paul replied. "You had a great ride."

9

Northboro Redux

After all the cheers and tears, it was time to move on to the next stage of life. For the first time in Mark's twenty-nine years, his future would not include playing baseball. The initial months were difficult. "I got so mad at the reporters," says Lorie. "They were constantly calling him or just showing up. They wouldn't leave him alone."

"Mark hasn't talked about baseball," Virginia told one in early July, explaining that he hadn't bothered to watch the All-Star Game. "He's still very upset about it."

"He was really depressed," says Lorie. "I felt bad for him. I wanted to yell at them, 'Just give him a break. He's been through enough; just give him a little time to sort things out.' Of course you're going to be depressed at that point. My parents felt bad for him. They tried to be there for him. But it was one of those things where he just needed some time."

There was a lot of time now. The closeness of family and friends helped. His buddies had always been there. To them, he had always been Fid, not The Bird. They didn't want anything from him; didn't expect anything from him except for him to just be Fid. That had always been enough.

Initially, Mark stayed with his parents and Lorie in the house in Northboro he had bought for them after his first big year. "He was a very protective big brother," laughs Lorie, who was in her late teens by then. "He would have to look over every boy who came to take me out. And he was very blunt with them. He would tell them, 'You want to live until tomorrow, you keep it in your pants, pal.'" Lorie's older sister remembers her complaining of a time Mark sent her back in the house to change clothes because he thought her tank top was not quite appropriate for a date.

Eventually Mark plunged back into life as Fid from Northboro. The energy and blue-collar work ethic were too strong for him to sit around. Fortunately, he had not blown his baseball money—he had invested it wisely while still in the game. He had bought a 123-acre mostly wooded farm on some of the last available land in Northboro. When he had spoken of owning a farm and driving trucks as a twenty-one-year-old rookie with the world at his feet, writers had laughed and used it as more proof of his supposed flakiness, but he had been serious all along. "Mark had always wanted land," says longtime friend and occasional business partner Wayne Hey, "even from way back. When he got some money from baseball, he took advantage of it and bought the property. Then he added another section a few years later. He sold a little of it off at a nice profit and ended up with around 120 acres. There's not hardly any land like that around here anymore. Everything else has been developed."

Mark bought cows, pigs, turkey, and sheep. The farm work kept him busy. There was always something that needed to be done; something that needed to be fed, something that needed to be cleared away, cut down, or graded. Sometimes, when he was feeling down, he would take his chainsaw and cut wood for hours to work out the frustration. It's a slow process, giving up something you have worked at and loved all your life. It's not easy to let go. But baseball had never defined Mark Fidrych. He enjoyed playing it—he loved it—but he had never been just a baseball player. The time slowly passed, and he adjusted to life as Fid from Northboro once more.

Mark lived simply and didn't need a lot of money—only about 6,000 dollars to pay the taxes on his land. He told a reporter, "Why do I need big money? You got a thousand dollars, you got a thousand problems. I've always been small. I just want to stay small." But even as he said that there were thousands of ideas going on in his head of what to do. "Initially, we played around raising cows, cutting firewood—trying to do something on the land," says Hey. "But it never became anything big. We always needed to have our regular jobs. But we did a bunch of things. We put in swimming pools for a few years. When we were putting in pools, it was always rush, rush, rush because it was the middle of summer and people wanted their pools before it turned cold. Then when they found out Mark Fidrych was putting in the pool we had to allow some extra time to go see the neighborhood kids and sign autographs. He would take half an hour or an hour a day and greet all the kids and the parents. I never saw him turn down anybody who wanted an autograph—he always appreciated them coming up and asking him. He always took time to talk to them." Mark would sometimes also give impromptu backyard pitching lessons to the family's kid after a job.

Detroit sportswriter Jim Hawkins dropped in unannounced one day in the early 1980s and found Mark chopping wood on the farm. "See what a guy's gotta do when he gets out of ball?" Mark joked. Mark welcomed Hawkins warmly and introduced him to his seven cows, named Babe, Zorro, Adam, Hiawatha, Alfon, Bronson, and Fred. He introduced his thirteen pigs. They had names also. "I call them Porkchop 1, Porkchop 2, Porkchop 3," Mark said. He refused to show any bitterness to the game or his fate. "Ball got me this," he said looking around at the farm. "Do you think I would have gotten this if I'd stayed pumping gas at Pierce's Gas Station? People ask me, 'Don't you think it's tragic, what happened to you?' I say, 'No, it's not tragic. What I had in Detroit, you couldn't ask for anything better. I've got no regrets. I can't have any regrets because I did what I wanted to do.' . . . The Tigers did as much for me as they possibly could.

"The only thing I'd change," he concluded, "if I would change

anything, would be to listen to Rusty Staub that day in spring training when he said, 'Slow down, boy.' "

Mark was moving past thirty years of age. Life was changing. Most
of his friends were married. The Cut Off, his favorite hangout
in Northboro, was condemned and became an empty lot. Pinball
games were replaced with Pac-Man and video games. People didn't
need gas station attendants to pump their gas—every station was
self-pump now. Nobody even wore leisure suits anymore. The
world was changing. The decade of the seventies was becoming a
distant memory.

There were occasional activities that kept Mark involved with
baseball. He was an extra in the Neil Simon movie *The Slugger's
Wife* in 1985. He joined the Screen Actors Guild and traveled to
Atlanta along with other former major leaguers such as Bucky
Dent, Bernie Carbo, and Al Hrabosky to film the baseball scenes in
Atlanta-Fulton County Stadium. Mark made $100 a day and told
reporters, "I like doing this kind of thing. I'll take any part they
want to give me. I don't even have to speak any lines."

Mark teamed with Bucky Dent later that year on a baseball
camp for kids. He played in an old-timers classic baseball game and
golf tournament in Anchorage, Alaska, in July of 1986 to raise
money for the Special Olympics. He would sometimes see the
Tigers when they came to Fenway Park and visit with old friends
still on the team, but baseball slowly sank into the background of
his life.

Even as Mark was adjusting to life after baseball, there was
always the nagging question of what had gone wrong with his arm.
All those different exams and tests by all those different doctors—no
one had ever come up with an answer. Tendinitis in the shoulder,
weak muscles from changing his motion to compensate, muscle
spasms, scar tissue, a subconscious mental block—there never was
an appropriate explanation for what had ended his career. In 1985
some friends told Mark about a clinic in Georgia in which doctors
were using revolutionary technology in the form of an instrument
called an arthroscope. It was a small flexible tube with fiber optics

that could be inserted into joints to allow them to see exactly what was causing problems in knees and shoulders—space-age stuff. A brilliant, innovative young doctor at the clinic was rapidly pushing this technology into everyday use. The young doctor's name was Andrews. James Andrews.

Mark went to the Hughston Sports Medicine Hospital in Columbus, Georgia, where Dr. Andrews performed arthroscopy on his shoulder and made a startling discovery: there were two severe tears in the rotator cuff. Finally, there was an answer to the eight-year-old mystery. Mark had battled all those seasons, worked so hard to come back, all the while trying to pitch with a torn rotator cuff. The manipulations, the exercises, the hypnosis, none of it had helped because the rotator cuff hadn't been fixed. "It made me know I wasn't crazy," Mark later told reporters. "Now I know my problems weren't in my head." The rotator cuff was surgically repaired. Once again, Mark could open doors with his right arm and sleep through the night without waking up from pain in his arm if he rolled on it the wrong way.

Although the shoulder was now fixed, Mark was thirty-two years old and had been out of baseball for almost three years—it was too late for The Bird to make a professional comeback. He had moved on. Dr. Andrews would also soon move on—to Birmingham, Alabama, where he became the orthopedist to the stars, repairing more major athletes' injuries than anyone in the country; a doctor on agents' speed dials.

In 1986, Gary Smith of *Sports Illustrated* visited Mark in Northboro for a feature article, ten years after his rookie season. Mark told him of a recurrent dream he was having—of being on a baseball field alone, no crowd, no cameras, no reporters; just Mark Fidrych throwing strike after strike. Just Mark Fidrych playing baseball.

Smith followed Mark on his rounds at the farm, getting slop for the pigs, clearing land at the site of his future house. Mark told him, "You don't make any money doing this. You do it because it's something to do. You do it because it keeps you going." He added, "I'm in love with my land. I got it all from playing ball."

Mark spoke of his attempts to make a living after baseball, doing several different part-time jobs. He told Smith that, in addition to his income from the farm, a few times a year he earned money speaking at banquets, did a little promotional work for various companies, and shot a commercial for Miller Lite that never aired. He had lots of ideas, sometimes the ideas would just come flooding in, but he still hadn't found his niche. "I've never found another place as comfortable as a mound," he reflected. "Never."

Mark's friend Wayne Hey told Smith, "Deep down, I think he's been completely lost without baseball. A lot of people wouldn't know it, because he's got something to say to almost everyone."

Overall, it was a depressing piece—catching Mark in the middle of transition, still perhaps wondering what he was going to do with the rest of his life, still struggling somewhat to find regular income. But the phase didn't last long. Mark Fidrych did not wallow in pity.

"Sometimes I still daydream about ball, but it's over," Mark told a reporter in 1987. "Sure I cried [when not being able to pitch well anymore] and I used to get depressed. But if you're depressed, go to Children's Hospital in Detroit; that'll get you out of depression." Mark had often visited there as a player and had been affected and inspired by the attitude of the sick children with whom he had talked.

One of the temporary jobs Mark held was as a beverage salesman. He visited Chet's Diner in Northboro regularly as part of the route. Chet's was an old-fashioned one-piece diner out on Route 20. A Northboro institution since 1919, Chet's was one of the oldest diners in the northeast. The owner, Mr. Pantazis, was a hardworking man who had immigrated to the United States from Albania in 1936 and had fought for his new country in World War II. He had bought Chet's in 1960 and ran it as a family business with his wife and children, including his pretty daughter, Ann. Mark Fidrych and Ann Pantazis had attended high school together but scarcely knew each other. Ann had been a serious honor student back then, taking mostly advanced-placement classes—they had traveled in different circles. Ann had attended Fairfield University, majoring in biochemistry, and worked as a dietician at a local hospital in addition to helping out at the diner.

Now in their early thirties, Mark and Ann discovered each other at the diner. Ann seemingly did not know about Mark's famous past. To her he was just a nice guy with an engaging personality who had popped into her life; a guy who came by the diner and always made her laugh—there were no preconceptions of the famous athlete.

"He bugged me for a long time for a date," Ann told a reporter in 1987. "I was seeing someone else, but he said, 'When you get rid of him I'll be waiting.' My mother was skeptical." Soon, Mark and Ann were seeing each other seriously.

For the first three months, their relationship was kept secret in the small town. "It's my thrill," Mark told *Sports Illustrated*'s Gary Smith, "just her and me." Smith wrote that Mark was nervous about commitment. The first girl he had fallen for had left him (the one who sent him the Dear John letter he wrote about in *No Big Deal*). Smith also wrote that a two-year relationship in Detroit had ended when the woman wouldn't go with him to the minor leagues or to Northboro.

Ann was perfect for Mark. She was smart, levelheaded, hardworking and shared a lot of his values. "Mark never liked fake women," says Lorie. "He didn't like the big-city, showy, materialistic types with false fingernails and tons of makeup. He and Ann were different in a lot of ways, but their differences kind of complemented each other. I'll never forget when Mark pulled me out on the deck one day and told me he was going to propose to Ann. He showed me the ring and asked, 'What do you think?' Ann made Mark so happy." They were married on October 12, 1986.

"After they got married, Mark settled down—eventually we all settle down," says Wayne Hey. He still had time for his buddies and fun, but usually would say, "Let me talk to Ann first," when plans were discussed.

Mark and Ann had a daughter, Jessica, the next year. Mark embraced fatherhood like he did everything else in his life, telling reporter in 1987 that the birth of his daughter was "one of the greatest highs of my life."

A man with a family needs a steady job, and Mark was ready to pick one main source of employment. Soon after his daughter was born, Mark walked into a dealership and plunked down $80,000 cash for a new ten-wheel Mack truck. Initially, he didn't even know how to drive it, but with much practice he eventually learned to smoothly shift gears and maneuver the massive truck like a pro. He named the truck Jessica after his baby daughter and proudly put the name on a plate above the front bumper. He had a local artist paint a logo on the side of the truck of Mark pitching, and he became the president and CEO of Mark Fidrych Company, Inc.

As an independent trucker, Mark contracted to use his truck to haul asphalt and gravel for construction companies. There was nothing easy about the work—twelve-hour days often starting at 5:00 AM. He became a common sight at construction sites in central Massachusetts, building roads, driveways, parking lots, and sidewalks. Sometimes people would be surprised to spot him—not expecting to see Mark Fidrych in a truck named Jessica working at a sidewalk construction job on Route 12 in Leominster, Massachusetts. "People on the road wave at me," he told a reporter in 1987. "They say 'I didn't think it'd be you driving it.' I say, 'Why not?' I'm proud of this truck.

"A lot of people think that Mark Fidrych made enough money where he didn't have to work," he said. "Well, I made enough to get me a ten-wheeler and a piece of land and a house, and now I've got to support that. Baseball was a lot easier life. Now all of a sudden, I'm on 495 with two blown-out tires and a ton of asphalt sitting there. I'd rather face somebody with the bases loaded and no outs."

He always took time to stop, talk to fans, and sign autographs. Once traffic was at a standstill due to construction and his truck was stopped near a downtown area in a small town. The owners of a local sporting goods store reported that they ran out of baseballs due to people running in to buy balls to take out for him to sign.

They had to send an employee over to the nearest Walmart to bring back some more.

Mark enjoyed himself driving the truck just like he had told reporters he would back in 1976. He was happy being one of the guys on the job and then going out for a beer with the other workers when the job was done; putting in a hard day's work and then coming home and jumping in the pool with his clothes on. The company that contracted his truck most frequently was Amorello & Sons of Worcester. "We'll be working a job and a cop on duty will come over, then say, 'Is that really Mark Fidrych driving that truck?'" Anthony Amorello told a reporter in 2000. "He's such a down-to-earth guy you'd never guess he was a superstar."

Mark approached his trucking business with the same enthusiasm and attitude as he had baseball. "One day I was driving home on Route 20 and there was a little construction job going on there with trucks and stuff," says Robert Boberg. "And there was Mark, directing traffic, wearing the glow-in-the-dark vest. And he's waving at everybody, a huge smile on his face, having a grand old time."

There was "always a smile" on Mark's face, according to Joe Amorello. "The rain, the snow—he was the first one on the job every day. He'd dress in a flannel shirt, and he'd be the first one to grab a shovel and get to work. He was an incredibly hard worker, and we got it done, but we sure had some laughs along the way."

Together Mark and Ann built a beautiful four-bedroom contemporary house, designed by themselves with the help of an architect, on a hilltop that overlooked the farm and the town of Northboro. The house had huge picture windows that provided a spectacular view, vaulted ceilings, and the centerpiece of the living room was a twenty-nine-foot-high stone fireplace built with rocks Mark gathered from the farm. Mark called his land Blue Water Ranch. The ranch would eventually have a man-made lake for fishing and ice skating and a pool. "This is what baseball got me," he would proudly tell visiting reporters.

"The farm was really where Mark's heart was," says his

brother-in-law Rick Duda, Carol's husband. Mark loved working on the farm, walking over the land with his beloved dog Patches, sitting on the deck talking to friends while watching hawks lazily float above the trees—a huge smile on his face, rubbing his hands together as he discussed his latest big plan. He put out food for deer in his backyard and enjoyed showing the deer to any children who came by the farm visiting with their parents. "Look what I've got," he would say, pointing to the deer.

"I'm happy where I am," Mark explained to a reporter in 1987 while discussing his farm and new family. "The man upstairs—the Lord, not the general manager—had some other direction for me and this is it."

"I looked at myself and how I wanted to live my life, and so I'm here," he noted to another reporter in 1989, after explaining that he could have made more money by staying in Michigan or in a bigger city. "When I hurt my arm, I was fortunate that I had guys I was playing ball with that said, 'Prepare yourself for when you get out of the game.'"

Mark was involved with Jessica in youth sports as she grew. He helped coach her Little League baseball teams and youth soccer teams. "I picked Jessica to be on my farm team in baseball when she was five," says Joe Sullivan, who became a close friend over the years. "I asked Mark to help me coach. He was great with the kids. He signed twelve baseballs; there were twelve kids on the team. After each game we gave away one of the balls to our 'player of the game.' We made sure each kid got a ball by the end of the year. The kids on the team all loved him."

Mark was not a pushy sports parent; there was no screaming and yelling from the sideline or bullying referees. He noticed that girls tend not to be as competitive as he had been when he was young, and he adjusted accordingly. "He said to me, 'I'm not sure if I should say something,'" says Hey. "Girls approached the game differently."

Mark appeared happy just to be involved and help out. Other parents remember him having fun playing pickup basketball games with kids in the neighboring gym while waiting to pick Jessica up from gymnastics class. The Fidryches routinely had Jessica's soft-ball and soccer teams over for swimming parties.

"In my last years at Algonquin, his daughter Jessica was there," says Robert Boberg. "She was a nice kid. She played on the volley-ball team, and Mark would come to all the games. I would usually bump into Mark at the games. He would always ask how my son was doing because he knew he was umpiring. He was very inter-ested in his daughter—a good parent. He was very proud of his family."

Initially, there was little sign in the Fidrych house that the owner had once played professional baseball. Boxes of memorabilia were stored in the attic. Mark was moved immeasurably when, in her early teens, Jessica began taking items from his baseball career and bringing them down to decorate the basement. Initially, she hadn't been too impressed with her formerly famous father's ca-reer, but when she discovered that he had made the Aqua Velva commercial, she conceded that he must have been fairly big.

Mark had one more opportunity to scratch the itch of base-ball. In 1989, he joined the nearby Marlboro Orioles of the Stan Musial League, an amateur league consisting mostly of college kids. "I just wanted to play," Mark told a reporter. "I heard about this league."

"He called me up," said the Orioles' manager, Tony Navarro. "He said, 'This is Mark Fidrych. I wonder if you'd have a spot open on your team.' He didn't say, 'I want to play for your team.' He didn't want to take anybody else's job. He asked if there was a spot open."

At thirty-five years old, Mark was the oldest player on the team. The next oldest, Andre the mailman, was twenty-six. "I kept thinking about the game all day," Mark told a reporter before his first game. "I was just driving my truck, delivering asphalt, and thinking about the game. Just dying for the game to start. My wife . . . she's never even seen me play. . . . When we were first to-gether, there'd be all these phone calls, and she'd say, 'What's this all about?' I said, 'Oh, I used to play baseball.'"

Mark enjoyed the camaraderie of his new team. He tried to

act like a regular guy even though the younger players were in awe of him. "I'd take my teammates out for a beer after the game, but I'm not sure how many are legal age," he joked. He invited them to his house for a party at the end of the season. But it was hard to stay active in baseball while putting in sixty-hour weeks with his truck and helping with his growing daughter. Also, he had never properly rehabbed the arm after his surgery, which made it difficult. He eventually gave it up and relegated his baseball playing to occasional old-timer's appearances and fantasy camps.

It was at an old-timer's game that Ann Fidrych first saw her husband pitch in front of a crowd. "She told me, 'You're two different people. Your personality changed when you put on the uniform. You were running around, smiling from ear to ear, signing autographs for kids,'" Mark later said.

At another old-timer's game, he took along his brother-in-law Rick, who was a huge baseball fan. "He took me into the dugout with him and got a bunch of guys to sign a baseball for me," says Rick. "When they would start to sign it he would joke and say, 'You don't want that guy to write on your ball do you?' I got Ernie Banks, Bob Lemon, Joe DiMaggio, a bunch of great players." His brother-in-law got him a baseball signed by Joe DiMaggio? That, in and of itself, has to qualify as the world's greatest brother-in-law.

Mark took Rick with him to a couple of Tiger fantasy camps in Lakeland also. At the camps, middle-aged baseball fans would plunk down large chunks of cash for the chance to spend a week playing baseball with former major leaguers. At the Tiger camps, as well as the Red Sox camps in Winter Haven, Mark was one of the favorite coaches and appeared to have as much fun as the fans. "Mark loved those camps," says Rick. "He just had a blast with the campers, goofing off and telling stories. One time all the campers and players were up late on the last night—telling exaggerated stories of their heroics on the field; just laughing and having a good time. And, of course, the refreshments were flowing. The next morning, everyone looked terrible on the bus going to the airport. Everyone had a hangover. Mark gets on the bus and just lets out a huge yell, then busts out laughing while everyone is holding their heads."

In 1996, Mark made a foray into the publishing business. He came out with a children's coloring book based on his 1976 season, *The Bird of Baseball: The Story of Mark Fidrych*. The book was the brainchild of Rosemary Lonborg, wife of former Red Sox pitcher Jim Lonborg, who Mark had met and befriended at charity events. "Gentleman Jim" Lonborg, who became a dentist near Boston after his baseball career was finished, was involved in many charities, particularly the Jimmy Fund, the official team charity of the Red Sox, which has provided help for area children since the early fifties. Rosemary Lonborg had written two previous children's books, one based on her husband entitled *The Quiet Hero: A Baseball Story*. "He was a gentleman and a good sport, and I thought that was a good example for children," she explains. Rosemary has a passion for children and has worked for over twenty years at the Dana-Farber Cancer Institute in the Jimmy Fund Clinic, helping children who are going through cancer treatment, assisting them with fun activities, and providing morale support. She initially had wanted to make a series of inspirational children's books about baseball players who were good examples, but the players she contacted turned her down. Over the years, the Lonborgs and Fidryches became close as they attended many charity functions together, the Lonborg daughters often babysitting young Jessica while they were at the events. "I presented the idea of a children's book about himself to Mark, and he loved the idea. We decided to make it a coloring book for kids based on his 1976 season." Mark paid to have the book published himself. He also served as the distributor and marketer for the book. He had thousands of copies made and stored them in his garage.

"Whatever you do, just do it with joy," the book concludes. "The theme of the book was joy," Rosemary says. "Bringing joy to your life and giving joy to others. Be yourself and make other people happy. That's an important lesson for children, and Mark was a great example of that."

With his pickup loaded down, Mark drove to bookstores asking them to place the books. But it was not a money-making deal—he gave away many more books than he ever sold. He would later give out autographed copies of the book on Opening Days at the Northoboro Little League each year. He gave away hundreds of books to Rosemary's patients at the clinic. He gave away autographed copies all throughout the region over the years.

Mark remained close to his parents throughout their lives. Virginia died in the early 1990s as a result of several medical conditions and complications from a broken hip. Paul Fidrych died in Jacksonville in 1998 at the age of seventy-four. Mark had realized how much baseball had meant to his father, often telling reporters, "I lived his childhood fantasy." Baseball provided a lifelong bond between father and son. Once, Mark was able to introduce Paul and a friend to Ted Williams. Words can not describe how much it meant for a baseball fanatic who grew up within fifty miles of Boston to be introduced to Teddy Ballgame by his own son. "Now I can die in peace," Paul Fidrych was heard to say after Mr. Ballgame walked away. Although Mark was gracious in giving credit to all his former coaches from Little League through the majors, he always named Paul Fidrych as his greatest inspiration and best coach.

Over the years, reporters would seek Mark out with regularity for "where-are-they-now" type articles and special occasions. He always welcomed them and was open. He was easy for them to find—his number was in the phone book. *Sports Illustrated* ran articles on him in 1986, 1997, and 2001.

"That whole ride, it was probably the biggest roller coaster any human being could be on," he told one writer, speaking of his time in the limelight. "Anyplace you went there was press, television. Anyplace you went in the airport, people recognized you. You were like Mr. Clean (in the sixties). You know how Mr. Clean was a household word? Everyone knew Mr. Clean. Well, everyone knew The Bird. To me, it was great."

He always maintained that he wasn't actually talking to the ball, but only looking at the ball while reminding himself before each pitch to watch his mechanics and verbalizing what he wanted to do with the pitch. But he admitted, "It was pretty neat seeing the cartoons of me talking to the ball in the Detroit newspapers."

With a trace of nostalgia he would tell them how much he had enjoyed his time in the majors. "Every time they have an All-Star Game, I think of the time I was there," he said in 1996.

And, above all, he was upbeat. "You know, Mark Fidrych is a lucky guy," he summed up one interview. "I got a great life now," he told another reporter in 1999. "I got a family. I got a house, I got a dog. I would like my career to have been longer, but you can't look back. You have to look to the future." He told ESPN in 2000, "I have a family, I have a lot of things that, at fifteen, I thought I'd never have. Life is beautiful."

Is that how he truly felt? Really? By all accounts, yes—that's exactly how he felt according to those who knew him. If he had bitter feelings, he kept them to himself. Maybe it took a lot of effort, but he kept them to himself. Had he come along a few years later, he would have made untold millions of dollars in baseball. A few years later and medical care would have been able to diagnose and fix his rotator cuff and give him more years in the majors, but he never expressed regret to reporters, family, friends, or old teammates. "I talked a lot with Mark," says John Hiller. "He was never bitter. He was always a very happy man. He met a great woman and was very happy with his life. His career allowed him to do a lot of great things."

"He never even slightly suggested any regrets of his injuries," said Joe Amorello, a friend who worked with him for over twenty-five years. "He was just happy to have the time he had in sports. He considered himself a lucky man."

Mark did occasionally express regret to reporters that he didn't get more endorsement deals and, despite a desire to do public relations work for Major League Baseball, was never offered anything. Hadn't he done a little bit of good for baseball? It would have been nice to get a little something; you know, a little something for the effort. Who better than The Bird to represent Major League Baseball to a new generation of fans? Who better than The Bird to make them remember the fun in the game at a time when steroid scandals and chronic boorish behavior by stars were trying the resolve of fans? But the call never came.

Mark remained a Tiger fan, frequently going back to Detroit for games and events, or catching them when they came into Fenway Park. He kept a special place in his heart for Michigan and the people of the state who had treated him so well. "When I'm on that plane (returning to Detroit) I get goose bumps thinking about the games I played, thinking about what I did, how much fun I had," he told a reporter in 1996. "I'm lucky because when I go to Detroit, or basically anywhere, when people recognize me, they ask, 'How's it going? What's your life like?' They're always very, very concerned. That, to me, is like, Wow! A person who saw me twenty years ago is actually concerned. They want to know how Mark is doing. What a great feeling to have. I don't know if other ballplayers can have that feeling."

On another visit to Michigan he said, "It's neat [still being recognized]. I don't do that many appearances, but I enjoy it. I like seeing the children of the parents who followed my career with the Tigers. I like seeing the parents tell them about the time they saw me pitch. It's part of my life."

The first time Ann accompanied Mark to Detroit, she remarked at how many friends he seemed to have there, as everyone from baggage handlers at the airport to people on the street called to him and wished him well. "I don't know any of these people," he confessed.

"Do you have any idea how big your husband was?" Jim Hawkins asked Ann when Mark introduced them in 1999 while visiting Detroit.

"I've heard stories," she replied.

"You have no idea," said the man who wrote *Go, Bird, Go.* "You had to be there."

Mark, along with a number of former Tiger players, participated in the special activities associated with closing Tiger Stadium. On September 27, 1999, before the last game at the old stadium, Mark, wearing his Tiger uniform, got the largest round of applause as he ran to the mound. He dropped to his knees and smoothed the dirt, then took some soil from the mound and, with tears in his eyes, put it in a bag. Then, he ran off the field of his youth one last time.

It was during the late 1980s that Mark Fidrych discovered two things: (1) The Bird could make money for good causes, and (2) he had a blast doing it. Mark began to spend more and more of his time doing charity work. He attended countless charity events in the Detroit area and, as a policy, never accepted an appearance fee. He asked for only compensation of plane fare and hotel room.

He participated in a charity basketball game at Boston Garden. "Can you believe they let me on the parquet floor?" he asked a reporter.

He helped support the local diabetes walkathon in Northboro, attending and giving out copies of his book to all the walkers. He hosted a golf tournament for the American Heart Association in Oxford in 1994.

There was the golf tournament held by former high school teammate Bill Stapleton each year at Sandy Burr Country Club in Wayland to raise money to fight Parkinson's disease, the Special Olympics Golf Tournament each year at Bally Meade in Falmouth, the Baseball Assistance Team dinner in New York to raise money to help those in baseball who are in need, ex-teammate Steve Grilli's Cooperstown event for the Hospice organization of Central New York, the Globe Santa fund-raiser in Boston to benefit less fortunate children in Massachusetts at Christmas, a Wiffle-ball game for the Jimmy Fund in Worcester, the Cape Cod Fall Classic Genesis Fund Fishing Tournament to benefit sick children, and the annual Joe Cronin Fishing Tournament for the Jimmy Fund. There were many others.

A disproportionate amount of Mark's charity work was for disabled children. He regularly attended fund-raising events for special-needs children and even had an event at his farm for them that was attended by Big Bird. "Mark really had a soft spot for special-needs children," says his sister Paula. "He was so patient with them."

A reporter in 2000 described Mark participating in the annual

Dan Duquette Skills Challenge in Fenway Park in which he "gently helped handicapped children soft-toss a baseball into a circle and hit off tees and then played ball with children of sponsors." The event raised more than $100,000 for the Genesis Fund, which supports research into birth defects and aids the families of children with birth defects. "The kids don't know who I am, but their parents do," Mark explained. "It was a kick. In the bullpen, I told the kids how I warmed up out here many years ago. I enjoy giving back. I'd like to do a lot more, but it's tough when you're out trying to make a living."

"It's called giving back," he told another reporter in 2001. "If you can help a younger kid out that is a great thing to have because people helped me out."

The charity in which Mark had the biggest impact was the Wertz Warriors of Michigan. Organized in 1982 by former Tiger slugger Vic Wertz, the group uses an annual cross-country snowmobile ride across the state to provide complete funding for the Special Olympics Michigan State Winter Games. After Wertz died, other Tigers such as Bill Freehan and Dave Rozema helped out. Each of the fifty to seventy riders raises at least $3,500 for the seven-day, 900-mile snowmobile trip. In the early 1990s Mark met two members, Larry King (the truck driver not the television personality) and Bob Ernst, while at a celebrity duck hunting expedition in Arkansas and struck up a friendship. They told him about the work the Warriors did and Mark was hooked. He had never snowmobiled before, but that did not stop him. "We had to help teach him how to ride and keep an eye on him the first few years," says Warrior chairman Victor Battini. "But he did okay, there were no major wipeouts."

Beginning in Mt. Clemens, Michigan, and ending in Petoskey, each day the riders zigzagged their way across northern Michigan, stopping at restaurants, lodges, schools, and watering holes along the way. At each stop, Mark, as the group's headliner, would make a speech and greet visitors. He signed thousands of autographs and posed for thousands of pictures. A highlight event of the ride was the participation in opening ceremonies at the Special

Olympics Winter Games. They gave the athletes rides and interacted with the kids. "It's not the snowmobiles for me, it's the Special Olympics," Mark said in 2006. "It's the athletes. It's another
thing to help out where you can." The February 2009 ride was
Mark's seventeenth straight year of participation.

"Mark was the catalyst for the group," says Battini. "People
would come out to see him. He was the nicest athlete I've ever met—
just an unbelievably great guy. He had absolutely no ego; just an unassuming, humble, fun guy to be around. We loved the guy."

"One of the first years he rode with us, we got into Elba, Michigan, late one night," continues Battini. "It had been a long, cold
ride and we were all dead tired. My phone rang at the hotel, and a
guy said, 'There's a bunch of people waiting here for Mark Fidrych.'
There was a little place about fifty miles away that people were
expecting us that we hadn't known about. Mark was already in
his pajamas, but he jumped up and said, 'Let's go.' So we rode over
there, and he talked and stayed until the last person got a picture
and an autograph. To this day, we still get twenty to thirty thousand dollars out of that little place every year.

"Mark always had time for everyone," adds Battini. "I never
saw him turn down a request or walk away before everyone had an
autograph. And he was just great with the kids, the Special Olympians. He would give them rides and talk to them. They all loved
him. Mark just had a way of connecting with people. It didn't matter who you were, he had a way of making you feel like you were
the most important person in the world. He could spend a few
minutes with someone and make them feel like they were his best
friend."

Kathy Hinchman worked with the Special Olympics and witnessed Mark's effect on the kids. "The athletes were thrilled," she
says. "He would speak from the podium onstage, but he didn't speak
as a professional athlete, he spoke as someone who loved and respected those athletes. He was dressed in a plaid shirt, jeans, and a
Wertz Warrior jacket. When he walked around in the hallways, he
didn't walk with security or an entourage, he walked around as
Mark, the Wertz Warrior." The Special Olympians didn't know,

and most didn't care, that he had been a famous baseball player (although their parents certainly did). To them, he was just a guy who showed genuine interest in them as individuals, who made them laugh and encouraged them. The kids loved him as Mark Fidrych, not The Bird.

Over the years, Mark was a familiar face around Northboro and in the area. He attended town meetings, regularly hung out at the American Legion, and was frequently seen driving his truck (honking his air horn at kids in their yards) or walking in a store holding his daughter's hand. He was happy to donate time, autographs, pitching lessons, or, once, even a live pig to local charity auctions. He apparently always had some copies of his coloring book with him to hand out (did he never leave home without them?). In the winter he drove his Ford F350 pickup truck with a snowplow on the front and plowed streets and mailboxes, making a chalk mark on the dashboard for each mailbox he cleared because he got paid by the city per mailbox. "If he would see an old lady shoveling her driveway, he would stop his route and help her clear it," says Rick Duda. "Everything was, 'Yes ma'am, yes sir.' He was always polite to older people."

He was seemingly never in a bad mood, always having something to say to everyone, always with a joke or something funny and a quick easy conversation. There was no such thing as a routine greeting from Mark Fidrych. He might yell out across a crowded drugstore to the wife of a friend, "Hey, has your husband gotten over that case of herpes yet?" Or, seeing some acquaintances raking a huge pile of leaves, swerve his truck through the pile, scattering leaves everywhere, and drive off howling hysterically. He would meet people at charity events or in the stands at a game or simply in a restaurant, strike up a conversation, become friends, and invite them to visit or call. And he would mean it. He would remember a name and ask about the kids or wife of someone he had only briefly met before. He seemed to enjoy talking about construction, trucks, farms, and family even more than baseball.

If you had Mark Fidrych at a wedding reception, you didn't

need to worry about entertainment. His dancing became the stuff of legend. "Oh, he thought he was dancing, but it was horrible," said Nancy Amorello, who termed it The Fidrych Dance. "He'd be flailing his legs, limbs flying everywhere, leaving five or six people with a bruise."

"I had a double wedding with Kirk Gibson," says former Tiger Dave Rozema. "By the end of the night, Mark had danced with every single female in the place. All the old ladies loved him. He was just having a blast."

To friends, he seemed to never change. "Mark was the same from the time he was fourteen until he was fifty-four," says Brad Ostiguy.

"When you would see Mark after some years, it would always be just like you never left," says Dan Coakley.

"He always said he would come back to Northboro, and he did," says Ray Dumas. "And he never changed. He would come up to me and slap me on the back so hard it would almost knock me down—I'm eighty-seven years old now—he'd just walk up on the porch and say, 'Hey Mr. D, where's Mrs. Dumas,' just like he had never left the neighborhood."

"Fame never changed his personality," says Carol.

Fame may not have gone to Mark's head, but he recognized how much his fame meant to other people and how much happiness it could bring them. He would spend time talking with people who approached him—actually giving his time, not just a handshake and a greeting. He was able to talk to people and come across as the down-to-earth guy that he was, even to perfect strangers. He could make other people feel important. Fans often remarked to others that they were happy to learn that he was a special guy after meeting him.

Ronnie Pappas was one such man. Pappas was a sixty-six-year-old Cape Cod man dying of cancer in 2005. He was a huge baseball fan and loved Mark Fidrych. Mark was contacted by Ronnie's sons, and he took the time to visit him in Cape Cod, talking baseball and giving him an autographed baseball, bringing joy to his final days.

Tom Marino, manager at the Northboro Legion Post, recalled a time when a man came into the American Legion and asked Mark if he would autograph a baseball card for his son who was having an operation the next day. Mark looked at the card and said, "No." Everyone was shocked because they had never heard of Mark turning down an autograph request, especially for a kid. But then he said, "But I'll be there at ten o'clock in the morning and I'll bring it." Mark showed up the next day at the hospital in his Detroit Tiger uniform and visited with the kid for two hours before he had his operation.

"Mark never turned down a request for an autograph," says Carol. "And he never charged for autographs." At his first card show, Mark was signing autographs and the kids in line kept handing him tickets. Mark later explained, "I said, 'Whoa, time out. What are these tickets?'" Someone informed him that each of the kids had to pay an extra fee for tickets to get his signature. "I said, 'Forget that.' If they want me at the show, they pay me, but they can't charge extra for tickets. It's my say, so I say it. If they won't do it that way, I say, 'Fine, you don't want me then.'"

He told another reporter in 1996, "I only do card shows when the promoter gives free autographs. The promoter can pay the ballplayer and then the ballplayer can do his thing for two hours. That's just the way I'm handling that."

He had always enjoyed interacting with fans, especially kids, and continued to enjoy that into middle age. As he got older, he appreciated the attention and the chance to step back and relive the glory. "The best thing I loved about playing ball was seeing a little kid's happy face," Mark said. "I went to a Bruins game, and a kid came up to me and said, 'Mr. Fidrych, can I have your autograph?' And I said, 'Little buddy, you just made my day.'"

He gave people the impression that he never realized how special he had been. "He was so unassuming, he actually told me once that he couldn't believe people got so excited about what he did as a Tiger," says Victor Battini of the Wertz Warriors. "He said, 'I was just having fun.' But I think he enjoyed it. I think he liked the recognition."

Fans would see him in a seat at a Tigers game or at Fenway Park and he would strike up a conversation that would last for innings. On a plane from Boston to Detroit for the 2006 World Series, a man discovered that the dark-haired lady in the middle seat was also going to Detroit for the Series. "My husband used to play for the Tigers," she said casually. "Oh really, who?" the man asked. With that the tall curly headed man in the window seat leaned forward and introduced himself.

But around Northboro, Mark downplayed his fame. "It was funny," said Northboro selectman Jeff Amberson, "people not from Northboro would see Fid and go, 'Hey, that's Mark Fidrych, the former major league pitcher,' while people from town saw a really good, really nice guy who was a pig farmer and owned a trucking company and, oh yeah, way back when played baseball."

One story goes that someone came into Chet's and saw Mark working there. "I know you from somewhere. Your face is familiar," the stranger said. "Well," Mark replied, "I used to work at the gas station after high school."

"My son was a big baseball fan," says Joe Sullivan, "but it was a long time before he would believe that Mark had actually played in the majors. He just didn't think he acted like a former professional player. He thought Mark was just a guy who had gone to school with Mom and was good friends with Dad. My son finally went down to the baseball card store and asked the guy if he had a Mark Fidrych card, and he pulled out a whole stack. But a few years later, when he was older, he joked with Mark, 'I bought your rookie card—it only cost a dollar.'"

Mark became a regular working at Chet's Diner every Saturday morning. Chet's, like everything else in his life he valued—his family, his farm, his dog, his truck—fit Mark perfectly. There was no pretense. A sign near the grill still states, "Prices subject to change according to customer's attitude," as regulars in flannel shirts, jeans, and old baseball caps belly up to the counter on stools. Chet's was the only diner in Northboro that had a framed copy of *Rolling Stone* with a picture of one of its workers on the cover. Mark cooked, cleaned tables, poured coffee, laughed, and talked to everyone, thoroughly enjoying himself, with Mother Pantazis cooking up her famous hash, Ann working behind the counter, and Jessica waiting tables—frequently reminding her dad to quit talking so much because he was falling behind.

One spring morning Mark was working the breakfast shift and an eight-year-old boy and his father recognized him. The kid asked Mark if he was going to Florida to try out for the Red Sox that year. "Well," Mark replied, "I'm not sure, do you think I should?"

"Oh yes," the kid answered. "The Sox could really use your pitching."

Mark flashed the kid and his dad a big smile and said, "Well, then I just may head down to spring training."

The kid beamed. "Dad! Mark is going to try out for the Sox!"

Mark stayed involved with local baseball. He gave free clinics to youths in town and sometimes threw batting practice to the high school team at Algonquin. He showed up for Opening Day of Northboro's Little League every year. He was always friendly to the Little Leaguers, tried to greet each one, and handed out auto-graphed copies of his coloring book. As the kid who had made good, he enjoyed returning to the same Little League field he had played on and encouraging the kids. Little Leaguer Michael Upton recalled getting an autographed baseball from him: "He handed me the baseball and said, 'Always keep up your dreams and you'll succeed.' That was an awesome day for me."

Mark allowed the Boy Scouts of local Troop 101 to use his farm for their campouts. He had met the Scouts and their leaders when they would stop at Chet's for breakfast before outings. He kept telling the leaders they should use his farm for campouts, telling them how beautiful it was there at night. After they took him up on the offer, they enjoyed it so much it became an annual event. He would give them stuff to burn, let them play with the pumpkins that had gone bad, let them take hikes in the woods, and sit around the evening campfires with them and tell stories. They got the feeling that he enjoyed the weekends more than they did. One of the scouts, Daniel Rowe, will never forget his first camping outing at the Fidrych farm. "We were getting ready to make a bonfire and the adults told me and a few of my friends to go make a fire, so we did," he says. "We made a bonfire out of long spears of wood and pallets and, of course, put some lighter fluid on it. We lit it up, and forgot to have some water buckets nearby, so it quickly became a very big fire. Someone ran up to get him and told him, while we were trying to get water from the nearby stream. He came down and said something along the lines of, 'Oh that is nothing. When someone told me there was a huge fire, I thought it was going to be burning halfway across the field. This is what I expected you guys to do.' He even invited us back the next year."

People sometimes put on a certain act for cameras, to maintain a carefully crafted image. Friends sometimes remember someone only in good terms. A true measure of a man's personality and character can be found in his behavior away from the camera; in how he acts when the media are not there, and how he treats total strangers. John Sanderson of Reading, Michigan, had a chance encounter that perfectly illustrates the true Mark Fidrych. "We go up to the upper part of Michigan every year over Thanksgiving deer hunting," Sanderson explains. "On Friday nights we used to go to Newberry to a big restaurant for dinner—it was about the only place to eat in town that time of the year. For several years we would see the same group of people there. One of them was a tall guy with curly hair, always wearing a Detroit Tigers baseball cap with his hunting clothes. He was always cutting up and laughing. He stood out in the crowd because he was so tall and had that curly hair. One year I asked the waitress who he was because he looked familiar, and she said, 'I'm not sure what his name is, but he used to be a famous baseball player.' One of my friends said, 'Mark Fidrych?' And she said, 'Yea, I think that's it.'

"So she talked to him, you know, some celebrities don't want to be bothered, but he jumped right up with a big smile and came over to our table and talked for a long time. He joked and talked about his baseball days. I hadn't been that big of a baseball fan, but I remembered watching him on TV. He didn't have any hard feelings or grudges about his career. He said that what had happened to his arm could have probably been fixed easily nowadays. He joked about how little money he made his first year. He said even though he later played on another team he always wore a Tiger hat out in public.

"When we got home, I mentioned it to my grandson who was about fourteen at the time. He was shocked. He's a big baseball fan. He gave me some baseball cards to see if I could get them autographed when we went back the next year. So the next time we went back, November of 2007, I took them. He was real nice about giving autographs. He joked with me, 'You're not going to sell them are you?' He said, 'I want you to promise that he'll get them to keep and not to sell.' He signed them 'To Brad.' Brad's cards were wrinkled and creased. He reached into his pocket and pulled out a perfect card in a little plastic case and gave that to me. He said, 'Just bring me back a letter from Brad next year.' He really lit up like a lightbulb; he seemed happy that we recognized him. I offered to buy his meal, but he said, 'No thanks. I'm just glad you remembered an old guy like me.' He was one of the nicest guys I've ever met. The world needs more people like that. The next year when we went back, I had the letter from Brad, but the restaurant had closed and I never did get to see him and give him the letter."

Monday, April 13, 2009, Mark Fidrych woke up early and started to work, just like every day of the previous twenty-six years. He had spent the day before, Easter, with family, having the Fidrych traditional Easter egg battles with his sisters. He had given Carol a load of autographed Mark Fidrych coloring books to pass out to the kids in her grade school class.

Mark had a job scheduled with his truck, Jessica, for Monday morning, but the site wasn't ready when he arrived, so he returned home. On the way, he passed a friend. They talked truck to truck for a few minutes with Mark mentioning that he was going to take advantage of the down time to do some needed repairs; then he drove back to the farm and crawled under the truck to work on it.

And that's where his friend, Joe Amorello, found him when he stopped by later.

The coroner would rule that a piece of Mark's clothes got caught in a rotary part of the engine. He was fifty-four years old.

Epilogue

As the baseball career of Mark Fidrych is reexamined, it becomes apparent that, lost in all the hoopla over his antics, he was a very good pitcher. How good of a career would he have had if he hadn't gotten hurt? One can only speculate. What is fact is that before the sixth inning of that Baltimore game in 1977, Mark Fidrych had a career record of 25–11 and an ERA of 2.19. It is also a fact that since 1920, only four men, Dizzy Dean, Mark Fidrych, Fernando Valenzuela, and Dontrelle Willis, have started 8–1 while being under twenty-two years old.

"The best young pitcher I've ever had in my career," Ralph Houk said in 1986. "There's no question in my mind that if he hadn't gotten hurt he could have been one of the great ones," Houk added in 1987. "He really challenged hitters . . . I tell you, if you ever got into the eighth inning with Mark, the game was over. There was just no way you were going to beat him in the last two innings."

It would be a mistake to look only at his colorful personality on the baseball field and assume that he was not a serious baseball player. He was a tremendous competitor; he just had a blast while he was competing. Similarly, it would be a mistake to assume that he did not take baseball and the preparation for the game seriously. Few players worked as hard as he did. He was a near fanatic about running. It was his conditioning and competitiveness, much more than any misuse by management, that was responsible for the large number of complete games he pitched as a rookie; that and the fact that his control allowed for unusually low pitch counts.

To look only at Mark Fidrych's statistics in assessing his baseball career would be like looking only at the measurements of the Sistine Chapel in assessing its beauty—some things are just impossible to judge by numbers alone. Much more important than his talent on the field was his impact on the game of baseball and its fans. This is what Mark Fidrych will always be remembered for. The following comments give voice to the sentiment that he inspired:

"Fidrych was the greatest thing I ever saw in baseball," said Rusty Staub in 2000.

"He was the most charismatic player we had during my time with the Tigers," said Ernie Harwell, whose time with the Tigers spanned almost fifty years.

"Never was there one person who dominated fans, for one year, the way he did," said Dan Ewald, who worked as the Tigers public relations director after writing for the *Detroit News*. "He was the most dominant fan force I'd ever seen in my life."

"You can talk about Ty Cobb or anyone else, but for one year, he was the biggest impact star in the history of the Tigers," said Jim Leyland in 2009. "For that one year he was bigger than anybody in the history of the game."

"Never in my thirty-seven years of baseball have I seen a player like him, and never will I again," Jim Campbell said in 1986. "My gosh, I don't know why we don't see more people like Mark Fidrych. He was what he was. All natural. So hyper, so uninhibited. A minute after he came into my office, he'd have one cheek of his butt on the corner of my desk. Before you knew it, he'd be lying on my desk, his head resting in one hand, the other hand gesturing in the air."

"I've been fortunate to have spent a good part of my life near the ballpark in Detroit," says Steve Thomas of the Detroit Athletic Company. "To this day, if I ask any old-timer what the most exciting thing he ever witnessed at 'the corner,' the answer is always the same: Mark 'The Bird' Fidrych during his rookie year. What amazes me is how much people relate to Mark Fidrych as a person, not just as a ballplayer. He had a charisma that just never shut off—whether he was on the mound or on the street. People genuinely admired him as a human being. That's something you don't see very often in the sporting world anymore."

Jack Wallace recently retired after thirty-nine years of teaching and coaching at Algonquin Regional High School. Over the years he came to pride himself on trying to teach kids to do things the right way and emphasizing the importance of academics and character. "You know something," he says, contemplating his most famous ex-player, "I'm more proud of Mark for being such an exemplary citizen after baseball than I am of anything he did on the field in the pros. He really was a great example of how a person can impact his community as he grows up. He gave back a lot to the community. He was a wonderful man, a great father. He did so much around here. A big part of Northboro died when he passed on."

Over a thousand people showed up at the First Parish Unitarian Church in Northboro to pay their respects to Mark Fidrych. The line lasted more than four hours. The Boy Scouts of Troop 101 waited patiently in line to give their last thanks to the man who allowed them to use his farm for campouts. One of the Scout leaders voiced what many in the area knew: "He's been incredibly generous."

Over twenty members of the Wertz Warriors, wearing their green jackets, drove in from Michigan. "We didn't even ask, they called me," says Victor Battini about the Warriors who volunteered to make the twelve-hour drive to Northboro on a day's notice. Once they arrived, they found that the feeling for them in Northboro had been established long ago by Mark Fidrych. "If you were wearing a green jacket, you couldn't pay for anything anywhere in that town," said one Warrior.

A little girl brought a small jar of cherries and placed them on the altar, explaining that she had always asked for a cherry for her ice cream at Chet's and Mark always gave her, not one, but several. Jim Lonborg attended with his wife, Rosemary, and told reporters about the many charity activities they had participated in together over the years. "He was all about giving back in any way he could."

Willie Horton gave a heartfelt eulogy. He noted that a few years earlier his daughter had needed a double-lung transplant. Mark had cancelled plans and joined Horton for a fund-raiser. "He was a trailblazer," Horton said. "Everyone playing in the major leagues today owes a debt of gratitude to Mark Fidrych. He brought baseball back to the people. He made it popular again. He helped save the game."

The Northboro Little League dedicated the 2009 season to Mark Fidrych, with the players all wearing a special black patch with "Mark Fidrych 20" on their sleeves. A large banner honoring Mark led the annual Opening Day parade. Mark's good friend and Northboro Little League president Joe Sullivan made an emotional speech to mark the occasion. Earlier, he had helped to raise over $7,000 in Mark's name to support the local American Legion baseball program in what would become an annual event. "He did what so many athletes these days don't do," said Sullivan. "He gave back to his community, his fans, his friends, and, above all, his family."

All over Northboro, saddened townspeople looked for ways to remember their favorite citizen. "After he died, I wanted to put up his picture at the American Legion," says Sullivan. "In the past, sometimes it's been hard to get people's pictures up, because there are so many deserving veterans. When I walked in with Mark's picture, the commander just said, 'Put it anywhere you want.'" Algonquin Regional High School named its baseball field in honor of Mark Fidrych. A Mark Fidrych Children's Fund was established with an annual softball tournament in Northboro to raise money to help sick children.

The Detroit Tigers had a special ceremony before their game on June 18, 2009, in which Ann and Jessica Fidrych combined to

throw out the first pitch to catcher Jim Leyland. During the emotional ceremony, they smoothed the dirt on the mound before throwing the pitch.

It had become popular myth over the years to view Mark Fidrych
as only a flake. He was a regular in baseball books and articles on
the subject, such as *Oddballs: Baseball's Greatest Pranksters, Flakes, Hot
Dogs and Hotheads* in 1989 by Bruce Shlalin, or *Cult Baseball Players:
The Greats, the Flakes, the Weird and the Wonderful* in 1990 by Danny
Peary, or the 2003 article in *Baseball Digest* entitled "Baseball Aches
for Flakes," or *Baseball Eccentrics: The Most Entertaining, Outrageous
and Unforgettable Characters in the Game* by Bill Lee in 2007. While
these were all written in a spirit of fun and are entertaining, it
would be a mistake to take these too seriously in judging him. In
talking to those who knew him and played with him, it is apparent that Mark Fidrych was not a flake. He was a character. He was
definitely different. He was enthusiastic, uninhibited, open, and
sometimes unable to see anything other than good in other people.
He had simple, nonmaterialistic needs that seemed totally foreign
to sportswriters and others, especially in the "me" decade of the
seventies. He possessed a rare ability to connect with people. He
inspired intense loyalty among the many people who considered
him a good friend. But he was not a flake.

And Mark Fidrych never really was The Bird either. He was
always Fid. Regardless of the hype, the media exposure, the unimaginable fame, he remained—throughout his life—Fid from
Northboro, the small-town guy. The Bird was a creation of the media. Fid never seriously talked to baseballs. He went along with the
gag and allowed the media to build The Bird to such outlandish
proportions because it was fun, and, certainly, baseball and the
nation in general needed fun in those days. And Fid always loved
to have fun.

In his later years, he realized how much The Bird meant to
people. He seemed to understand the feelings of middle-age men
who wanted to be able to shake his hand and try to express how
much he meant to them so many years ago, and maybe introduce

their children to the hero of their childhood. He certainly enjoyed doing that. He brought The Bird back to make people feel good on occasions. He brought The Bird back to raise money for good causes. But he was always still Fid.

Each season, new rookies appear in the major leagues. Some of them do very well and attract fans. Some become phenoms and cause writers to search past history for comparisons. But none can ever measure up to the phenomenon of The Bird in 1976, however. The times are different. With the money, the media, and the general attitude of the population, an atmosphere like that can never exist again. And that's unfortunate. For all of us.

In May of 2010, the newest pitching phenom, Stephen Strasburg, played a minor league game in Syracuse. A huge crowd turned out, the largest in the history of the stadium. The game was broadcast on regional television. Gazing over the enormous crowd, the play-by-play man asked his partner on the air if he had ever seen a pitcher draw such a crowd all by himself. The color commentator, ex-Detroit Tiger pitcher Steve Grilli, answered without hesitation, "Yea, Mark 'The Bird' Fidrych—every time he went out."

When fans of a certain age think of Mark Fidrych they are invariably taken back to a magical time when a young, impossibly energetic, talented, floppy-haired pitcher lit up the baseball world and took thousands of fans along for the ride. They can close their eyes and see him on the mound, standing with his feet together, holding the ball in front of his face, his lips moving as he contemplates the next pitch. They remember the crowds, the excitement, the unbelievable atmosphere of the whole summer. They had never seen anything like it.

And they never did again.

Acknowledgments

Every nonfiction author must rely on the goodwill of others in order to provide as complete a picture as possible, and I am sincerely thankful for the graciousness shown to me by the people mentioned here. Obviously, this book would not have been possible without the cooperation and memories of Mark Fidrych's friends, family, teammates, and fans. I have never met anyone who had more people who considered themselves to be close friends. This fact alone suggests something about Mark's remarkable personality and ability to connect with people.

I would like to especially thank Mark's sister, Carol Fidrych-Duda, and her husband, Rick, for their great hospitality on my trip to Northboro and for the tour of Northboro and the old neighborhood. Thanks also to Jack Wallace for showing me the baseball fields of Mark Fidrych's youth and to Mark's good friend Joe Sullivan for the tour of his "Bird garage" and for sharing his opinions and memories.

I would like to thank the following people who were kind enough to speak or exchange e-mails with me: Victor Battini, Paul Beals, Jack Billingham, Tom Blackburn, Robert Boberg, Neil Burke,

Dan Coakley, Rick Duda, Kevin Dumas, Ray Dumas, C. Michael Eliasz, Carol Fidrych-Duda, Laura Floetke, Fred Gladding, Charlie Glodas, Steve Grilli, Paula Grogan, Glenn Gulliver, Jeff Henningson, Wayne Hey, John Hiller, Kathy Hinchman, Jeff Hogan, Ralph Houk, Doug Howard, Jim Jablonski, Lori Karolowicz, Bruce Kimm, Dave Lavoice, Fred LeClaire, Rosemary Lonborg, Frank MacCormack, Dave Machemer, Keith MacWhorter, David Miles, Chuck Murphy, Brad Ostiguy, Mark Peerman, Daniel Rowe, Dave Rozema, John Sanderson, Greg Scupholm, Vivian Shyu, Thalia Stambaugh, Sherry Stover-Conley, Joe Sullivan, Gary Sutherland, Bob Sykes, Jane Syzdek, Steve Thomas, David Veinot, Jack Wallace, Rod Wharram, Diane Horn Whitaker, Kenneth White, Jim Willard, John Wockenfuss, Patrick Zier, and Tom Zocco.

It is a special treat to talk to former professional baseball players, and I am very appreciative to all of them for their time. I felt particularly honored, and lucky, to be able to talk to Ralph Houk, whose connection to Major League Baseball encompassed the DiMaggio and Mantle years of the New York Yankees. He was very helpful and enjoyed talking about Mark Fidrych, who he stated was one of his all-time favorites. I was greatly saddened to learn of Mr. Houk's death a few months after our conversation.

I would like to thank the staff of the Northboro Historical Society, the Worcester Public Library, and the Bartholomew County Library in Columbus, Indiana particularly for Tyler Munn and Denise Wirrig, their invaluable assistance.

I would like to thank the following people who provided pictures (sorting through them and deciding which to include proved to be one of the most difficult tasks): Carol Fidrych-Duda, Jack Wallace, Lorie Karolowicz, Brad Ostiguy, and Sue Digiorgio of the Wertz Warriors. Also thanks to Kevin O'Sullivan of AP images for his rapid assistance and John Horne at the National Baseball Hall of Fame Library.

This project may not have been possible without my agent, John Talbot, who immediately recognized the importance of telling Mark Fidrych's story to the present generation. Similarly, my editor, Rob Kirkpatrick, and his assistant, Nicole Sohl, provided invaluable assistance.

I would like to thank my mother for her continuing support and my brother, Ed, for sharing technical know-how and literary advice.

Finally, I would like to thank my beautiful wife Kathy for her never-ending support. Her presence on our trek to Northboro made the whole trip much more enjoyable.

Notes

1. Northboro

6 Paul Fidrych was of Polish heritage . . . Interviews with Carol Fidrych-Duda, May 16, 2010; Paula Grogan, May 14, 2010; and Lorie Fidrych Karolewicz, June 3, 2010.

7 Situated on land . . . Interviews with Carol Fidrych-Duda, Paula Grogan, Lorie Fidrych Karolewicz, Ray Dumas, April 24, 2010; Kevin Dumas, May 7, 2010; Jim Jablonski, April 26, 2010; Brad Ostiguy, June 7, 2010; Paul Beals, April 24, 2010; Charlie Glodas, April 29, 2010; and David Miles, April 29, 2010.

9 "My dad was always going . . ." Mark Fidrych and Tom Clark, *No Big Deal*. Philadelphia and New York: J. B. Lippincott, 1977.

9 "I stopped raising . . ." Gary Smith, "The Bird Fell to Earth," *Sports Illustrated*, April 7, 1986.

9 "Later in life . . ." *ESPN SportsCentury*, "Mark Fidrych," originally aired August 14, 2000.

9 "Teachers always seemed . . ." Fidrych and Clark, *No Big Deal.*

11 "There's something kind of . . ." Robert McKimson (director), "Little Boy Boo," *Looney Tunes,* Warner Brothers Studios, Los Angeles, 1954.

11 "It was a neighborhood . . ." Interview with Jim Jablonski.

11 "He was always a happy little . . ." Interview with Ray Dumas.

12 "His dad was always out . . ." Interview with Jim Jablonski.

12 "He knew a lot about baseball . . ." Interview with Kevin Dumas.

12 "He was a tough guy . . ." Interview with Dan Coakley.

13 Paul Fidrych's boy . . . "Make your own hole," Interviews with Paul Beals, Jim Jablonski, David Miles, Kevin Dumas, and Ray Dumas.

15 The Fidrych house held a close family . . . Interviews with Jim Jablonski, Ray Dumas, Kevin Dumas, Paul Beals, Dan Coakley, Wayne Hey, Carol Fidrych-Duda, Paula Grogan, and Lorie Fidrych Karolewicz.

19 "Mark was one of the hardest . . ." Interview with Brad Ostiguy.

19 "Mark was great in Babe Ruth . . ." Interview with Fred LeClaire, May 6, 2010.

20 "It came in curly . . ." Interview with Paula Grogan.

20 Mark showed up at Algonquin . . . Interviews with Brad

Ostiguy, Dan Coakley, Jeff Henningson, April 27, 2010; Jim Jablonski, Paula Grogan, Carol Fidrych-Duda, Kenny White, May 3, 2010; Robert Boberg, April 22, 2010; and Jack Wallace, June 13, 2010.

23 "Why didn't you tell me . . . ?" Bob Duffy, "A Two-hitter in His First Major League Start Sent Mark 'The Bird' Fidrych Soaring and He Landed in the Role of All-Star Starter as a Rookie, He Took Wing," *Boston Globe*, July 12, 1999.

23 "Mark was very unique . . ." Interview with David Veinot, June 11, 2010.

23 "He was a real good pitcher . . ." Jim Benagh and Jim Hawkins, *Go, Bird, Go!* New York: Dell, 1976.

24 "Coach Ted Rolfe's Northborough . . ." *Enterprise-Sun*, July 5, 1972.

24 "Those were tough years . . ." Interview with Jack Wallace.

24 "Of course, everybody had a little trouble . . ." Interview with Brad Ostiguy.

24 "Mark Fidrych, a junior righthander . . ." *Enterprise-Sun*, April 14, 1973.

25 "Any lingering doubts . . ." Richard Plante, "Fidrych Really Back!" *Enterprise-Sun*, July 9, 1973.

25 "I throw the knuckler . . ." *Enterprise-Sun*, July 14, 1973.

25 "There were some games in Legion . . ." Interview with David Veinot.

26 Fortunately, there was just the place . . . Interviews with

Tom Blackburn, April 30, 2010; and Tom Zocco, April 29, 2010; Fidrych and Clark, *No Big Deal*; Benagh and Hawkins, *Go, Bird, Go*.

30 "Hey, tell them . . ." Dave Marsh, "The Tale of the Bird," *Rolling Stone*, May 4, 1977.

30 "The whole family was just shocked . . ." Interview with Carol Fidrych-Duda.

30 "I met him at the door . . ." Marsh, "The Tale of the Bird."

2. Bristol

31 The Bristol Tigers were playing . . . T. J. Lewis, *A View From the Mound*, Lulu.com, 2007.

32 Mark Fidrych had joined . . . Interviews with Bob Sykes, August 12, 2010; and Jeff Hogan, May 4, 2010; Fidrych and Clark, *No Big Deal*; Lewis, *A View From the Mound*.

33 "I lucked out . . ." Fidrych and Clark, *No Big Deal*.

35 "Joe had the kind of personality . . ." Lewis, *A View From the Mound*.

35 "Joe was a tough . . ." Ibid.

36 "A lot of guys came . . ." Brad Wilson, "Fidrych Provides Thrill for Former Mentor," *Daytona Beach Morning Journal*, Sept. 14, 1976.

36 "You don't want my help . . ." Fidrych and Clark, *No Big Deal*.

37 Grodzicki watched each of the pitchers . . . Ibid.

37 "Mark really latched on to Grod . . ." Interview with Bob Sykes.

38 "I said, 'Fine, I've got a job . . .'" Fidrych and Clark, *No Big Deal*.

38 In one of Mark's first games . . . Lewis, *A View From the Mound*.

38 "My buddy Melvin Ray . . ." Edie Clark, "The Bird Is Still the Word (former All-Star pitcher Mark Fidrych, now farmer)," *Yankee Magazine*, June 2001.

39 "I don't even know . . ." Duffy, "A Two-hitter . . ."

39 "Mark pitched great for us . . ." Interview with Jeff Hogan.

39 "Bird was the fiercest competitor . . ." Interview with Bob Sykes.

39 "He talked like the devil . . ." Benagh and Hawkins, *Go, Bird, Go*.

40 One harrowing trip . . . Fidrych and Clark, *No Big Deal*.

41 "Getting this paycheck," Ibid.

41 "It was exciting playing professional baseball . . ." Interview with Bob Sykes.

41 Mark got fined a few times . . . Interview with Jeff Hogan.

41 "I remember Alleycat Johnson . . ." Gary Smith, "The Bird Fell to Earth."

41 Mark initially shared a cramped trailer . . . Fidrych and Clark, *No Big Deal*; Interviews with Bob Sykes and Jeff Hogan.

43 Despite the occasional off-field adventure . . . Lewis, *A View From the Mound*; Interview with Jeff Hogan.

44 Once in 1974 . . . Lewis, *A View From the Mound*; Fidrych and Clark, *No Big Deal*; Interview with Jeff Hogan.

44 There was one memorable night . . . Lewis, *A View From the Mound*; Fidrych and Clark, *No Big Deal*; Interviews with Jeff Hogan and Bob Sykes.

46 Mark had performed well . . . Interview with Jeff Hogan.

46 "We had five pitchers . . ." Benagh and Hawkins, *Go, Bird, Go.*

3. Lakeland, Montgomery, and Evansville

47 Frank MacCormack was hanging out . . . Interview with Frank MacCormack, July 20, 2010.

48 Mark had gotten his buddies to drive . . . Interview with Wayne Hey, May 13, 2010.

49 The players spent much free time . . . Benagh and Hawkins, *Go, Bird, Go*; Fidrych and Clark, *No Big Deal*; Interviews with Frank MacCormack and Patrick Zier, August 1, 2010.

49 Patrick Zier was a young sports reporter . . . Interview with Patrick Zier.

50 For all his fun off the field . . . Patrick Zier, *Lakeland Ledger*, October 8, 1981.

51 "In some ways, perhaps, Stubby . . ." Patrick Zier, "Nice Guys Don't Always Finish Last," *Lakeland Ledger*, March 4, 1977.

52 "My father owned several businesses in Lakeland . . ." Interview with Diane Horn Whitaker, August 7, 2010.

52 "We went everywhere . . ." Interview with Lorie Fidrych Kar-olewicz.

52 "Mark had a really neat relationship . . ." Interview with Bob Sykes.

53 At Lakeland, Mark became a starting pitcher . . . Patrick Zier, "Fidrych Fidgets L-Tigers to Win," *Lakeland Ledger*, April 18, 1975.

53 "When we first got him . . ." Benagh and Hawkins, *Go, Bird, Go.*

53 "The Bird did basically . . ." "Polk Personalities" *Lakeland Ledger*, November 15, 1977.

53 Patrick Zier called him "Fidgety Fidrych" . . . Zier, "Fidrych Fidgets L-Tigers to Win."

53 Opposing manager Rac Slider . . . Mike Cobb, "Fidrych Sharp in Lakeland's Win over Sox," *Lakeland Ledger*, June 20, 1975.

53 "I drank too much cold water . . ." Zier, "Fidrych Fidgets L-Tigers to Win."

53 Mark began the season . . . Fidrych and Clark, *No Big Deal.*

54 "I was down at Lakeland . . ." Benagh and Hawkins, *Go, Bird, Go.*

54 Montgomery was managed by Les Moss . . . Fidrych and Clark, *No Big Deal.*

56 He made an immediate impression . . . Interviews with Bruce Kimm, June 21, 2010; Fred Gladding, July 13, 2010; Mark Peerman, July 8, 2010; Frank MacCormack and Steve Grilli, May 8, 2010.

58 "A pitcher who talks to himself . . ." Pete Swanson, "Cinderella Triplets Top Tide for JWS Title," *Sporting News*, October 4, 1975.

59 "Everybody is talking about those pitchers . . ." Larry Paladino, "Tigers Considering Many More Changes," Associated Press in *Argus-Press*, September 22, 1975.

59 "If we had been in a pennant race . . ." Benagh and Hawkins, *Go, Bird, Go.*

59 "I threw the ball and . . ." Fidrych and Clark, *No Big Deal.*

60 "Me and Mark went fishing a lot . . ." Interview with Dave Rozema, May 18, 2010.

4. Detroit

61 Mark Fidrych was definitely known . . . Interviews with Ralph Houk, May 10, 2010; Fred Gladding, Gary Sutherland, June 24, 2010; and Jack Billingham, July 12, 2010.

62 "Very few pitchers make a staff . . ." Jerry Green, "Why Wasn't Bird Used Earlier? Houk Gets Answer From Book." *Detroit News*, July 9, 1976.

62 "We certainly intended to keep him . . ." Benagh and Hawkins, *Go, Bird, Go.*

63 "I walked into that big league clubhouse . . ." Steve Rushin, "Mark Fidrych," *Sports Illustrated*, July 2, 2001.

64 "The big thing I remember . . ." Interview with John Hiller, May 11, 2010.

64 "He was a kind of eccentric . . ." Interview with Gary Sutherland.

64 "This kid is from Boston? . . ." Duffy, "A Two-hitter . . ."

65 "Because of his enthusiasm . . ." Interview with Ralph Houk.

65 "Rare Bird . . ." Dan Ewald, "Rare Bird: Tiger Rookie Pitcher Fidrych Livens up Camp," *Detroit News*, March 22, 1976.

66 "We had to hit off him . . ." Interview with Gary Sutherland.

66 "He didn't really know a lot of the guys . . ." Interview with Frank MacCormack.

66 "Who was that . . ." Benagh and Hawkins, *Go, Bird, Go*.

67 "I was watching that preseason game . . ." Interview with David Veinot.

67 Mark's friends at home . . . Bill Clark, "Fidrych Finds Out Bosox Are Different," *Lakeland Ledger*, April 1, 1976.

68 Red Sox coach Don Zimmer . . . *Sporting News*, June 5, 1976.

68 Ralph Houk was not . . . Associated Press report in *Argus-Press*, March 29, 1976.

68 "There's something about this Fidrych . . ." Clark, "Fidrych Finds Out Bosox Are Different."

68 Mark found himself . . . Green, "Why Wasn't Bird Used Earlier?" Rushin, "Mark Fidrych"; Dan Ewald, "Tiger Rookie Elated," *Detroit News*, April 6, 1976.

69 Mark soon came down when he learned . . . Fidrych and Clark, *No Big Deal*; Rushin, "Mark Fidrych."

77 Red Sox pitcher Bruce Hurst . . . Ian Browne, "Former Red Sox Remain Fond of Houk," MLB.com, July 22, 2010.

77 Dave Rozema . . . Interview with Dave Rozema.

79 Early in the season, Horton told . . . *Sporting News*, May 22, 1976.

79 On the trip into Cleveland . . . Fidrych and Clark, *No Big Deal*; Interviews with John Hiller, Frank MacCormack, and Dave Rozema.

80 During an April trip to California . . . Jim Hawkins, "Fidrych Is Not Flaky . . . It's the Rest of Us." *Detroit Free Press*, June 7, 1976.

80 After an early season loss . . . Fidrych and Clark, *No Big Deal*.

82 Coming out of spring training . . . Interviews with Ralph Houk, John Hiller, and Gary Sutherland.

83 "If the rookie righthander . . ." Hal Schram, *Detroit Free Press*, May 11, 1976.

83 The major league starting debut . . . Interviews with Ralph Houk, Fred Gladding, Bruce Kimm, John Wockenfuss, August 10, 2010; and Doug Howard, June 6, 2011.

86 Michael Happy, who would grow up to write . . . Michael Happy, "The Bird Flies Up to Heaven," Detnews.com, April 13, 2009.

87 "I'll never get over this . . ." *Detroit Free Press*, May 16, 1976.

87 "You know what's really neat . . ." Benagh and Hawkins, *Go, Bird, Go*.

88 "The first time I got up . . ." *Sporting News*, June 5, 1976.

88 "My mind was more . . ." *Detroit Free Press*, May 16, 1976.

88 "How can you hit . . ." Benagh and Hawkins, *Go, Bird, Go.*

88 Indian outfielder John Lowenstein . . . Benagh and Hawkins, *Go, Bird, Go.*

88 "Mark Fidrych, an eccentric . . ." AP/UPI wire report in *St. Peterburg Times,* May 16, 1976.

88 When asked about the game . . . Patrick Zier, "Fidrych Two-hits Tribe in Major League Debut," *Lakeland Ledger,* May 16, 1976.

89 It was a thrill . . . Interviews with David Veinot, Paul Beals, and Kevin Dumas.

89 "It's really nice . . ." *South Middlesex Daily News,* May 26, 1976.

90 "Mark was so keyed up . . ." Interview with Fred LeClaire.

90 Later, Virginia Fidrych . . . Dave Anderson, "Detroit's Bird Capturing Hearts," *New York Times,* in *Miami News,* July 5, 1976.

90 He took time to stop by . . . *Enterprise-Sun,* May 27, 1976.

90 "Whoa, I struck out Hank Aaron!" Fidrych and Clark, *No Big Deal.*

91 "I like it . . ." *Detroit Free Press,* June 2, 1976.

91 "Far out . . ." Benagh and Hawkins, *Go, Bird, Go.*

93 "Fidrych Is Not Flaky . . ." Hawkins, "Fidrych Is Not Flaky . . . It's the Rest of Us."

94 "Having a ball . . ." Dan Ewald, "Having a Ball: 'Bird' Likes Lofty Perch," *Detroit News,* June 11, 1976.

94 "After I got older . . ." Interview with John Hiller.

95 "There was a buzz . . ." Interview with Bruce Kimm.

95 "He was an easy pitcher . . ." Phil Pepe, *Catfish, Yaz, and Hammerin' Hank: The Unforgettable Era that Transformed Baseball.* Chicago: Triumph Books, 2005.

95 "I took my son, who was ten . . ." Interview with Robert Boberg.

96 "It looked like Rocket City . . ." *Detroit Free Press*, June 25, 1976.

96 Virginia was fingering a broken string . . . Dave O'Hara, AP in *Lewiston Evening Journal*, June 24, 1976.

96 When he arrived at The Cutoff . . . Anderson, "Detroit's Bird Capturing Hearts."

5. Birdmania

98 "My phone started ringing . . ." *Detroit News*, June 29, 1976.

99 "Did you ever see baseball . . ." Joe Falls, "The Bird Makes It Look Like Old Days," *Detroit Free Press*, June 29, 1976.

99 Veryzer said, "these people aren't . . ." Rushin, "Mark Fidrych."

99 In the enlisted barracks . . . Interview with Jim Jablonski.

99 Back in Massachusetts . . . Interviews with Paul Beals, Kevin Dumas, Ray Dumas, and Robert Boberg.

100 On Chesterfield Avenue . . . Paul Craigue, "Northboro Goes

National with 'Markie' Fidrych," *Evening Gazette,* June 29, 1976; Interviews with Paula Grogan, Carol Fidrych-Duda, and Lorie Fidrych Karolewicz.

100 "As we got to the stadium . . ." *ESPN SportsCentury,* "Mark Fidrych."

100 "No one knew . . ." Fred Bierman and Benjamin Hoffman, NYtimes.com, April 18, 2009.

101 "I've never seen anything quite like him . . ." *Evansville Courier,* July 7, 1991.

101 "Fidrych was brilliant . . ." Pepe, *Catfish, Yaz, and Hammerin' Hank.*

103 "By the end of the game . . ." Interview with Paula Grogan and Brad Ostiguy.

103 "In the seventh inning . . ." Interview with Fred Gladding.

104 "I was the right fielder . . ." Pepe, *Catfish, Yaz, and Hammerin' Hank*; Jay Lovinger (editor), *The Gospel According to ESPN: Saints, Saviors, and Sinners.* New York: Hyperion, 2002.

105 "I don't think I can ever remember . . ." Interview with Bruce Kimm.

105 "Thanks. I may never get to play . . ." Rushin, "Mark Fidrych."

105 "I just kept telling myself . . ." Charlie Vincent, "Bird: The People Really Get Me Up," *Detroit Free Press,* June 29, 1976.

106 "These guys are making . . ." "Bird Is Talk of Town and He's Just Loving It," *Detroit Free Press,* June 30, 1976.

106 Later, at his locker . . . Rushin, "Mark Fidrych."

106 "Everywhere I went . . ." Joe Falls, "Fidrych Charges Up Even the Opposition," *Detroit Free Press*, July 5, 1976.

107 "I kept cooking ham . . ." Paul Craigue, "Northboro Goes National with 'Markie' Fidrych."

107 "all the officers could talk about . . ." Ibid.

107 "When I noticed all . . . Interview with John Hiller.

108 "He's not flaky," Jim Benagh, "A Rare Bird Flies High Above Baseball's Flock," *Detroit Free Press*, July 2, 1976.

108 "He's not quite . . ." Jim Hawkins, "Go, Bird, Go! Fidrych Kills New York 5–1," *Detroit Free Press*, June 29, 1976.

108 "He's not nutty," Frank Dolson, "Fans Coo-Coo Over the Bird," Knight Newspapers in *Evening Independent*, August 4, 1976.

109 "I only have four," Jerry Green, "Cuckoo Over a Rara Avis," *Sports Illustrated*, July 12, 1976.

109 "That ball has a hit in it . . ." Bob Rubin, "Bye-bye Birdie, You'll Be Missed," *Miami Herald*, July 8, 1983.

109 "If I don't talk . . ." Hubert Mizell, "Big Bird: A Little Loony, Perhaps, but Entertaining," *St. Petersburg Times*, June 30, 1976.

109 "If I want it to . . ." Ibid.

109 "The only time that happens . . ." Benagh, "A Rare Bird Flies High Above Baseball's Flock."

109 Dave Anderson wrote an article . . . Anderson, "Detroit's 'Bird' Capturing Hearts."

110 Detroit Hero Fidrych Does It All . . . " Detroit Hero Fidrych Does It All for $16,500 a Year," *L.A. Times-Washington Post* Service, in *Tri City Herald*, July 8, 1976.

111 "Only I know my real value . . ." Benagh, "A Rare Bird Flies High Above Baseball's Flock."

111 "Forgotten in the fuss . . ." Joe Falls, "Not Giving Bird Raise Is Smart Move," *Detroit Free Press*, June 30, 1976.

111 "no player, on any . . ." Joe Falls, *Detroit Free Press*, July 2, 1976.

111 "Mark Fidrych has taken . . ." Ibid.

111 "Let's hope he . . ." Ibid.

111 "I have to say . . ." Patrick Zier, *Lakeland Ledger*, July 4, 1976.

111 "He's (Mark) the only reason . . ." Larry Paladino, Associated Press in *Argus-Press*, July 1, 1976.

112 "Saturday night will be . . ." Joe Falls, *Detroit Free Press*, July 2, 1976.

112 "I really haven't been . . ." Steve Kaufman, "Bird's the Word at Box Office," *Detroit News*, July 4, 1976.

112 "That's all we were . . ." Joe Falls, "Fidrych Charges Up Even the Opposition."

113 "In the ninth inning . . ." Interview with Greg Scupholm, August 6, 2010.

114 "We had our greatest . . ." Benagh and Hawkins, *Go, Bird, Go.*

114 "Mickey Mantle used to draw . . ." Jim Hawkins, *Detroit Free Press*, July 4, 1976.

114 "I saw Sandy Koufax . . ." Joe Falls, "Fabulous Fidrych: He Gives Off Sparks," *Detroit Free Press*, July 4, 1976.

114 "He was sincere . . ." Joe Falls, "Fidrych Charges Up Even the Opposition."

114 "I don't think he talks to the ball . . ." Ibid.

114 "I talk to the baseball too . . ." Ibid.

114 "I'll never get used to this . . ." UPI, *Wilmington Morning Star*, July 8, 1976.

114 Larry Paladino of the Associated Press . . . Larry Paladino, Associated Press in *Argus-Press*, July 1, 1976.

115 "I couldn't ask for anything better . . ." *Newsweek*, July 12, 1976.

116 "Anybody want a cookie?" Benagh and Hawkins, *Go, Bird, Go.*

116 "There has never been a love affair . . ." Joe Falls, "And So The Bird's Only Human After All," *Detroit Free Press*, July 10, 1976.

116 "The Bird made a tactical error . . ." Ibid.

117 "I'm only using it during the season . . ." Doyle Dietz, *Reading Eagle*, July 13, 1976.

117 "It's everybody's goal . . ." Duffy, "A Two-hitter . . ."

117 Mark was so elated . . . Rubin, "Bye-bye Birdie, You'll Be Missed."

117 "The 1976 All-Star Game . . ." Ibid.

118 He switched identities . . . Duffy, "A Two-hitter . . ."

118 At the scheduled news . . . Benagh and Hawkins, *Go, Bird, Go*; Joe Falls, AP in *Tuscaloosa News*, July 13, 1976; Bob Smizik, "All-Star Game Changes into Bird Sanctuary," *Pittsburgh Press*, July 13, 1976.

119 "Pete didn't like him . . ." ESPN.com, May 14, 2008.

120 "He came over to me . . ." Rushin, "Mark Fidrych."

120 Before the game . . . Fidrych and Clark, *No Big Deal*; Benagh and Hawkins, *Go, Bird, Go*.

120 "Oh, I'm sure I will," Associated Press in *Ocala Star Banner*, July 14, 1976.

121 "Seventy thousand people here . . ." Duffy, "A Two-hitter . . ."

121 "No," Johnson replied, "because I know . . ." Ibid.

122 "Don't worry . . ." Fidrych and Clark, *No Big Deal*.

122 "He gets more mail . . ." Jim Hawkins and Dan Ewald, *The Detroit Tigers Encyclopedia*. Champaign, IL: Sports Publishing, 2003.

122 "Initially when Ralph Houk . . ." Interview with John Hiller.

122 Paul Fidrych was in heaven . . . Interviews with Carol

Fidrych-Duda, Lorie Fidrych Karolewicz, Paula Grogan, and Laura Floetke, September 15, 2010.

123 Mark soon discovered . . . Patrick Zier, "Fidrych Difference from Spring to Spring," Lakeland Ledger, February 27, 1977; Marsh, "The Tale of the Bird"; Fidrych and Clark, *No Big Deal*; Interviews with Lorie Fidrych Karolewicz, Carol Fidrych-Duda, Paula Grogan, and Frank MacCormack.

128 "It's a good thing . . ." Interview with Frank MacCormack.

129 "Me, Tom Veryzer, Mark, and Ben Oglivie . . ." Interview with Frank MacCormack.

129 "We would stomp and yell . . ." Interview with Laura Floetke.

130 "It was like Samson and Goliath," Hawkins and Ewald, *The Detroit Tigers Encyclopedia*.

130 "The first time we came to Detroit . . ." Joe Falls, "Fidrych Charges Up Even the Opposition."

130 "That year was unbelievable . . ." Interview with Fred Gladding.

131 "As the game was ending . . ." E-mail communication with Rod Wharram, July 2, 2010.

132 Someone in the Twins . . . Fidrych and Clark, *No Big Deal*; Ron Fimrite, "He's Not a Bird, He's Human," *Sports Illustrated*, April 11, 1977.

132 "Who's Oliva?" Dave Wright, "Remembering Mark Fidrych: Who's Oliva?" *MinnPost.com*, April 14, 2009.

133 After the game, a television interviewer . . . Fidrych and Clark, *No Big Deal*.

134 "He is fresh. He is funny . . . Jim Hawkins, "One Strange Bird," *Sporting News*, August 14, 1976.

134 Meanwhile, Mark was enjoying . . . Fidrych and Clark, *No Big Deal.*

135 "Mark would come in after every inning . . ." *Worcester Telegram and Gazette*, April 22, 2009.

135 "When he hit that I felt so happy . . ." AP in *Spokane Daily Chronicle*, August 12, 1976.

136 "Naw, he hasn't contacted me . . ." Richard Shook, "Fidrych Wins No. 15," UPI in *Ludington Daily News*, August 25, 1976.

136 "Babe Ruth didn't cause that much excitement . . ." Larry Paladino, Associated Press in *Argus-Press*, August 26, 1976.

136 "Nobody ever pulled them in . . ." Joe Falls, "F as in Fidrych and Fright," *Sporting News*, September 11, 1976.

136 "The first thing . . ." *Sporting News*, July 10, 1976.

137 "Times have changed . . ." *Sporting News*, October 2, 1976.

137 "He heard the kids were disappointed . . ." UPI in *Rome News-Tribune*, August 29, 1976.

137 Mark gave a slightly different account . . . Fidrych and Clark, *No Big Deal.*

137 Ken White, a friend from Northboro . . . Interview with Kenneth White.

138 "It's a bird. It's a plane . . . Benagh and Hawkins, *Go, Bird, Go.*

138 "selling like hotcakes . . ." *Worcester Telegram*, September 5, 1976.

139 "If they had asked me . . ." Fidrych and Clark, *No Big Deal.*

139 *Sports Illustrated* reported . . . Smith, "The Bird Fell to Earth."

140 promotor Allan Carr . . . *Sporting News*, September 4, 1976.

140 Late in the year . . . Earl McRae, "A Rare View of The Bird," *Sport*, July, 1977; Patrick Zier, "Fidrych: Difference From Spring to Spring," *Lakeland Ledger*, February 27, 1977.

141 "I think Mark Fidrych . . ." Interview with Bruce Kimm.

141 "He loved to win . . ." Interview with Ralph Houk.

141 Campbell paid to fly . . . *Sporting News*, October 30, 1976; Fidrych and Clark, *No Big Deal.*

142 "The whole season was . . ." *Sporting News*, October 30, 1976.

143 Not to be outdone . . . UPI in *Ludington Daily News*, October 16, 1976; Stan Grossfeld, "As the Bird Flies, a Decade after Mark Fidrych Amazed and Amused Baseball Fans Everywhere, He Is Content in His Post Baseball Life," *Boston Globe*, December 27, 1987.

144 "They know I'm no good . . ." Marsh, "The Tale of the Bird."

144 "You never felt . . ." Interview with Paul Beals.

144 "The hype was sort of overwhelming . . ." Interview with Wayne Hey.

144 Those close to him . . . Fimrite, "He's Not a Bird, He's Human."

145 "We want to make it a day . . ." *South Middlesex News*, August 24, 1976.

145 The more than 500 tickets . . . Interviews with Carol Fidrych-Duda, Paula Grogan, Jack Wallace, and Bruce Kimm; *Worcester Telegram*, October 19, 1976.

146 "He seemed just a little too pat . . ." Dave Nightingale, "Mark Fidrych Remains a Refreshing Change," *Chicago Daily News* Service in *Miami News*, December 9, 1976.

146 During the banquet . . . Dave Anderson, "Success Hasn't Made The Bird Less Cuckoo," *New York Times*, January 31, 1977; Fidrych and Clark, *No Big Deal*.

148 "No player in our time . . ." Joe Falls, "F as in Fidrych and Fright," *Sporting News*, September 11, 1976.

149 "What we've really got . . ." Joe Falls, "The Bird with the Golden Arm," *Palm Beach Post*, September 4, 1976.

149 "In an era of self-important . . ." *Newsweek*, July 12, 1976.

149 "Sports fans have become . . ." Larry Eldridge, "Mark (The Bird) Fidrych: A New Folk Hero Arrives," *Baseball Digest*, October, 1976.

149 The Lindell AC's owner . . . Benagh and Hawkins, *Go, Bird, Go.*

150 "This is the greatest . . ." *Sporting News*, September 25, 1976

150 "He electrifies the fans . . ." Eldridge, "Mark (The Bird) Fidrych: A New Folk Hero Arrives."

150 "When he pitched . . ." *Sporting News*, April 16, 1977.

150 "He just caught . . ." Lovinger, *The Gospel According to ESPN*.

150 "He was so popular . . ." Interviews with Bruce Kimm, John Hiller, John Wockenfuss, and Frank MacCormack.

151 "The strange thing . . ." Pepe, *Catfish, Yaz, and Hammerin' Hank*.

6. "Slow Down"
153 "I don't ever have to worry . . ." UPI in *Bryan Times*, January 31, 1977.

154 "smoothed out . . ." Anderson, "Success Hasn't Made The Bird Less Cuckoo."

154 "The Bird is flaky . . ." Jim Hawkins, "Success hasn't changed Fidrych, or pair of socks, *Sporting News*, February 19, 1977.

155 "It got so I felt . . ." Fimrite, "He's Not a Bird, He's Human."

155 "It's even got curtains . . ." McRae, "A Rare View of the Bird."

156 "What's the sophomore jinx . . ." Jerry Green, "Will Mark Fidrych Defy the 'Sophomore Jinx'?" *Baseball Digest*, April 1977.

156 "It's enough . . ." Marsh, "The Tale of the Bird."

156 "You never saw . . ." Milton Richman, "Fidrych Rarin', Ready, Houk, Tigers optimistic," UPI in *Ludington Daily News*, March 16, 1977.

156 "I've never seen . . ." Will Grimsley, AP in *Gettysburg Times*, March 10, 1977.

157 March 21, 1977, was a beautiful . . . Interview with Bob Sykes; *ESPN SportsCentury*, "Mark Fidrych."

158 "They said it was . . ." *Lakeland Ledger*, March 23, 1977.

158 "It does not appear . . ." AP in *TriCity Herald*, March 27, 1977.

159 "They told me the worst . . ." Larry Paladino, AP in *Argus-Press*, March 29, 1977.

159 "There was a large tear . . ." *Sporting News*, April 16, 1977.

159 "Most of them wanted . . ." AP in *Spokane Daily Chronicle*, April 1, 1977.

160 In order to give . . . McRae, "A Rare View of the Bird."

160 As if there wasn't enough . . . Joe Falls, *The Detroit Tigers: An Illustrated History*. New York: Walker and Company, 1989; Joe Falls, *Fifty Years of Sportswriting*. Champaign, IL: Sagamore, 1997; Jason Beck, "Detroit's Falls has seen it all," MLB.com, July 18, 2002.

161 "In 1977, when he hurt . . ." Interview with Ralph Houk.

162 "So I got hurt . . ." McRae, "A Rare View of the Bird."

162 "When this happened . . ." Ibid.

162 "It was hard on him . . ." Interview with Bob Sykes.

162 "He's so young . . ." Peter Gammons, "The Bird Flaps Again and Doesn't Flop," *Sports Illustrated*, June 6, 1977.

163 "I asked the Louisville Slugger . . ." Ibid.

163 "My agent went . . ." *Lakeland Ledger*, May 13, 1977.

163 "I'm supposed to be . . ." Fimrite, "He's Not a Bird, He's Human."

163 Clark explained . . . Fidrych and Clark, *No Big Deal.*

165 "It's even shocking . . ." Joe Pollack, *Sporting News*, August 13, 1977.

165 "[Fidrych] is a very, very . . ." Jonathan Yardley, *Sports Illustrated*, October 10, 1977.

165 "I don't want to hear . . ." Richard Shook, UPI in *Ellensburg Daily Record*, May 27, 1977.

166 "I've done the best . . ." Marsh, "The Tale of the Bird."

166 "Two things keep . . ." Gammons, "The Bird Flaps Again and Doesn't Flop."

167 Jim Hawkins reported . . . Jim Hawkins, *Sporting News*, June 18, 1977.

167 "I feel like I let . . ." Gammons, "The Bird Flaps Again and Doesn't Flop."

168 In early July, Dave Anderson . . . Dave Anderson, "Out in Left Field with The Bird," *Pittsburgh Post-Gazette*, July 4, 1977.

169 "I was watching him . . ." Interview with Dave Rozema.

169 "All of a sudden . . ." Interview with Bruce Kimm.

170 "a slight muscle pull . . ." AP in *Spokesman-Review*, July 14, 1977.

170 "The hurt is still . . ." Patrick Zier, "It Hurts! The Bird Sidelined," *Lakeland Ledger*, July 25, 1977.

171 The cause of Mark's . . . Interviews with Bob Sykes, John Hiller, Frank MacCormack, Dave Rozema, Ralph Houk, Patrick Zier, and Bruce Kimm.

171 "They pitched every fifth . . ." Patrick Zier, "Detroit's Arm Woes, Part I," *Lakeland Ledger*, March 16, 1978.

172 "I don't buy that . . ." Patrick Zier, "Campbell Disputes Arm Theory, Part II," *Lakeland Ledger*, March 17, 1978.

172 "Naw, I don't think . . ." Patrick Zier, "Pitchers Feel They Haven't Been Mistreated," *Lakeland Ledger*, March 18, 1978.

173 ABC hired him . . . Associated Press, September 9, 1977; John Vallerino, *Lakeland Ledger*, September 9, 1977; *New York Times*, August 9, 1990.

175 "That was neat . . ." Mike Feely, "Detroit's Fidrych Is First 'Bird' to Fly South for the Winter," *Sarasota Herald-Tribune*, November 3, 1977.

175 "I don't think any . . ." Jim Hawkins, "The Bird Goes to Roost, but Hopes Still High," *Sporting News*, September 17, 1977.

176 "I never really had . . ." Feely, "Detroit's Fidrych Is First 'Bird' to Fly South for the Winter."

176 "It was just a little . . ." Interview with Dave Rozema.

176 Later that winter . . . Will Grimsley, AP in *Ludington Daily News*, November 25, 1977.

7. The Long Road Back

178 Jim Hawkins reported . . . Jim Hawkins, "Tigers Give Fidrych 100 Pct Mark," *Sporting News*, April 15, 1978.

179 "I was a different . . ." Larry Keith, "Roar? No Tigers Go 'Tweety,'" *Sports Illustrated*, April 24, 1978.

180 "I expect him . . ." Jim Hawkins, "Tigers Sing Sad Bye-bye to Bird, So What's New?" *Sporting News*, May 13, 1978.

180 "I'm going to take . . ." Ibid.

181 "I'd like to contribute . . ." Patrick Zier, "Fidrych Is on His Own in Comeback Bid," *Lakeland Ledger*, June 11, 1978.

181 "How would you like . . ." Jim Hawkins, "The Bird Warbles Another Sad Song," *Sporting News*, April 14, 1979.

181 "Look at me . . ." Zier, "Fidrych Is on His Own in Comeback Bid."

182 "muscle spasm . . ." *Sporting News*, June 24, 1978.

182 "I agree . . ." AP in *Daytona Beach Morning Journal*, June 29, 1978.

183 "But the older guys . . ." *Lakeland Ledger*, August 6, 1978.

183 "Mark was just such . . ." Interview with Jack Billingham.

183 "When he was on . . ." Interview with Bob Sykes.

184 "It's not so bad . . ." Patrick Zier, *Lakeland Ledger*, July 22, 1978.

184 "This time . . ." *Lakeland Ledger*, August 6, 1978.

184 "Sure I've worried . . ." *Daytona Beach Morning Journal*, August 6, 1978.

185 The Associated Press reported . . . AP in *Argus-Press*, August 15, 1978.

185 "It was supposed . . ." Patrick Zier, "Is The Bird Really Back?" *Lakeland Ledger*, March 19, 1979.

185 "Hey, who's he . . ." *Sporting News*, January 6, 1979.

185 "Right now . . ." Patrick Zier, *Lakeland Ledger*, December 8, 1978.

186 "I'll be in the rotation . . ." Jim Hawkins, "The Bird Hops on Cloud Nine," *Sporting News*, March 17, 1979.

186 "Thank God my arm feels better . . ." Jerry Green, "What's the Word on The Bird?" *Sports Illustrated*, May 28, 1979.

186 Jim Hawkins later reported . . . Jim Hawkins, "To Keep His Spirits High Bird Reads the Good Book," *Sporting News*, July 28, 1979.

186 "I feel fine . . ." Green, "What's the Word on The Bird?"

187 "He's throwing about . . ." Ibid.

187 "He will go through . . ." AP in *Argus Press*, May 24, 1979.

187 "My confidence will . . ." Ibid.

188 "It is sure to help . . ." Tom Loomis, *Toledo Blade*, July 31, 1979.

188 "Essentially you can forget . . ." *Lakeland Ledger*, July 31, 1979.

189 "It's like I haven't been . . ." AP in *Sarasota Herald-Tribune*, March 2, 1980.

189 "Sure I was disillusioned . . ." AP in *Kingman Daily Miner*, March 2, 1980.

189 "The Fidrych comeback . . ." Tom Gage, "Tigers Listen to Bird's Chirps," *Sporting News*, March 22, 1980.

189 "When Jimmy says . . ." *Lakeland Ledger*, March 29, 1980.

189 "All this is doing . . ." AP in *Toledo Blade*, April 4, 1980.

190 "I think all the crutches . . ." AP in *St. Petersburg Times*, April 6, 1980.

190 "He's a spoiled . . ." *Lakeland Ledger*, April 9, 1980.

190 "Hey, it was a . . ." *Lakeland Ledger*, April 23, 1980.

190 "Going back . . ." *Sporting News*, April 19, 1980.

191 "I'm still the same . . ." *Lakeland Ledger*, April 23, 1980.

191 "He put horse liniment . . ." *Evansville Courier & Press*, August 3, 2009.

191 "He was working . . ." Interview with Chuck Murphy, July 13, 2010.

191 "There wasn't a pitcher . . ." Interview with Dave Machemer, July 8, 2010.

192 "It was awesome . . ." Interview with Glenn Gulliver, July 9, 2010.

192 "He was happy-go-lucky . . ." *Evansville Courier & Press*, April 14, 2009.

192 "Back then . . ." Interview with Glenn Gulliver.

193 "Everywhere we went . . ." Interview with Chuck Murphy.

193 "He was unbelievable . . ." *Evansville Courier & Press*, April 14, 2009.

193 "Hey pal . . ." Scott Simon, "Mark Fidrych, Always Gracious," www.npr.org, April 18, 2009.

193 "I'd had hopes . . ." Leigh Montville, "The Lone Rider," *Sports Illustrated*, August 27, 1990.

194 "Leyland expected . . ." Interview with Dave Machemer.

194 "Leyland had fun . . ." Interview with Glenn Gulliver.

194 "I refuse . . ." *Sporting News*, April 19, 1980.

194 "He would sit down . . ." *Worcester Telegram and Gazette*, October 15, 2006.

195 "Mark was such . . ." Interview with Dave Machemer.

195 "Jim Leyland and Mark . . ." UPI in *Palm Beach Post*, May 14, 1980.

196 "Mark was really down . . ." Interview with Dave Machemer.

196 "That was probably . . ." *Lakeland Ledger*, August 12, 1980.

197 "He was really throwing . . ." Interview with Glenn Gulliver.

197 "We filled the park . . ." Interview with Chuck Murphy.

197 "Hi Jim . . ." *Lakeland Ledger*, August 12, 1980.

198 "He's as good . . ." AP in *Gettysburg Times*, August 13, 1980.

198 "I've never seen . . ." *Sporting News*, August 30, 1980.

198 "When I came up . . ." Interview with Bruce Kimm.

199 "I wanted this . . ." AP in *Kentucky New Era*, September 3, 1980.

199 "I know . . ." *Toledo Blade*, September 2, 1980.

199 "I think I can . . ." *Boston Globe*, March 4, 1981.

200 Joe Falls reported that . . . Joe Falls, "Now-or-Never Again Spring Makes For Unflapping Bird," *Sporting News*, March 14, 1981.

200 "Sending Mark down . . ." AP in *Spokesman Review*, April 5, 1981.

200 "I consider myself . . ." UPI in *Sarasota Journal*, April 2, 1981.

200 "I'll be there . . ." AP in *Tuscaloosa News*, April 2, 1981.

201 "Feel sorry . . ." Paul Meyer, *New York Times* Wire Service, "Fidrych Still Refuses to Feel Sorry about State of Hill Career," in *Toledo Blade*, July 13, 1981.

201 "The Tigers have done . . ." AP in *Times-News*, October 6, 1981.

202 "I told Campbell . . ." AP in *Reading Eagle*, October 15, 1981.

8. Pawtucket

203 He consulted . . . Peter Richmond, "Fidrych Keeps on Flingin," *Miami Herald*, March 18, 1983.

204 "If he was going . . ." Ibid.

204 "I fed . . ." AP in *Bangor Daily News*, March 31, 1982.

205 "I can't think . . ." *Toledo Blade*, June 6, 2000.

206 "No, I owe a lot . . ." *Toledo Blade*, June 15, 1982.

206 "He was a competitor . . ." Interview with Keith MacWhorter, June 22, 2010.

207 "If we had . . ." Jim Donaldson, Projo.com (*Providence Journal*), April 16, 2009.

207 The matchup between . . . Jack Cruise, "Fidrych-Righetti packed McCoy," *The Day*, July 17, 1992.

208 "About the seventh inning . . ." *Worcester Telegram and Gazette*, April 14, 2009.

208 "One guy gets on . . ." Leigh Montville, "A Minor Miracle: Fidrych Wins Honor; Righetti Passes Test," *Boston Globe*, July 2, 1982.

208–209 "Mark was actually timed . . ." Interview with Keith MacWhorter.

209 "When it was over . . ." Jim Donaldson, Projo.com (*Providence Journal*), April 16, 2009.

209 "The scene after . . ." *Reading Eagle*, July 6, 1983.

209 "I get gooseflesh . . ." Interview with Keith MacWhorter.

210 "the baseball gods . . ." Personal correspondence with Keith MacWhorter, June 23, 2010.

210 "When he got . . ." AP, April 14, 2009.

210 "He was tremendously . . ." Peter Richmond, "Fidrych Keeps on Flingin," *Miami Herald*, March 18, 1983.

210 "Forget all that bull . . ." Ibid.

211 "He (God) gave it . . ." Ibid.

211 "The thing about Mark . . ." Michael Madden, "The Bird Tests His Wing—And It Flaps Again," *Boston Globe*, March 12, 1983.

211 "I didn't even want . . ." Richmond, "Fidrych Keeps on Flingin."

212 "I have no doubts . . ." *New York Times*, March 27, 1983.

212 "He just wasn't . . ." Interview with Ralph Houk.

212 "I'm just glad . . ." *Sporting News*, April 25, 1983.

212 "His control . . ." Dave Anderson, "Sweet Bird of Baseball," *New York Times*, July 4, 1983.

212 "You could see . . ." Interview with Carol Fidrych-Duda.

212 "It was frustrating . . ." *ESPN SportsCentury*, "Mark Fidrych."

212 "Everybody . . ." *Schenectady Gazette*, October 11, 1986.

213 "He was one . . ." Peter Gammons, *Boston Globe*, June 30, 1983.

213 "When I left . . ." Patrick Zier, *Lakeland Ledger*, February 4, 1984.

213 "My father . . ." Dan Shaughnessy, "Fidrych, a Rare Bird, Is Well Grounded," *Boston Globe*, June 1, 1996.

213 "How do you know . . ." Interview with Keith MacWhorter.

213 "I told someone . . ." Leigh Montville, "Fidrych Has no Regrets about Baseball Career," *Boston Globe*, July 1, 1983.

213 "Mark called . . ." Interview with Paula Grogan.

214 "I've had enough . . ." *ESPN SportsCentury*, "Mark Fidrych."

9. Northboro Redux

215 "I got so mad . . ." Interview with Lorie Fidrych Karolewicz.

215 "Mark hasn't talked . . ." Rubin, "Bye-bye Birdie, You'll Be Missed."

215 "He was really . . ." Interview with Lorie Fidrych Karolewicz.

216 "Mark had always . . ." Interview with Wayne Hey.

217 "Why do I need . . ." Smith, "The Bird Fell to Earth."

217 "Initially, we played . . ." Interview with Wayne Hey.

217 "See what . . ." Jim Hawkins, "The Bird Was a Class Act," *Oakland Press*, April 15, 2009.

218 "I like . . ." *Palm Beach Post*, June 9, 1984.

219 "It made me know . . ." Shelby Strother, *Detroit News*, May 25, 1986.

219 "Now I know . . ." Smith, "The Bird Fell to Earth."

219 In 1986, Gary Smith of *Sports Illustrated* . . . Smith, "The Bird Fell to Earth."

220 "Sometimes I still . . ." Grossfeld, "As the Bird Flies . . ."

221 "He bugged me . . ." Grossfeld, "As the Bird Flies . . ."

221 "It's my thrill . . ." Smith, "The Bird Fell to Earth."

221 "He never liked . . ." Interview with Lorie Fidrych Karolewicz.

221 "After they got . . ." Interview with Wayne Hey.

222 "one of the greatest . . ." Grossfeld, "As the Bird Flies . . ."

222 "People on the road . . ." Ibid.

222 "A lot of people . . ." Dan Shaughnessy, "Fidrych, a Rare Bird, Is Well Grounded."

223 "We'll be working . . ."John Gearan, "Fidrych Still Trucking After All These Years," *Worcester Telegram and Gazette*, August 11, 2000.

223 "One day . . ." Interview with Robert Boberg.

223 "always a smile" . . . Nicholas Dawidoff, "Fidrych," *New York Times Magazine*, December 27, 2009.

223 "He'd dress . . ." John Walker, "The Bird: Mark Fidrych Meant so Much to so Many," www.mlive.com, April 15, 2009.

223 "This is what . . ." Bill Doyle, "The Bird: 20 Years Later, Fidrych Enjoying Life Away From The Game, *Worcester Telegram & Gazette*, May 19, 1996.

223 "The farm . . ." Interview with Rick Duda.

224 "I'm happy . . ." Grossfeld, "As the Bird Flies . . ."

224 "I looked at myself . . ." Mary Frain, "Fidrych Sticking on Farm with Two Roster Additions," *Worcester Telegram & Gazette*, June 25, 1989.

224 "I picked Jessica . . ." Interview with Joe Sullivan, May 27, 2010.

224 "He said to me . . ." Interview with Wayne Hey.

225 "In my last years . . ." Interview with Robert Boberg.

225 "I just wanted to . . ." Leigh Montville, "Fidrych a Long Way from Big Leagues but He's Back in the Game," *Boston Globe*, June 3, 1989.

226 "She told me . . ." Joe Gergen, *Newsday in St. Louis Post-Dispatch*, February 24, 1991.

226 "He took me . . ." Interview with Rick Duda.

227 "He was a gentleman . . ." Interview with Rosemary Lonborg, June 20, 2010.

227 "Whatever you do . . ." Rosemary Lonborg, *The Bird of Base-ball: The Story of Mark Fidrych*. Northboro, MA: Fidco Distributors, 1996.

227 "The theme of the book . . ." Interview with Rosemary Lonborg.

228 "I lived his . . ." Grossfeld, "As the Bird Flies . . ."

228 "That whole ride . . ." Mike O'Hara, "Everyone Still Knows 'The Bird,'" *Detroit News*, July 11, 2005.

229 "It was pretty neat . . ." Doyle, "The Bird: 20 Years Later."

229 "Every time . . ." Ibid.

229 "You know . . ." *Evansville Courier*, November 3, 1996.

229 "I got a great . . ." Duffy, "A Two-hitter . . ."

229 "I have a family . . ." *ESPN SportsCentury*, "Mark Fidrych."

229 "I talked a lot . . ." Interview with John Hiller.

229 "He never . . ." Dave Nordman and Elaine Thompson, "Fidrych Found Dead," *Worcester Telegram & Gazette*, April 14, 2009.

230 "When I'm on . . ." "Spotlight Has Dimmed but The Bird Is Still a Charmer," *Evansville Courier*, November 3, 1996.

230 "It's neat . . ." *Grand Rapids Press*, July 10, 2006.

230 "I don't know . . ." Rushin, "Mark Fidrych."

230 "Do you have any idea . . ." Jim Hawkins, "Bird's Legend Will Live Forever," *Oakland Press*, April 14, 2009.

231 "Can you believe . . ." Rushin, "Mark Fidrych."

231 "Mark really . . ." Interview with Paula Grogan.

232 "It's called . . ." *Worcester Telegram & Gazette*, July 8, 2001.

232–233 "We had to help . . . Mark, the Wertz Warrior," Interview with Victor Battini, October 7, 2010; E-mail communication with Kathy Hinchman, August 6, 2010.

234 "If he would see . . ." Interview with Rick Duda.

235 "Oh, he thought . . ." Chad Finn, Boston.com, April 13, 2009.

235 "I had a double wedding . . ." Interview with Dave Rozema.

235 "Mark was the same . . . never changed his personality," Interviews with Brad Ostiguy, Dan Coakley, Ray Dumas, and Carol Fidrych-Duda.

236 Tom Marino . . . *Worcester Telegram & Gazette*, April 15, 2009.

236 "Mark never turned down . . ." Interview with Carol Fidrych-Duda.

236 "I said, 'Whoa . . .'" Vic Ziegel, "Former Tigers Goofball Fidrych Remains a Different Sort of Bird," *New York Daily News*, July 23, 1993.

236 "I only do . . ." Shaughnessy, "Fidrych, a Rare Bird, is Well Grounded."

236 "The best thing . . ." Smith, "The Bird Fell to Earth."

236 "I went . . ." Grossfeld, "As the Bird Flies."

236 "He was so . . ." Interview with Victor Battini.

237 "It was funny . . ." Ken Powers, "Saturday's Northborough American Legion Baseball Fundraiser to Honor the Memory of Mark Fidrych," www.thedailynorthborough.com, April 29, 2011.

237 "My son . . ." Interview with Joe Sullivan.

238 One spring morning . . . www.teampaulc.org, April 17, 2009.

238 "He handed me . . ." *MetroWest Daily News*, May 2, 2009.

238 "We were getting ready . . ." E-mail communication with Daniel Rowe, July 2, 2010.

239 "We go up . . ." Interview with John Sanderson, June 24, 2010.

Epilogue

242 "The best young . . ." Smith, "The Bird Fell to Earth."

242 "There's no question . . ." *Lakeland Ledger*, October 7, 1987.

243 "Fidrych was the greatest . . ." *ESPN SportsCentury*, "Mark Fidrych."

243 "Never was there one . . ." Walker, "The Bird: Mark Fidrych Meant so Much to so Many."

243 "He was the most . . ." Walker, "The Bird: Mark Fidrych Meant so Much to so Many."

243 "You can talk . . ." Hawkins, "The Bird Was a Class Act."

243 "Never in my . . ." Smith, "The Bird Fell to Earth."

243 "I've been fortunate . . ." E-mail communication with Steve Thomas, September 10, 2010.

244 "You know something . . ." Interview with Jack Wallace.

244 "He's been . . . any way he could," Paul Jarvey, "Last Respects, Thousands Attend Wake for Generous and Joyful Fidrych," *Worcester Telegram & Gazette*, April 17, 2009.

245 "He was a trailblazer . . ." Dave Nordman, "Fans, Friends Bid 'Bird' Farewell," *Worcester Telegram & Gazette*, April 18, 2009.

245 "He did . . ." Michael Morton, "Northborough Recognizes

Fidrych, Rolfe," *MetroWest Daily News*, May 3, 2009; "After he died . . ." Interview with Joe Sullivan.

247 "Yea, Mark 'The Bird' Fidrych . . ." Interview with Steve Grilli.

Bibliography

Benagh, Jim, and Jim Hawkins. *Go, Bird, Go!* New York: Dell, 1976.

Epstein, Dan. *Big Hair and Plastic Grass*. New York: Thomas Dunne Books, 2010.

Ewald, Dan. *John Fetzer: On a Handshake*. Champaign, IL: Sagamore, 1997.

Falls, Joe. *The Detroit Tigers*. New York: Walker and Company, 1989.

———. *Fifty Years of Sportswriting*. Champaign, IL: Sagamore, 1997.

Fidrych, Mark, with Tom Clark. *No Big Deal*. Philadelphia and New York: J. B. Lippincott, 1977.

Gutman, Bill. *Mark Fidrych*. New York: Tempo Books, 1977.

Harwell, Ernie. *Ernie Harwell: Stories From My Life in Baseball*. Detroit, MI: Detroit Free Press, 2001.

Harwell, Ernie, and Tom Keegan. *Ernie Harwell: My 60 Years in Baseball*. Chicago: Triumph Books, 2002.

Hawkins, Jim, and Dan Ewald. *The Detroit Tigers Encyclopedia*. Champaign, IL: Sports Publishing, 2003.

Houk, Ralph, and Robert Creamer. *Season of Glory*. New York: Pocket Books, 1988.

Kell, George, and Dan Ewald. *Hello Everybody, I'm George Kell*. Champaign, IL: Sports Publishing, 1989.

Lewis, T. J. *A View From the Mound: My Father's Life in Baseball*. Raleigh, NC: LuLu.com, 2009.

Lonborg, Rosemary. *The Bird of Baseball: The Story of Mark Fidrych*. Northboro, MA: Fidco Distributors, 1996.

Lovinger, Jay (editor). *The Gospel According to ESPN: Saints, Saviors and Sinners*. New York: Hyperion, 2002.

Peary, Danny. *Cult Baseball Players: The Greats, the Flakes, the Weird and the Wonderful*. New York: Simon and Schuster, 1990.

Pepe, Phil. *Catfish, Yaz, and Hammerin' Hank: The Unforgettable Era that Transformed Baseball*. Chicago: Triumph Books, 2005.

Index

Aaron, Hank, 71, 90

acting, 218

Algonquin Regional High
   School, 20–21, 26, 225

All-Star Game (1976), 117–22

Amberson, Jeff, 237

American Association playoffs,
   58

American legion baseball, 22–25

Amorello, Anthony, 223

Amorello, Joe, 229, 241

Anaheim Angels, 135–37

Anderson, Dave, 168

Anderson, Sparky, 188, 190, 198

Andrews, James, 219

Angel, Dan, 129–30

Appalachian League pennant
   (1974), 45–46

Arroyo, Fernando, 176

Association of Professional
   Baseball Physicians, 185

autographs, 57, 108, 131,
   137–38, 193, 235–36

awards, 143–44, 146–47, 152

Ball Four (Bouton), 203

Baltimore Orioles, 111–13, 169

Barden, Glen, 158

Bare, Ray, 63

Barrett, Marty, 208

"Baseball Aches for Flakes," 246

Baseball Digest, 108, 246

*Baseball Eccentrics: The Most
   Entertaining, Outrageous and
   Unforgettable Characters in the
   Game* (Lee), 246

Baseball Players Association, 72

Basic Agreement, 72

basketball, 22, 27

Battini, Victor, 232–33, 236, 244

Bauer, Paul, 188

Beals, Paul, 103

Behm, Bill, 158

Belanger, Mark, 169

Benaugh, Jim, 138, 230

Bench, Johnny, 121

Berra, Yogi, 76, 168

Billingham, Jack, 62, 183

"Bird Day," 143

The Bird of Baseball: The Story of Mark Fidrych (Lonborg, R.), 227–28

Birnbaum, Bob, 44

birth, 7

birthday, 135

Blackburn, Tom, 26

Blue, Vida, 172–73

Blue Water Ranch, 223–24

Blyleven, Bert, 91, 172

Boberg, Robert, 95, 99–100, 223

Bogart, Peggy, 130

Bonnell, Diane, 21

Boston Red Sox, 67–68, 89–90, 95–96, 156, 198

Boswell, Dave, 81

Bouton, Jim, 203

Boy Scouts, 238–39, 244

The Bristol Tigers, 35–44

  demographic of, 33–34

  mound behavior at, 31–32

  1974 Appalachian League pennant, 45–46

Brown, Gates, 75

bubble gum, 80

Bucks for the Bird, 130

Bumbry, Al, 169

Busticaris, Jimmy, 149

Campaneris, Bert, 128

Campbell, Jim, 49, 55, 61, 69–70, 171–72, 196–97

  background of, 74

  on Fidrych, M., 188, 200, 243

Carbo, Bernie, 67

Carew, Rod, 168

Carty, Rico, 87–88

CBS. *See* Columbia Broadcasting System

Chambliss, Chris, 101

charity work, 155, 231–34

Chet's Diner, 220, 237–38

Chicago White Sox, 136, 156–57, 180, 198

childhood, 6. *See also* schooling

  baseball, 11–15, 22–25, 27

  behavior, 9–10, 16–17

  birth, 7

  friends, 89, 99, 205

  hairdo, 20, 24

  injuries, 16–17, 25

  jobs, 18–19

  personality, 8, 10, 21–22

  social life, 22

Christian Science Monitor, 149

Cincinnati Reds, 68

Clark, Bill, 68

Clark, Tom, 137, 163–64

Cleveland Indians, 84–87, 133

Coakley, Dan, 17, 235

Coleman, Joe, 63

Columbia Broadcasting System
(CBS), 71–72

comeback, 179, 189, 196–97,
199–200. *See also* recovery

Concepcion, Dave, 121

Coombs, Mike, 53

Cosby, Bill, 139

Cowen, Maurice, 182

Cowens, Dave, 36

Cuellar, Mike, 114

curtain calls, 105, 113, 115, 128,
168

Cusick, Joe, 29–30

The Cutoff, 96, 218

Cy Young Award, 143–44

Dan Duquette Skills Challenge,
232

Dana-Farber Cancer Institute,
227

dancing, 234–35

death, 240–41, 244

DeBarr, Dennis, 57

Decker, Frank, 181

Dempsey, Rick, 169

Denman, Brian, 213

Dent, Bucky, 218

depression, 215, 220

Detroit, 75–76, 149–50, 154, 166

Detroit Free Press, 116, 138

"Detroit Hero Fidrych Does it
All for $16,500 a Year,"
110–11

Detroit News, 65, 69, 86

Detroit Tigers, 29–30, 61–62.
See also spring training
accommodations with, 63
Anaheim Angels *vs.*, 135–36
attendance of fans, 76, 98–99,
105, 112, 142, 156
Baltimore Orioles *vs.*, 111–13,
169
Boston Red Sox *vs.*, 89–90,
95–96, 156, 198
ceremony for Fidrych, M.,
245–46
Chicago White Sox *vs.*, 136,
156–57, 180, 198
Cincinnati Red *vs.*, 68
Cleveland Indians *vs.*, 84–87,
133
contract with, 141–42, 188
decline of, 75
downtime with, 81
end of career with, 201–2,
213
fans of, 94, 98–99, 114, 115
Fetzer ownership of, 73–74
Kansas City Royals *vs.*, 115
loyalty to, 239–40
Milwaukee Brewers *vs.*,
90–91
Minnesota Twins *vs.*, 132
mound behavior at, 66,
85–86, 88, 101–3
New York Yankees *vs.*,
98–107
Oakland A's *vs.*, 127–28
pitching staff, 63–64

Detroit Tigers (*continued*)
  press tour, 154–55
  record at, 94, 96–97, 114, 140,
    187, 242
  Red Sox *vs.*, 67–68
  rookie season with, 64–66
  salary at, 110–11, 114–15,
    129–30, 141–42, 186
  Texas Rangers *vs.*, 91, 135
  Toronto Blue Jays *vs.*, 179,
    199
  treatment of rookies, 79
"Detroit's 'Bird' Capturing
  Heart," 109
discipline, 43–44, 51
draft (1974), 29–30
Duda, Rick, 224, 234
Dukakis, Michael, 143
Dumas, Ray, 11, 235
Dwyer, Jim, 198
dyslexia, 9

endorsements, 139, 144, 220,
    225, 229–30
Evansville Courier & Press, 193
Evansville Triplets, 55, 189–92
  fans, 57
  final appearance with, 197
  mound behavior at, 56
  record at, 56, 58
  salary at, 192–93
Evers, Hoot, 32, 49
Evert, Chris, 120
Ewald, Dan, 65, 93–94, 243
exploitation, 137–38

Falls, Joe, 92, 111, 116–17,
    148–49, 160–61
fame, 122–31, 144–45, 228,
    235
fans, 3, 5–6, 237
  Anaheim Angels, 137
  attendance of Detroit Tigers,
    76, 98–99, 105, 112, 142,
    156
  autographs, 57, 108, 131,
    137–38, 193, 235–36
  Bucks for the Bird, 130
  chants of, 100–101, 103,
    104–5, 115, 209
  curtain calls for, 105, 113,
    115, 128, 168
  Detroit Tigers, 94, 98–99, 114,
    115
  effect on, 131–32, 148, 247
  encouragement of, 189
  Evansville Triplets, 57
  fame and, 122–31
  growth of, 95, 107–8
  kids, 57, 126, 193
  love of, 128–29, 247
  mail, 108, 111, 122
  Pawtucket, 205, 209–10
  reaction to hospitalization,
    159–60
  after retirement, 230
farm, 204, 216–17, 219, 224,
    238–39. *See also* Blue Water
    Ranch
fashion, 64, 69–71
fatherhood, 221–26
Fetzer, John, 73–74

Fidrych, Ann (wife), 245–46
  engagement to, 220
  marriage to, 221
  on personality, 226
  relationship with, 220–21
Fidrych, Carol (sister), 8, 212
Fidrych, Jessica (daughter),
  221–22, 224–26, 245–46
Fidrych, Lorie (sister), 8, 15, 52,
  216
Fidrych, Paul (father), 12, 107
  background of, 6–7
  contract negotiations of,
    141–42
  death of, 228
  merchandise collection of,
    123
  pride of, 52, 122–23
  reaction to retirement, 213–14
  relationship with, 15–16, 20,
    28, 68–69
  superstition of, 100
Fidrych, Paula (sister), 7, 17–18,
  103, 213–14
Fidrych, Virginia (mother), 90,
  100, 145
  background of, 6–7
  death of, 228
  on injuries, 202
  interview reactions of, 165–66
  relationship with, 16
The Fidrych Dance, 235
Fidrych Frizzies, 130
"Fidrych Is Not Flaky . . . It's the
  Rest of Us," 93
"Fidrych Is the Only One Not

Worried About a Raise,"
  114–15
"The Fidrych Syndrome," 176–77
Finley, Charlie, 72–73
Fisk, Carlton, 68
Floetke, Laura, 123, 129
Florida Instructional League,
  46, 59–60, 181–82
Ford, Dale, 88
Ford, Gerald, 117, 120
Ford, Jack, 120
Ford, Whitey, 78
Ford Thunderbird, 116–17, 156
Foster, George, 121
free agency, 1, 72–73
Freehan, Bill, 64–65, 75, 232
Frey, Jim, 106
funeral, 244

Gage, Tom, 189
Game of the Week, 2
Garland, Wayne, salary of, 156
Garr, Ralph, 151
Garvey, Steve, 121
Gedman, Rich, 203–4
Genesis Fund, 232
Gibson, Kirk, 235
Ginsberg, Allen, 163
Gladding, Fred, 56–57, 62,
  130–31
Glynn, Ed, 57
Go, Bird, Go (Hawkins &
  Benaugh), 138–39, 230
Green, Jerry, 92, 108–9
Grilli, Steve, 57–58, 247

Grodzicki, John, 31, 36–38, 187
Guise, Edwin, 159, 187
Gullett, Don, 182–83
Gulliver, Glenn, 192, 197

hairdo, 20, 24, 64
Happy, Michael, 86
Harwell, Ernie, 137
Hatfield, Fred, 55
"Having a Ball: 'Bird' Likes Lofty Perch," 94
Hawkins, Jim, 92–93, 108–9, 134, 138, 217, 230
Hegan, Jim, 106
Henry Ford Hospital, 159
heroics, 43
Hey, Wayne, 48, 216, 220
Highlands University, 29
Hiller, John, 55, 64, 75, 78, 150–51, 229
Hinchman, Kathy, 233
Hobson, Butch, 168, 209
Hogan, Jeff, 31, 32, 36, 39
Homel, Jack, 182
Horton, Willie, 75, 78–79, 245
hospitalization, 159–62
Houk, Ralph, 7, 59, 61–62, 76–78, 161
    on Fidrych, M., 141, 242–43
    on injury, 171
Howard, Doug, 85
Hriniak, Walt, 203
Hunter, Catfish, 72–73, 182–83

Iltch, Mike, 139
injuries, 229
    arm/shoulder, 169–75, 180–85
    back spasms, 186–87
    childhood, 16–17, 25
    diagnosis of, 175, 218–19
    effect of, 175–76
    Fidrych, V., on, 202
    Houk on, 171
    knee, 157–62
    recovery, 162–63, 195–97
    rumors about, 173
    surgery, 159–60, 162, 219
interviews, 110, 133, 165–66

Jablonski, Jim, 99, 103
Jackson, Reggie, 71, 114
James, Art, 58
Jim Dandy Trailer Park, 41–43
Jimmy Fund Clinic, 227
Jobe, Frank, 180
jobs
    childhood, 18–19
    after retirement, 217, 220–23, 237–38
John, Elton, 134
Johnson, Alleycat, 39, 41
Johnson, Darrell, 117
Johnson, Dave, 195
Jones, Randy, 118
Junior World Series, 58–59, 61

Kaat, Jim, 211
Kaline, Al, 71, 86

Kansas City Royals, 115
Karras, Alex, 81
Kell, George, 86, 136
kids, 126, 231–34
Killebrew, Harmon, 71
Kimm, Bruce, 59, 67
  on Fidrych, M., 56, 95, 141,
    150, 169–70, 173
  relationship with, 83–84, 89,
    198
King, Larry, 232
Kuhn, Bowie, 73, 133–34,
    176–77

LaBrecque, Mark, 160
LaGrow, Lerrin, 63–64, 68, 128
Lajoie, Bill, 46
Lakeland Ledger, 49, 140
Lakeland Tigers, 48–50
  conditions at, 51–52
  losing streak at, 53–54
  management of, 51
  mound behavior at, 53
Lamont, Gene, 58
LaRussa, Tony, 58
learning disabilities, 9–10
LeClaire, Fred, 90
Lee, Bill, 246
LeFlore, Ron, 120
legend, 61, 67, 91–92, 108
Leibovitz, Annie, 166
Lemongello, Mark, 56, 57
Leonard, Dennis, 115
Lewis, Joe, 31, 32
  disciplinary actions of, 44–45

morning workouts of, 40
motivational speeches of,
    35–36
personality of, 34–35
Leyland, Jim, 181–82, 189, 243
  background of, 193–94
  on Fidrych, M., 197
  friendship with, 193, 194, 196
  parents of, 199
Lindell AC, 81–82, 112, 149
Little League, 13, 238, 245
  daughter in, 224
  Fidrych, M., influence on,
    128
  mound behavior, 14–15
Lolich, Mickey, 74, 75, 172
Lonborg, Jim ("Gentleman
    Jim"), 227, 245
Lonborg, Rosemary, 227–28,
    245
Lowenstein, John, 88
Lucken, William, 149

MacCormack, Frank, 47–48,
    56–57, 67, 124, 171
Machemer, Dave, 191–92, 195
MacWhorter, Keith, 206–7,
    209–10, 213
Madsen, Virginia. *See* Fidrych,
    Virginia
Major League baseball, 68–69.
    See also specific teams
Man of the Year Award, 146–47
Mantle, Mickey, 71
Manual, Jerry, 58

March of the Dimes, 154

Maris, Roger, 125

Mark Fidrych Children's Fund, 245

Mark Fidrych Company, Inc., 222

The Mark Fidrych Syndrome, 4

Marlboro Orioles, 225–26

marriage, 42, 221

Martin, Billy, 66, 75, 81

Massachusetts High School Athletic Association, 26

Matlin, Lew, 107, 113–14, 158

Matthau, Walter, 147–48

Mauch, Gene, 133

May, Lee, 168

May, Milt, 83

Mays, Willie, 71

McAfee, Bill, 48

McLain, Denny, 92, 136

McNally, Dave, 73

McRae, Hal, 121–22

media, 189–90
 interviews, 110
 negativity of, 188
 1976 All-Star Game, 118–19
 popularity in, 4–6, 60, 91–92, 106–8, 114, 122, 168–69
 retirement and, 215, 230

merchandise, 123, 129, 167

Messersmith, Andy, 73

Mexico, 176

Michaels, Al, 174–75

Middlesworth, Hal, 107

Miles, David, 14

Miller, Marvin, 72

Milwaukee Brewers, 90–91

Minnesota Twins, 132

Minor League baseball. *See also specific teams*
 life in, 40–41
 promotion to AA, 54–55
 promotion to AAA, 55
 road trips in, 40–41
 salary in, 41
 statistics of, 34
 transfer back to, 184, 189, 200

Mitchell, David, 159

Mitchell, Joni, 164–65

Molinaro, Bob, 198

Monday Night Baseball, 2, 71, 98

Monday Night Football, 71, 98

Mondor, Ben, 205

money, 18, 147, 192–93. *See also* salary

Montefusco, John ("The Count"), 118, 122

Montgomery Rebels, 54–55

Morgan, Joe, 119, 121, 208

Moss, Les, 54, 186

mound behavior/dialogue with baseball, 62, 109. *See also* personality
 Bristol Tigers, 31–32
 cartoons about, 228–29
 Detroit Tigers, 66, 85–86, 88, 101–3
 Evansville Triplets, 56
 Fidrych, M., on his, 87
 Lakeland Tigers, 53
 Little League, 14–15
 Pawtucket, 206

Rose and, 119
Scott on, 91
Zier on, 53
Munson, Thurman, 106,
    119–20
Murphy, Bob, 48
Murphy, Chuck, 191
Murray, Eddie, 169

Navarro, Tony, 225
Nettles, Craig, 151
New York Baseball Writers
    Association of America,
    153–54
New York Times, 109
New York Yankees, 71
    Detroit Tigers *vs.*, 98–107
    Hunter contract with, 72–73
    at World Series, 2–3
Newsweek, 149
nickname, 1, 25, 33, 65, 100,
    246
No Big Deal (Fidrych, M. & Clark,
    T.), 137, 163–64, 165
Northboro, 5–6, 9–18, 20–30
    population of, 7–8
    return to, 215–41
    Steelers, 19–20
    visits to, 205

Oakland A's, 127–28
*Oddballs: Baseball's Greatest
    Pranksters, Flakes, Hot Dogs
    and Hotheads* (Shalin), 246

Oliva, Tony, 132
optimism, 183–84
Ostiguy, Brad, 19, 22, 235
"Out in left field with The Bird,"
    168
Overmire, Stubby, 51

Paladino, Larry, 114–15
Palmer, Jim, 143
Pappas, Arthur, 203–4
Pappas, Ronnie, 235
Parrish, Lance, 32
Patchin, Steve, 191
Paul, Gabe, 136
Pawtucket, 203–4, 207–8,
    211–14
    fans, 205, 209–10
    mound behavior/dialogue
        with baseball at, 206
    record at, 210
Peary, Danny, 246
Peerman, Mark, 57
pension, 195
People, 109
personality, 48, 50, 164, 226.
    See also mound behavior/
        dialogue with baseball
    in baseball books, 246
    bubble gum, 80
    charisma, 94–95, 125, 134,
        244
    childhood, 8, 10, 21–22
    enjoyment, 2, 58, 112
    enthusiasm, 64–65, 82, 150,
        161, 183, 192, 206

personality (*continued*)
  fame and, 235
  Fidrych, A., on, 226
  hairdo, 20, 24, 64
  heroics, 43
  legend, 61, 67, 91–92, 108
  mannerisms, 58, 64–65,
    79–80
  sense of humor, 92
  on television, 174–75
Piniella, Lou, 101
pitching standards, 172–73
Pittsburgh Press, 117–18
players
  salary of professional, 72–75
  strike of, 72
popularity, 57, 148
  growth of, 126–27
  in media, 4–6, 60, 91–92,
    106–8, 114, 122, 168–69
  in Mexico, 176
practical jokes, 41
privacy, 123–25
Providence Journal, 210

The Quiet Hero: A Baseball Story
    (Longborg, R.), 227

"Rare Bird: Tiger Rookie Pitcher
    Fidrych Livens Up Camp,"
    65
Ray, Melvin, 38
recovery, 162–63, 195–97,
    203–4. *See also* comeback

religious life, 186, 211, 224
retirement. *See also* farm
  depression and, 215, 220
  fans after, 230
  Fidrych, P., reaction to,
    213–14
  jobs after, 217, 220–23,
    237–38
  life in, 216–17
  media and, 215, 230
Richards, Paul, 136
Rickey, Branch, 36
Rickles, Don, 146–47
Righetti, Dave, 207–9
Roarke, Mike, 208, 212
"Roast the Bird" banquet,
    145–46
Roberts, Dave, 63, 162
Robinson, Brooks, 130
Rolfe, Ted, 22–23
Rolling Stone, 165–66
Rookie of the Year Award, 144,
    152
Rose, Pete, 119, 121
Rozema, Dave, 60, 66, 77–78,
    169, 186, 232, 235
Ruhle, Vern, 59, 63

salary
  bonus, 116, 147
  Detroit Tigers, 110–11,
    114–15, 129–30, 141–42,
    186
  Evansville Triplets,
    192–93

in Minor League baseball, 41

pension qualification, 195

professional players, 72–75

Saleski, Stan, 25

Sanderson, John, 239

Sawyer's Bowladrome, 11

schooling
elementary, 8–10
grades, 9
high, 20–21, 26
learning disabilities, 9–10

Schram, Hal, 83

Schwechheimer, Lou, 207

Scott, George, 13, 91

Scrivener, Chuck, 56

Scully, Vin, 147

Scupholm, Greg, 113

Seaver, Tom, 211

Sechen, Sue, 185

Seollin, Pat, 112

Shlalin, Bruce, 246

Silen, Lee, 195–96

Simon, Neil, 218

Singleton, Ken, 169

Sisson, Frank, 112

Slider, Rac, 53

The Slugger's Wife, 218

Smith, Gary, 219

Smizik, Bob, 117–18

Special Olympics, 232–34

Sport, 160, 162

Sporting News, 58, 92–93, 108–9, 134, 148, 165

Sports Illustrated, 108, 139, 161–63, 165, 179, 228

spring training
1976 Detroit Tigers, 62–64, 161
1977 Detroit Tigers, 156
1978 Detroit Tigers, 178–79
1979 Detroit Tigers, 186

Stan Musial League, 225

Stange, Lee, 211

Staniec, Ed, 149

Stanley, Mickey, 75, 124

Starr, Bart, 71

Staub, Rusty, 2, 101–2, 211, 243

Stengel, Casey, 77

Stover-Conley, Sherry, 125

Strasburg, Stephen, 247

strike, players, 72

Sullivan, Joe, 224, 237

surgery, 159–60, 162, 219

Sutherland, Gary, 62

Sykes, Bob, 33, 37, 39, 42, 162

Syzdek, Jane, 125–26

Tanana, Frank, 136, 173

Telegram-Gazette, 69

television appearances, 139–40

Texas Rangers, 91, 135

Thomas, Steve, 24

Thompson, Jason, 55–56, 106–7

Tiant, Luis, 90, 122

Tiger fantasy camps, 226–27

"Tigers Sing Sad Bye-Bye to Bird, So What's New?", 180

Torchia, Tony, 213

Toronto Blue Jays, Detroit Tigers *vs.*, 179, 199

Trammell, Alan, 35, 179

Ulecker, Bob, 100
Unitas, Johnny, 71

Valenzuela, Fernando, 201
Veinot, David, 23
Veryzer, Tom, 80, 99, 105
Vitale, Dick, 136

Wagner, Mark, 67
Wallace, Jack, 24, 244
Washington, Claudell, 127–28
Weaver, Earl, 114, 151
Weaver, Roger, 213
Weber, Jim, 205–6
Wertz, Vic, 232
Wertz Warriors, 232
Wesson, Daniel, 145
Wharram, Rod, 131–32
"When Fidrych Talks, Baseball
    Listens," 93
Whitaker, Diane Horn, 52
Whitaker, Lou, 179
White, Ken, 137–38
White Pines, 145–46

William Morris Agency, 127,
    139, 144
Williams, Ted, 228
Wilson, Dennis, 135
Wilson, Earl, 74–75
Wockenfuss, John, 86, 151
Wolf, Warner, 100
Woolf, Bob, 74–75
Worcester Academy, 26–28, 70
Worcester Center Galleria,
    153
Worcester Telegram, 138
work-ethic, 27, 50–51, 173
World Series·
    Junior, 58–59, 61
    New York Yankees at, 2–3

Yastrzemski, Carl, 13, 67–68,
    90, 96, 210–11

Zier, Patrick, 49–50, 53, 88
Zimmer, Don, 68
Zimmerman's Bar, 49, 50
Zocco, Tom, 27